Against the Flow

Against the Flow

Rafferty-Alameda
and the
Politics of the Environment

George N. Hood

Fifth House Publishers
Saskatoon, Saskatchewan

Layout and design by Donald Ward/Ward Fitzgerald editorial design
Cover design by John Luckhurst and Sandra Hastie/GDL
Cover photograph by Gerard Kwiatkowski/gk Photographics
Map on page 10 by George Duff

The publisher gratefully acknowledges the support received from The Canada Council, Communications Canada, and the Saskatchewan Arts Board.

Printed and bound in Canada
94 95 96 97 / 5 4 3 2 1

Canadian Cataloguing in Publication Data

Hood, George N. (George Newton), 1955–

Against the flow

Includes bibliographical references and index.
ISBN 1–895618–35–5

1. Rafferty-Alameda Project. 2. Dams-Environmental aspects-Souris River Watershed. 3. Dams-Political aspects-Souris River Watershed. 4. Water resources development-Environmental aspects-Souris River Watershed. 5. Water resources development-Political aspects-Souris River Watershed. I. Title.

TC426.5.S2H66 1994   333.91'0097124'4   C94–920012–3

FIFTH HOUSE LTD.
620 Duchess Street
Saskatoon, SK
S7K 0R1

CONTENTS

George Hood was a civil servant under the Blakeney and Devine governments in Saskatchewan and worked exclusively on the Rafferty-Alameda Project from 1985 to 1991, first as director of planning and then as vice-president of the Souris Basin Development Authority. He holds Masters degrees in Public Administration and Political Science from Queen's University and the University of Western Ontario. He is currently the Director of the Centre for Resource Studies at Queen's University.

List of Abbreviations

CCAFT	Citizens Concerned About Free Trade
CWF I	*Canadian Wildlife Federation Inc et al v. Canada (Minister of the Environment) and Saskatchewan Water Corporation* (1989)
CWF II	*Canadian Wildlife Federation Inc et al v. Canada (Minister of the Environment) and Saskatchewan Water Corporation* (1990)
CRTC	Canadian Radio-Television and Telecommunications Commission
EARP	Environmental Assessment Review Process
EIA	Environmental Impact Assessment
EIS	Environmental Impact Statement
EPA	Environmental Protection Agency (U.S.)
FEARO	Federal Environmental Assessment Review Office
HEP	Habitat Evaluation Procedure
IEE	Initial Environmental Evaluation
IJC	International Joint Commission
IRIA	*International River Improvements Act*
NAWAPA	North American Water and Power Alliance
NEPA	*National Environmental Policy Act*
PFRA	Prairie Farm Rehabilitation Administration
PURC	Public Utilities Review Commission
ROD	Record of Decision
SBDA	Souris Basin Development Authority
SCRAP	Stop Construction of the Rafferty-Alameda Project
SEPS	Saskatchewan Environment and Public Safety
SID	Supplementary Information Document
SWF	Saskatchewan Wildlife Federation

PREFACE

It was journalist and author Walter Stewart, holder of the Max Bell chair at the University of Regina, who advised me that providing a view from the inside was potentially the most interesting perspective I could bring to writing about the Rafferty-Alameda project. I gave a great deal of thought to this, and became convinced that there was no other way to do justice to the topic. That none of the principals are any longer involved in the issue and that few of them still hold public office has also made this possible. Even the organization responsible for building the project has disappeared.

Choosing this format meant relying on information that has, until now, not been in the public domain. What I have attempted to do, successfully I hope, is deal sensitively with these matters without betraying confidences. I have let the determining factors be whether the information included helps explain what happened on Rafferty-Alameda and why, and whether it is relevant to the broader field of environmental policy. If in doubt, I have erred on the side of exclusion. I am not a historian, and have no pretensions in that regard. While this account relies on both primary and secondary sources, it is also anecdotal, personal, and impressionistic.

As an undergraduate at Queen's University in the Department of Political Studies during the 1970s, I read the diaries of British Member of Parliament Richard Crossman as well as the journals of David Lilienthal, written during his tenure at the Tennessee Valley Authority.[1] Both influenced my decision in the early days of the Rafferty-Alameda project to keep a journal and make regular entries about my impressions of events. These journals have been helpful both in refreshing my memory and in restraining me from presenting a revisionist interpretation of events.

Although the journals were invaluable in the preparation of the manuscript, the period spent writing this book was even more essential. I could not have written this while I was involved in the project, nor while I lived in Saskatchewan. I needed the time to put many things into perspective: time away from Saskatchewan to sort out my own feelings about its people and space (which I miss a lot) and about its insidious politics (which I miss not a bit); time to realize that the art of government as practised is fundamentally different from the preconceived and idealistic notions I had when I first arrived in Saskatchewan to work for the Blakeney government in the early 1980s. Eventually I realized that the most frequently learned lessons in government are in how not to do something, and that the deferential respect I once had for all elected politicians was naive; they suffer from the same frailties as the rest of us.

The world, the country, and Saskatchewan do not revolve around Rafferty-Alameda. At one time I thought they did, and I behaved accordingly. I needed time to distance myself from things I took too seriously; time to rationalize my own feelings about something that had irrevocably changed my life; time to retool because the project, the government, and the province had combined to inflict a severe case of burnout. To some, this account might have had greater utility had it been completed closer to the actual event. To them, I give the assurance that the wait was necessary—at least for me.

Work on the Rafferty and Alameda dams was not always pleasant. Despite difficult circumstances, there were many who rallied to the cause, and provided me with invaluable professional and personal support. Early on I discovered that almost everyone involved in the project knew more about what we were doing than I did. For their patience and understanding I was, and am, most appreciative.

Gordon Crerar, Jim Dobson, Hilding Franson, Dick Henders, Al Kirk, Scott Manson, Ted Mather, Dave McDonald, Gordon Mills, Godwin Phillips, Fran Rieder, Gregg Trout, and Kevin Young provided sound technical advice and moral support during the development of the project, for which I am grateful. Daphne Budding, Sheila Harlos, Carol Hill, Julie-Ann Loustel, and Lil Wanner supplied essential administrative services—more often than not under less-than-ideal circumstances. Barry Bridges, D.E. "Tom" Gauley, Q.C., Lawrence Portigal, Bob Kennedy, Cliff Wheatley, and David Wilson rendered solid legal counsel as we navigated in uncharted legal waters. Others within the Saskatchewan government were also immeasurably helpful. Wayne Dybvig and Tony Moser of the Saskatchewan Water Corporation, Carmen Dybwad and Darren Foster of SaskPower, and Don Fast of Saskatchewan Environment and Public Safety all made significant contributions.

In the United States, Jack Beard of the Department of the Army, Louis Kowalski of the St. Paul, Minnesota, office of the U.S. Army Corps of Engineers, Bruce McKay from U.S. Senator Quentin Burdick's office, Bob Schempp, city manager of Minot, North Dakota, and David Sprynczynatyk, North Dakota state engineer, were willing to ignore convention in order to see the project through. It is difficult to overestimate their devotion to public service and their contribution to Rafferty-Alameda.

Being involved in an issue as controversial as Rafferty-Alameda in a province as political as Saskatchewan meant that a close association with those in the political arena was inevitable. If anything, the experience left me with a somewhat jaundiced view of the world of politics and its occupants. But it was not an altogether unpleasant experience, for I discovered there are dedicated people in politics. From the Conservatives, Eric Berntson, Joanne Tenold, Connie Young, Chris Dekker, and John Weir did everything they could to support those of us working on the project. And they remained supportive long after it became common practice in the provincial government to do otherwise. I am also indebted to Jack Messer and Carole Bryant, both well-known members of the NDP. After the defeat of the Devine government in the 1991 general election, Messer and Bryant proved that not everything in Saskatchewan had to be dealt with in a partisan way. Both treated me with respect and, though uncertain of the outcome, they encouraged me to write about Rafferty-Alameda.

Writing, by its very nature is a catharsis—the writing of this book probably more so than most. The members of the Political Studies department at Queen's University, through the Skelton-Clark Fellowship, provided me with the opportunity to pursue this book project. Cynthia Alexander, Fred Drummie, Stewart Fyfe, Mary Louise McAllister, Hugh Thorburn, and Peter Trueman made the task of writing a pleasant one.

Initially, when I began writing, I was motivated more by a desire to exorcise the demons that were haunting me from six years on the project. It took Tara Ariano of Brock University, Dale Eisler of the *Regina Leader-Post*, and Andrew Sancton of the University of Western Ontario, in addition to others listed elsewhere here, to convince me there was at least a remote possibility that others might be interested in what I had to say. I appreciate their comments and hope they were right.

On a more personal note, I am indebted to John E. Hood of Gananoque, Ontario, for his critical eye in reviewing a very rough and vitriolic first draft. I appreciate his wise counsel and fellowship. The other half of "The Two Georges," George Hill, was truly the *sine qua non* of the Rafferty-Alameda project. While many individuals made valuable contributions, Hill's alone were indispensable. His unstinting support throughout the travails associated with Rafferty-Alameda was appreciated.

Notwithstanding the encouragement and efforts of all those listed, responsibility for what follows and for any errors or omissions is solely mine.

Finally, to Debbie, who bore the brunt of the Rafferty-Alameda experience, and Mallory and Cole, both children of Saskatchewan, I will forever be grateful.

INTRODUCTION

My involvement in the Rafferty-Alameda experience began by accident on September 20, 1985. I was working in the Intergovernmental Affairs Branch of Premier Grant Devine's own department, the Executive Council, when I was asked to fill in for an ailing colleague and attend a meeting on the Rafferty Dam with the U.S. Army Corps of Engineers in North Dakota.

I grabbed the file on the project as I left the office. At the Regina airport I introduced myself to the engineers from SaskPower, who seemed less than overjoyed at having what I'm sure they thought was a political hack from Devine's office tagging along. During the hour-long flight from Regina to Minot, I reviewed the file—a mishmash of handwritten notes and minutes of meetings—in an attempt to familiarize myself with the project. All I really learned was that the Souris River has a horseshoe-shaped course, flowing south from Saskatchewan into North Dakota, then north into Manitoba where it eventually joins the Assiniboine, which, in turn, joins the Red at Winnipeg.

The engineers told me that there were two Saskatchewan dams under consideration: the Rafferty Dam on the main stem of the Souris near Estevan, and the Alameda Dam, sixty kilometers to the east on Moose Mountain Creek, a tributary of the Souris. They gave me an aerial tour of the river as we headed southeast toward Minot, pointing out the dams that were already in place. It was obviously a heavily managed river. It was equally obvious that it had almost no water in it.

The meeting in Minot was with representatives of the United States Army Corps of Engineers, the State of North Dakota, and the City of Minot. Its purpose was to determine whether there would be any American interest in a joint venture to build the two dams in Saskatchewan. To my surprise, on our arrival we were furtively shepherded into a small, windowless room in the basement of the tiny Minot airport. This was certainly not typical of any bilateral meeting I had attended. When I asked for an explanation, I was told that all meetings involving state officials in North Dakota were, by state law, open to the public. The implication was clear: this was a meeting the public should not know about.

The discussion was quite technical, and I found it increasingly difficult to follow as the parties, virtually all of them engineers, launched into a complex deliberation of the separable costs and recoverable benefits of potential structures on the Souris. My entire knowledge of Rafferty-Alameda was barely an hour old; the other options they were talking about were all new to me. The Army Corps of Engineers, arguably the preeminent dam builders in the world, told us that it would take them eighteen years to build the Rafferty and Alameda dams. This time frame, they pointed out, allowed for the lawsuits that were now attendant on practically every dam project in the United States, and would be inevitable with Rafferty-Alameda as well. Such litigation was unheard of in Canada at the time, and the Saskatchewan engineers responded with more than a little bravado and smug nationalism that it would only take us three years.

They were wrong.

Never before or since has a dam project in Canada faced the litigation that confronted Rafferty-Alameda. Within half a year of that meeting in the basement of the Minot airport, I had left the Executive Council to work full-time on the project, first as director of planning and operations and then as vice-president. What follows is a first-person account of what occurred, and why.

The story should have relevance for students of public policy who are interested in how wrong-headed decisions get made by government, and then get justified and defended. It is a timely story for people who are interested in the changing politics of the environment. It will also provide a window on the country's fragmented decision-making process—a result of the entrenched power of the bureaucracy in Ottawa—the increasing influence of special interest groups, and the growing irrelevance of those we elect at both the provincial and federal levels.

Much about Rafferty-Alameda does not fit the usual pattern of major projects. It has never been a NIMBY, for instance, a "Not In My Back Yard" project. In fact, it has consistently enjoyed overwhelming support from the people it affects the most. The reasons for this support are regionally and culturally determined; they are steeped in history and the perpetual struggle against the vagaries of a harsh climate, yet were all but ignored during the controversy.

The initial political spin on the project was determined by factors internal to Saskatchewan—its fierce partisan politics on the one hand, and the unstable relationship between the Devine government and its civil service on the other. The difficulties the project encountered with the federal environmental assessment process perhaps constitute its most notorious dimension, but there were also self-induced problems as the project wound its way through the provincial regulatory processes. Yet during all the litigation and work stoppages, it was still possible to negotiate an agreement between Canada and the United States to permit American participation.

This is a record of what happened between the Minot meeting in 1985 and the agreement with the last hold-out landowners in 1993, which finally allowed the project to be completed. It is an account of how a small and relatively obscure water project can be propelled to national prominence through bureaucratic incompetence and political maneuvering. It is the chronicle of a project that involved complicated litigation through almost every level of court in the country, including the Supreme Court, and became a symbol for environmentalists and major project developers alike. It is the story of a project whose political fate was sealed even before the government of Grant Devine was elected in 1982. It is a tale of infighting within governments and their bureaucracies. Finally, for the residents of southeastern Saskatchewan, it is the story of a nightmare that seemed endless.

CHAPTER ONE

OLD WATER

Understanding the Rafferty-Alameda issue requires an appreciation of the prairie condition, the physical factors that define the essence of this part of Canada. The elements have a profound and lasting impression on the people who live on the prairies. The vagaries of the weather as well as the geographic isolation have helped create a province with a sparse and declining population and a sense of political disenfranchisement.

These factors have influenced how prairie-dwellers look at the world, and they provide the filters through which they view the Souris River and the Rafferty and Alameda dams. When all the rhetoric and hyperbole are stripped away, any analysis of the Rafferty-Alameda issue must begin with the century-long struggle waged by those who have been most adversely affected by its flows: the residents of the Saskatchewan portion of the Souris River basin.

In Saskatchewan, it is impossible to drive down any rural road and not be struck by how recent the history of the province is. In virtually every field are monuments to a way of life once lived: piles of rocks picked by hand, abandoned farm machinery once pulled by horses, rusted hulks of 1930s-vintage automobiles, old wooden granaries, weather-beaten and deserted homes. In the small towns the struggle against harsh economic forces is evident in the shuttered stores and the abandoned gas stations. Unpaved roads predominate. Most roads that are paved have their interminable straightness interrupted every dozen kilometers or so by another town. Large stretches occur where towns have disappeared altogether. In many areas, the distance between towns is still a function of the water storage capacity of steam-powered locomotives, or the speed of a horse-drawn wagon loaded with grain travelling from the farm and back in a day. Many people in Saskatchewan can still remember the anxieties of using a chamber pot in the middle of winter, and the excitement when electricity first came to the farm.

I vividly recall my first trip outside Regina after I had moved to the province from Ontario in 1981. Driving through towns of less than 500 people—Kronau, Lajord, Sedley—I was surprised at the rectangular façades of abandoned buildings that I had previously seen only in television westerns. I remember thinking I had moved to a place that was, at best, thirty years behind the times and, at worst, somewhere near the end of the earth. What did these people, living out in the middle of nowhere, do? It took me six years, but eventually I found the answer.

What they do is live frugally and honestly in close cooperation with their neighbors, their lives shaped by their closeness to the land and the elements.

The predominating unit of time in Saskatchewan is not the minute or the hour, or even the day, but the season: seeding in spring, harvest in fall. These annual rites occur according to the schedule set by nature, and they influence the pace of life of the entire province. The weather is a universal preoccupation because it influences the economic fortunes of everyone who lives here. More than any other natural factor, rain—at the right time and in the right amount—is the key to economic prosperity. Certainly, temperature, snow, and hail are important factors as well, but the ubiquitous source of concern is rain. Too much, too soon, too little, too late: all have their consequences.

In many respects a year in the life of the province can be divided in two: farming and everything else. Significant public events are generally not scheduled during seeding or harvest. Ironically, the first litigation on the Rafferty-Alameda project involved the propriety of an environmental panel holding public meetings during the harvest months of August and September, which are among the busiest times of the year for farmers and ranchers in the province.[1]

Some people might argue this way of life is backward. In 1992, after I came to Queen's University to write this book, I was asked by someone from Ontario who should have known better how it felt to be back in civilization. I bristled at the insensitivity. After some thought I concluded that whatever else life in Saskatchewan may be, it is not uncivilized. It is basic and often elemental, but it is this proximity to the elements and their influence that gives the province and its people their distinctiveness.

In many respects, Saskatchewan is the quintessential Canadian province. Its predominant image is still formed from the elements and from the relationship of its people to the land, the sky, and the water. I suspect this is why the province has produced more than its share of writers and artists who have gone on to national and international success interpreting the physical images of the country to others.

All these images combine to leave an indelible impression on me of what Saskatchewan is. It is an image I hated when I first moved to the province. I remember the acute pangs of homesickness I felt one day, sitting on the outskirts of Regina and gazing out at the interminable flatness of it all. I still recall my amazement at the discovery that you couldn't drive in any one direction in Regina for fifteen minutes without hitting bald prairie. I was living on a prairie island.

In the six years I spent working on Rafferty-Alameda I came first to appreciate, and then love, the beauty of the prairies, in particular its people and what the land does to them; for it makes them more humane than they would be in almost any other part of the country. As I have discovered since I left, these feelings are not unique. Others share them, including Peter Gzowski, who spent some time in Saskatchewan working for the *Moose Jaw Times-Herald*:

But it is the land that has stayed with me, the land and its hold on life. In the next decade, when the CCF—the NDP, as it had become—finally fell, *Maclean's* sent me back to Saskatchewan to try and find some patterns. The most Canadian of provinces, as I called it then, and though that phrase may have been too glib, I know now what I meant—a place where people tried to hold together in a harsh climate, and weave a social fabric in answer to their common needs.[2]

This is the crucial premise for any discussion of the Rafferty-Alameda issue. If one is to understand the project and the controversy it generated, one must understand the historical forces that combined to create it. In Saskatchewan, there is no more critical factor than water.

Weather on the prairies occurs in cycles, the most significant (that we know about) being those that are decades long.[3] The droughts of the thirties and the eighties are two of the most recent and prominent examples, but they are by no means the only ones. During the nineteenth century, two expeditions exploring the Canadian west reached radically different conclusions about climatic conditions in the region. In 1857 Captain John Palliser described a significant portion of southern Saskatchewan—some twenty million hectares, now known as Palliser's Triangle—as being too dry to support farming. As one historian has noted, Palliser was "not altogether wrong in some of his observations made in what was probably a period of drought."[4] Beginning in 1872 and continuing over the next decade, John Macoun, a naturalist, toured the same region but, unlike Palliser, concluded that "the prairie was fertile, that the seasonal distribution of rainfall rather than the total amount was significant, and that the soil once broken would produce good crops."[5]

Both Palliser and Macoun were astute observers, and there can be no doubt that they each kept accurate records. The discrepancy in their accounts provides the first reliable historical record of the climatic differences that affect this area. Such swings in the weather have left their mark on the province and its inhabitants. Edward McCourt wrote of the drought of the 1930s that

> the rains fell at last and the erstwhile desert rejoiced and blossomed like the rose; but no amount of rainfall could ever wash away dreadful memories of the agonizing struggle to survive. For the people of Saskatchewan that nine year sojourn in a dust-darkened wilderness was a genuinely traumatic experience which left its mark not only on those who actually lived through the Dirty Thirties, but to some degree on their descendants.[6]

The images are as powerful today as they were sixty years ago. Black-and-white photographs from the 1930s reveal what at first glance appears to be snow drifting in ditches and against fences, but on closer examination turns out to be topsoil. There are countless stories of people jamming wet rags into doorjambs and window frames in a vain effort to keep out the blowing dust. A common joke concerns the Saskatchewan farmer who, during the thirties, goes out to cultivate his land, and heads to Manitoba to find his topsoil.

In addition to the challenges imposed by the weather, the sheer physical expanse of the prairies presented its own constraints. The province would not have been settled as widely or as early as it was were it not for the construction of dams to provide water storage. The locomotives of the Canadian Pacific Railway could not have made it across the prairies were it not for the water supplied by reservoirs on many Saskatchewan streams.

To this day, the reality of life for residents of rural and urban Saskatchewan is one of managing water. Without the ability to manage their uncertain water supply, they could not live where they do. Reservoirs are common in cities, towns, and villages across the prairies. On farms an excavated pond, or dugout, is often a necessity of survival. Rivers here differ from rivers in other parts of the country in that their flows vary widely from season to season and year to year. These conditions have long been accepted by those who reside on the great plains, and it has resulted in their having a unique perspective on water:

> In the West, lack of water is the central fact of existence and a whole culture and set of values have grown up around it. In the East, to "waste" water is to consume it needlessly or excessively. In the West, to "waste" water is not to consume it—to let it flow unimpeded and undiverted down rivers.
>
> To easterners, "conservation" of water usually means protecting rivers from development; in the West, it means building dams.[7]

The distinction has great significance for the Rafferty-Alameda project, which was viewed differently in the various parts of the country largely on the basis of the public's varying image of water. On the prairies, there had long been a consensus regarding water conservation. It is what led Norman Ward, the distinguished Saskatchewan political scientist, to conclude, "the need for water on the prairies is a subject about which there can be little serious disagreement."[8] As will become apparent, the same views are not held elsewhere in Canada.

The drought of the thirties and the magnitude of the effort required to ease its effect meant that government action was necessary. Provincial governments on the prairies, suffering their own financial difficulties, had limited resources. Responsibility thus fell on the federal government, which formed the Prairie Farm Rehabilitation Administration. The PFRA constructed many of the larger impoundments on rivers and streams throughout the prairies. These structures helped see communities through the drought. The paradox is that periods of drought are often supplanted by periods of dangerous flooding; there is either too little water or too much.

This fact is crucial to any rational understanding of the issues around the Rafferty-Alameda project. An appreciation of the area is also necessary. Far from being a pristine country, untouched by human hands—a view put forward by several opponents of the project—this area, like the rest of the grain belt, is one of the most physically altered landscapes on the planet. Since it was first

settled, the land has been heavily cultivated. As the melt-water channel for glacial Lake Souris, the land on either side of the Souris River valley is characterized by an absence of topsoil and a preponderance of stones and rocks. Geogra-
phers estimate that glacial Lake Souris drained in eight or nine days approximately 11,700 to 11,300 years ago, likely at the rate of 100,000 cubic meters
per second—a far cry from the placid creeks that flow through the valleys now.
The contemporary evidence of such large flows can be seen from current land
forms such as uniform channel widths, high depth-to-width ratios, and the gravel
concentrations two kilometers wide on the adjoining margins.[9]

Largely devoid of trees, the landscape is lacking in natural beauty. It is
strewn with pump jacks, pipelines, and storage tanks—oil field facilities
developed at a time when concern for the environment or aesthetics was
minimal. Mounds of spoil material from the coal strip mines surrounding
the city of Estevan give the impression of a lunar landscape. Nearby, two
thermal-electric generating stations billow out smoke, frequently shrouding
the city in an acidic haze.

The farms near Estevan are dotted with piles of rocks that stand as testi-
mony to the never-ending price farmers seem willing to pay for the privilege of
growing cereal crops in this unforgiving environment. Many farmers to this day
are forced to pick rocks that are brought to the surface by the spring thaw and
cultivation. Area resident Edgar Sawyer recounts the difficulties:

> . . . it just seemed like you could pick and pick and pick, and then look
> back . . . you know, if you could see that you had accomplished some-
> thing, but you haven't. There's just as many stones out there. But we
> used to pick in the spring and in the fall, we used to pick stones with a
> team and wagon . . . if you pick five or six loads of stone in a day, well
> you think you've done something, you see. But then you look at night
> when you're done and, "Well, where did we pick them stones?" God, it
> was awful. And some people just bounced over them. Hard on machin-
> ery. Wasn't so bad with horses, you know. They would slow down. But
> on the tractor, you'd get some awful jolts.[10]

Touring the southeastern portion of the province, in particular the area adjacent to the Rafferty Reservoir, the inescapable conclusion is that nature did
not treat the area kindly. What limited beauty was bestowed upon it, humankind
has done its best to disfigure through agriculture, coal mining, and oil and gas
extraction.

The Souris River system in Saskatchewan is comprised of three principal
tributaries: Long Creek, situated west of the main stem of the Souris River and
adjacent to the Missouri Coteau, the Souris River itself, and Moose Mountain
Creek, which flows south from Moose Mountain to join the Souris near the
appropriately named town of Oxbow, sixty kilometers east of Estevan. Long
Creek already has one major impoundment on it: the Boundary Reservoir south
of Estevan is the source of cooling water for the coal-fired Boundary Dam Power

Station, which provides approximately 50 percent of the base load capacity for the province.

The main stem of the Souris River has its origin in the middle of the prairie northwest of the city of Weyburn, approximately eighty kilometers southeast of Regina. Above Weyburn, the river is characterized by low banks and a poorly defined valley. Below Weyburn the valley becomes more defined, with a slightly steeper slope. The Souris has an average fall of 0.3 meters per kilometer. The valley is shallow and flat, and the normal flow velocity of the river is slow. Wide, sweeping meanders, and the fact that the region as a whole only receives about forty centimeters of precipitation annually add to its lethargy. Close to Weyburn, above the upper reaches of the Rafferty Reservoir, there is a ribbon of light brush and scrub, but the majority of the eighty-kilometer reach of the river from Weyburn to Estevan is largely devoid of trees.

On any trip down the valley one would see evidence of past efforts to control the river. Levees, weirs, dikes, and dams are prevalent along the valley between Weyburn and Estevan. As a means of irrigating his hay land, one farmer near Estevan annually constructed a two-meter-high earth embankment, over one-half kilometer in length, across the entire Souris River valley, temporarily halting the spring runoff.[11] The impoundment behind this structure stretched for kilometers up the valley, and to his neighbors who were affected by it he would complain about "those damn beavers" again.

Downstream from Estevan, the Souris changes in both direction and character, flowing east, parallel to the international boundary, with more dense tree cover along the banks. The valley of Mountain Creek, which joins the Souris just west of the town of Oxbow, is considerably deeper than that of the Souris

Spoil piles left behind by the strip mining of coal in the Estevan area. Author photo

valley at Rafferty and is more clearly defined, particularly in the area inundated by the Alameda Reservoir. The land adjacent to Moose Mountain Creek valley has a greater concentration of trees and a higher quality of topsoil than that surrounding the Souris above Estevan. Below the confluence of Moose Mountain Creek, the Souris valley is heavily treed right down to where it crosses the forty-ninth parallel.

The valley upstream of the city of Minot, North Dakota, was described in 1853 by Isaac Stevens:

> Its valley is from half a mile to a mile wide, about 200 feet below the prairie level, and it is well wooded with maple, oak, ash and elm. The deep coulees run back from it for fifteen or twenty miles, and must be avoided by keeping far from the river itself.[12]

This portion of the valley was home to the largest reservoir on the Souris prior to the construction of the Rafferty and Alameda dams (Lake Darling). Below Lake Darling, Minot straddles the valley, with many buildings located in the flood plain. In 1969, religious parallels were drawn as the flooding Souris (referred to as the Mouse in the U.S.) bisected the city for forty days. This flood

The Rafferty and Alameda dams are located on the Souris (Mouse) River system, which flows through Saskatchewan, North Dakota, and Manitoba.

gained almost mythical status for the residents of Minot, leading to prolonged demands for flood protection.

Turning east and then north, the river and the valley maintain the same basic characteristics until they reach the town of Verendrye, North Dakota, where the benches disappear and merge with the valley. Near the border with Manitoba, the U.S. Fish and Wildlife Service operates a number of low-level dams and weirs, creating wetlands for the propagation of waterfowl.

In Manitoba, the valley becomes progressively steeper until it reaches the confluence with the Assiniboine River below the town of Wawanesa. Throughout its course, the river is placid. In 1880, however, coal from Estevan was transported by barge down the Souris and Assiniboine rivers to Winnipeg. During this expedition, which almost certainly took place during spring runoff, "turbulent rapids" were encountered near Souris, Manitoba.[13]

The Souris is entirely dependent on precipitation. Unlike other rivers on the plains, such as the Saskatchewan and the nearby Missouri, it is not fed by mountain runoff. The Souris has highly variable flows from season to season and from year to year. Generally the river is high during spring runoff, as approximately 80 percent of its flows are derived from snow melt. Occasional floods occur in late spring and early summer as a result of rains. Flows normally diminish to zero or near zero in the fall and winter. Despite the droughts of the thirties and the eighties, significant floods on the Souris occurred in 1882, 1904, 1949, 1956, 1960, 1969, 1975, 1976, and 1979, causing millions of dollars in agricultural and property damage not only in Saskatchewan but downstream in North Dakota and Manitoba. On average, the Souris River in Saskatchewan sustains significant floods two out of every ten years. In the remaining years, evaporation generally exceeds precipitation. Consequently, the Souris River basin is among the most water-scarce regions of Saskatchewan, with little water-based recreation, few irrigation projects, and frequent municipal water shortages.[14]

That few people understood the nature of the region's rivers was driven home to me in conversation with my sister, who resides outside Toronto. Learning of my involvement in a project of growing national controversy, she inquired, "Just how big is this river, anyway?" My response was, "It depends." During spring runoff the Souris near Estevan can be a kilometer wide and three meters deep. At other times there is no water in it at all. In disbelief, my sister asked, "How can that be?" She was not alone. When we took people on tours of the project at the height of the controversy, their inevitable response was, "You mean, this is it?" But unless they saw the river in both incarnations, it was difficult to believe. It also rendered the already difficult task of explaining the project virtually impossible.

The widely varying flows of the Souris have led to major problems for those who inhabit the region. Without exception, there was too much water or not enough. Grant Devine, never shy about speaking in a homespun tenor to a Saskatchewan audience, captured the essence of the river when he referred to it as "either mud or flood."

The voices of the people can best tell the story of life beside this most unpredictable river. When they are heard in chorus, they tell of common hardships resulting from periods of flood and drought, and the very human and simple desire to make something better of their world:

In 1930–31 the river . . . was so dry, we even planted potatoes and barley in the river bottom . . . The river itself was the problem. The unpredictable flow of the river seemed to get worse. It seems it was either flooding or drought, with seldom a good year in between. In 1953 we had over twenty inches of rain in June. The river overflowed its banks for many miles and stayed that way throughout the summer.[15]

Jack Muirhead, area rancher

. . . I have argued that it has been drier these last few years in this country than it ever was in the thirties. Because in the thirties . . . all down in the flats and around there, there was stock running. And you was riding a saddle horse pretty near belly deep in snow. Well that snow all melted and ran into the river. And you haven't had such a thing for the last six years. No snow around here at all . . . The only thing we haven't had that we had in the thirties is wind.[16]

Gerald Pick, area farmer

The history of the Souris is clear: residents have believed for many years that the river was in desperate need of management. The fact that there are forty dams on the system, ten of which are in Saskatchewan, confirms this. The magnitude of the water management problem, however, was such that any long-term solution was beyond the means of local interests. This was recognized as early as the 1940s.

You see, in the thirties, the late thirties, they came in and they built those dykes. And they built Midale Dam, and there was a big scheme to irrigate—flood irrigate. And it never worked, because in 1943, the first time they ever got any water, they washed the dam out. Yeah, '43 was a big flood. They had a hell of a storm here in March. But they repaired the dam afterwards, and '48—another big year, another big flood—it washed the dam out again . . . So they repaired it again, and they dug the spillway down, so the blamed thing doesn't hold water any more. That dam was supposed to back water up to where Mainprize Park is, I suppose.[17]

Jack Muirhead

Area residents obviously believed that, to the extent possible, the elements should be controlled for the betterment of humankind. This attitude was common among farmers who felt little compunction about filling in potholes or removing trees to increase their cultivable acres. This same attitude was applied to the Souris. It was there to be managed. But the cycles of flooding were far enough apart—ten to fifteen years between the peaks and valleys of flood and drought—that it must have been difficult to mount a sustained campaign to solve the problems the river presented.

One of the first recorded calls for water management in the Souris basin came from the town of Alameda in 1907.[18] A large dam immediately above Estevan was called for in 1932, when the *Minot Daily News* reported that interests on both sides of the international border were considering cooperative construction of a dam on the main stem of the Souris River near Estevan:

> Construction of a huge dam in the Souris (Mouse) River near Estevan, Sask., would assure a steady, even flow of water in the stream thru [*sic*] Minot, thus solving a sewage problem which exists, and would reduce the flood hazard here to a minimum, was the assertion of members of an Estevan delegation which came to Minot late yesterday . . .
>
> President A.J.H. Bratsberg of the Minot city commission, who presided at the dinner meeting, sketched the history of the flood relief work in Minot, and told of the progress that has been made. He assured the Estevan delegation of Minot's interest in the proposal and promised them a full and complete study will be made . . .
>
> [Minot] City Commissioner Thomas said that he and City Engineer Peterson had studied the engineering plans laid before them by the Estevan delegation and that from a hurried checking of them, he believed the conclusions as to the amount of water that would be held back were correct.[19]

The Souris River valley had many small weirs and dikes: monuments to futile efforts to manage this unpredictable river. Courtesy Estevan Mercury

In spite of these early Canadian calls for water management, no significant effort appears to have been made until 1940. This prolonged period of
waiting must have been difficult for Saskatchewan and Manitoba residents
of the basin to accept, given two factors: the devastating effects of the drought
of the 1930s, and that, just a few kilometers to the south, their American
neighbors had gone ahead with an ambitious and successful multiple-dam
program on the Souris.

The International Joint Commission (IJC) conducted its first formal
transboundary review of the Souris River in 1940. As a bilateral tribunal
with no decision-making powers of its own, the IJC historically has acted as
a fact-finding and recommendation-making body to the governments of
Canada and the United States. In 1940, the IJC met in an attempt to establish
an apportionment of the Souris River waters between Saskatchewan, North
Dakota, and Manitoba. Representatives of the Saskatchewan government
proposed a comparatively small amount of water that could be fully utilized.
Dams would be required, and impoundments were proposed in Saskatchewan to help alleviate both the effects of drought and of flooding.[20] In 1940,
though, the federal government and the IJC played a far more prominent role
in the development of a province's water resources than it could in the 1980s.
This is evident in the remarks of the counsel for the Canadian government
before the IJC:

> ... due to war conditions, it had become necessary to curtail the ac-
> tivities of the Prairie Farm Rehabilitation Act [sic] (PFRA) organiza-
> tion and to divert the available funds and engineering staff to an en-
> tirely different government purpose. When the present situation had
> disappeared, he said, the policy of completely utilizing the equitable
> portion of the Souris River within the Provinces of Saskatchewan and
> Manitoba would be resumed by the Dominion and the two provinces.[21]

In appearing before the 1940 IJC hearings on the Souris River, J. Clark
Salyer, chief of wildlife refuges for the United States Biological Survey, noted
the conditions in the basin and the rationale for the construction of water storage facilities on the Souris on the American side during the 1930s:

> It was apparent that the storage was to be one of the most important
> features of the project. Our experience during the drought years taught
> us that if we wanted continued protection we would have to store dur-
> ing the wet years in order to keep going during the dry years. A study of
> the stream flow records seem to prove that we could have a successful
> project here on a major scale. So we purchased the land, made our
> surveys, built the storage dam and the adjoining dams across the valley
> to make irrigation marshes for waterfowl and to protect our expendi-
> ture of some three million dollars to secure adequate protection of our
> water supply and our water rights.[22]

Salyer's views indicate that the Americans felt they had sufficient hydrologic data, even in the midst of the drought of the 1930s, to justify the
construction of a series of dams on the Souris River. Similar conclusions
were reached by municipal officials from Estevan and Minot in 1932. The
IJC, however, reached a much different conclusion about the Souris in 1940
when it examined the question of apportionment. The commission noted the
difficulty of its task because of the highly variable flow and the inadequacy
of the flow records:

> So far as the records go, and they are very inadequate, the mean monthly
> discharge in second-feet as measured at Minot, North Dakota, has var-
> ied from 1.3 in 1937, 1.3 in 1931, 7.8 in 1932, and 8.7 in 1935, to 324.4
> in 1923, 339.7 in 1916, and 434.5 in 1927, the total acre-feet for the
> same years running from 939 and 940 and 5,605 and 6,410 acre-feet to
> 235,958 and 247,129 and 315,600 acre-feet.[23]

The commission also noted the obvious jurisdictional complexity, and that
there were widely varying interests vying for use of the water throughout the
basin. Since the area had recently been subjected to drought, competing claims
for use of the water were intense, and contributed significantly to the commission's hesitancy in establishing a permanent apportionment. There is no question, however, that the commission understood both the problems posed by the
variability in flow and the most practical solutions available. In its report, the
commission acknowledged that the North Dakota reservoirs on the Souris were

> . . . valuable as long range means of regulating the flow on this unusu-
> ally variable stream. Without this means of conserving water all these
> interests would suffer in periods of natural low water flow, and it would
> not be possible to release water to Manitoba even to the limited extent
> needed for human consumption and stock watering.[24]

The commission did not recommend the establishment of a permanent apportionment for the Souris, citing inadequate stream flow data as the reason. In
making this recommendation to the Canadian and American governments, the
commission deemed it advisable to continue the investigation for such period of
time as seemed necessary. It also suggested the establishment of a joint Canada-
U.S. body of engineers to administer the interim measures it was recommending, measures that were accepted by the respective federal governments.

This acceptance had the effect of short-changing Canadian interests. Saskatchewan was permitted to continue its current use of the waters of the Souris
River, which, compared to the capacity the United States had with its twenty-
one dams, was comparatively small. Permission to construct a small-capacity
reservoir at Weyburn did not add significantly to Saskatchewan's storage capacity. North Dakota, on the other hand, was permitted not only to continue its
current use of the Souris but to construct a 200 acre-foot capacity reservoir on

one of its tributaries. While the latter was of no significant advantage to American interests, the maintenance of the *status quo* in terms of existing use certainly was. It constituted a tremendous advantage in favor of the United States since, in 1940, the entire reservoir capacity in the Saskatchewan portion of the Souris basin totalled only 17,000 acre-feet, or 7.5 percent of the total storage south of the border.

Although the Saskatchewan government had made representation to the commission that annual flows in excess of 440,000 acre-feet had been reported, and that Saskatchewan only contemplated storing 36,000, the IJC recommended an additional allocation of only 4,000 acre-feet.[25] The commission forecast that five years hence, in 1945, the flow records would be much more dependable and informative. The commission also recommended that if North Dakota and Saskatchewan wanted to construct additional storage facilities, application should be made to the IJC for permission.[26] The 1940s and the 1950s were relatively wet years in the Souris basin. In light of such conditions, pressure to establish a permanent apportionment between the three jurisdictions was, no doubt, less acute than if the drought had persisted. The five years envisaged by the IJC for the establishment of a permanent apportionment ended up lasting nineteen years, and even then the solution was not permanent.

The commission met again in the latter half of the 1950s, this time prompted by a request from the government of Saskatchewan for additional water allocation. The province proposed the construction of a dam to create an industrial reservoir to provide cooling water for a thermal-electric generating station on Long Creek near Estevan. The restrictions placed on Saskatchewan's water use by the 1940 apportionment meant that virtually no development requiring a large volume of water had been possible for the better part of two decades. Saskatchewan's frustration was evident from correspondence between the provincial and federal governments in 1957. The Saskatchewan CCF minister of agriculture wrote to the Department of External Affairs:

> Development of the Souris River basin in Saskatchewan makes it necessary that this province have the unrestricted use of the water flowing within its boundaries, which the interim measures referred to [1940] now prohibit. In an endeavor to facilitate a fair and just settlement of the matter under reference, the Province of Saskatchewan has made the following offer to the Commission; that it was prepared to pass fifty percent of the natural flow of the Souris River where it crosses the international boundary at Sherwood Crossing to take care of the requirements of the State of North Dakota, provided the State of North Dakota would, for its part, pass sufficient water to Manitoba to take care of that Province's requirements.
>
> Unfortunately, Saskatchewan's offer has not been accepted and no progress whatsoever appears to have been made toward a permanent solution. A reference to the Commission should not be used to defeat the rights of Saskatchewan under the Treaty of 1909. Saskatchewan has

been very patient and has made a most generous offer to facilitate a settlement. The Saskatchewan Government is prepared to stand by that offer, but is unwilling to delay further the development of its own natural resources in the Souris River basin.[27]

In order to develop its portion of the Souris River basin, the T.C. Douglas government was apparently willing to take matters into its own hands. Such an extraordinary step reflects the increased importance Saskatchewan placed on the matter. Its position no doubt reflected that, whereas in 1940 the proposed uses for the water were relatively minor, at issue in 1959 was a major industrial project critical to the entire province: the construction of the Boundary Dam Power Station.

An agreement between Regina and Ottawa in 1959 lifted the 1940 apportionment and permitted Saskatchewan to retain 50 percent of the waters of the Souris River, demonstrating that a bipartisan solution to water issues on the Souris was achievable in Saskatchewan. It also showed that it was possible to circumvent the role of the IJC, as contemplated in the commission's 1940 report. In August 1957, Prime Minister John G. Diefenbaker wrote to the secretary of the IJC:

> The Government of Saskatchewan states that the interim measures recommended by the Commission in 1940 are delaying development in the Souris River watershed in Saskatchewan.
>
> Accordingly it does not wish to be inhibited any longer by these interim measures. At the same time, the Provincial Government is willing to permit for the present the continued passage of fifty per cent of the natural flow of the water at Sherwood Crossing to allow the International Joint Commission a further opportunity to reach agreement upon recommendation for a permanent settlement of the matters contained in the 1940 reference.
>
> The Canadian Government considers that the application of the interim measures during the past sixteen years has provided opportunity to extend the period of streamflow data beyond that contemplated by the Commission or the governments and believes that the accumulation of further records is not essential to a solution of the questions before the International Joint Commission.
>
> The Canadian Government agrees with the view expressed by the Government of Saskatchewan that the interim measures of 1940 are an obstacle to the development of south-eastern Saskatchewan. Furthermore, the statement by the Province of Saskatchewan that it intends to permit fifty per cent of the natural flow of the water in Saskatchewan into North Dakota at Sherwood Crossing is a generous offer. In consequence, the Government of Canada requests that the interim measures recommended by the Commission be modified in accordance with paragraph 7 of the enclosed letter from the Province of Saskatchewan.[28]

The evolution of the Souris River apportionment is an interesting one in the context of the Rafferty and Alameda dams. For about two decades both Saskatchewan and Manitoba were prevented from developing their portions of the Souris River basin, despite the acknowledgement of the IJC that reservoirs on the water course made sense. The 1955 submission from the Saskatchewan government to the IJC concluded:

> . . . development practically was brought to a standstill in this drainage basin. This was entirely due to the order of the Commission, issued in the intervening period of the war limiting Saskatchewan to 1,000 acre-feet for small domestic use only.[29]

The United States was able to receive the majority of the waters from the Saskatchewan portion of the Souris River basin in the relatively wet years of the 1940s and 1950s, giving it a tremendous advantage in the sense that it was able to establish licensed uses—first in time, first in right. There is no question that Saskatchewan and Manitoba were adversely affected by the restrictive water allotments they were granted.

The interim apportionments of 1940 and 1959 are also interesting; they do not reflect the fact that the Saskatchewan government may have had a legal basis on which to argue that it had a right to all the Souris River waters originating in the province. The Saskatchewan letter to the Department of External Affairs in 1957 indicates that the province recognized it had broader rights than it had so far laid claim to. The Boundary Waters Treaty of 1909 allowed the upstream user complete control of river flow on its side of the border, provided that upstream interests would be liable for any downstream damages the upstream uses may cause.[30]

The IJC took an inordinate length of time to establish an arrangement even approaching an equitable division of the Souris River waters. The interests of Saskatchewan were at best tempered and at worst sacrificed because of the jurisdictional complexity of the river itself. If the upstream jurisdiction had an inherent legal right to all the waters originating within its borders, then Saskatchewan would store everything it could, North Dakota would do the same, and Manitoba would only receive the water that originated in its portion of the basin.[31]

While Saskatchewan may have had this legal right, the federal government and, by extrapolation, its representatives on the IJC, were not going to grant it. The resulting stalemate almost exclusively benefited the state of North Dakota. The big loser was the province of Saskatchewan, particularly the residents of the Souris River basin, who were not only denied what was legally theirs but, for nineteen years at least, were unable to manage the river at all.

From the establishment of the 1959 interim measures until the end of the 1970s, little of what happened in relation to the Souris River basin gave residents cause to hope that their problems with the river would be solved. The opposite, in fact, was true. All their governments seemed able to do was conduct studies. Over this twenty-year period, there were no less than four major studies involving the Souris River. In the early 1970s, the federal, Saskatchewan, and Manitoba governments conducted the Saskatchewan-Nelson Basin Study. This included the Canadian portion of the Souris, and involved a number of investigations for potential dam sites, including Rafferty. The study also included some rather interesting proposals, such as the possibility of constructing a canal to reroute the Souris River directly into Manitoba, thus preventing it from flowing into the United States. There was also a proposal to connect the Qu'Appelle River to the Souris via an excavated channel.

Extensive flood damage in the late 1960s and early 1970s provoked an immediate response from basin residents on both sides of the international border. In Saskatchewan, a nonpartisan group calling itself the Moose Jaw–Souris River Association was formed in 1969, constituting an amalgam of mayors from southeastern Saskatchewan communities. The association was formed in an attempt to bring pressure to bear on senior levels of government to do something about the water management problems of this portion of the province:

> We feel that an additional dam approximately seven miles upstream from Estevan would serve a number of functions.
> . . . No mention has been made of the plan to develop a reservoir along Moose Mountain Creek water course in the vicinity of Alameda. It is our understanding that some work has been done on this study which would result in better flood control in the Oxbow area as well as providing a supply of water to be used for livestock, irrigation, recreation and wildlife. It should be noted that the flooding of this water course has caused very high flood peaks with the resulting downstream damage.
> . . . we would like to point out that the estimates of the time required to fill both the Boundary Dam Reservoir and the Diefenbaker Dam were underestimated. We understand that Boundary Dam was supposed to be full in three years. In fact it was filled in less than two. Diefenbaker Lake was supposed to require seven years. We understand that it required only three years. Even if there was abnormal evaporation we feel we cannot wait any longer for something to happen. We must have immediate action to get the dam west of Estevan—we need it now or we will be too late.[32]

The nonpartisan nature of the organization is reflected in the fact that Moose Jaw mayor Louis "Scoop" Lewry, a well-known NDP supporter, was a member, as was Estevan mayor Gregg Trout, a PC supporter. According to Trout, the issue of water management as a partisan political issue never arose.[33] Water issues, by their nature, are not usually political in a partisan sense. As late as 1970, political parties in the Saskatchewan Legislature appear not to have taken positions on water management on the Souris.

Government response to demands for water management took the form of two federal-provincial studies: the Souris River Basin Study and the Qu'Appelle

River Study. The former had two effects as far as the Rafferty-Alameda project was concerned. First, a major public consultation component was built into it, with five task forces made up of citizens from various centers along the Canadian portion of the river. These groups were consulted by the staff of the study, itself comprised of consultants and officials from the federal, Saskatchewan, and Manitoba governments. An unanticipated result of the study was the creation of a network among residents of the valley in Saskatchewan, North Dakota, and Manitoba, each of whom found that the problems they faced in their reach of the river were similar to those experienced by the others. This network easily resurrected itself during the Rafferty-Alameda project.

Second, the Souris River Basin Study reaffirmed the need for water management on the Souris, but concluded that the Rafferty Dam could not be justified on flood control objectives alone; an industrial component would be required. This finding proved sufficiently nebulous to allow the province, some seven years later, to proceed with the Rafferty Dam. No detailed attention in the Souris River Basin Study was paid to the possibility of a dam at Alameda on Moose Mountain Creek.

In the United States, the driving force in the 1970s was the flood of 1969. Minot straddles the Souris, and approximately 13,000 of its citizens lived in the flood plain. Many of its arterial roads crossed the valley, as well. In 1969, the flood plain was inundated for forty days. This flood crystallized the efforts at water management on the Souris in North Dakota and led to the search for solutions north of the forty-ninth parallel.

Any project the size of a dam, or several dams, will tend to raise emotions

Orlin "Bill" Hanson, one of the key supporters of the U.S. purchase of flood protection on the Saskatchewan reach of the Souris. Courtesy Minot Daily News

and propel passionate individuals into the public light. This was certainly the case with Orlin "Bill" Hanson. A cowboy-hat-and-boot-wearing rancher, Hanson was raised on land adjacent to the Canadian border. Frequently citing that he attended his first Souris River flood control meeting in the 1950s, he parlayed the issue into a political career in the North Dakota House of Representatives and Senate. Hanson points out with pride that, in 1987, the *Grand Forks Herald* rated him the second most conservative state representative. "I don't believe in new laws and new rules or regulations," he says in a bottom-of-the-barrel voice and an accent that might be mistaken for Texan, "unless it's absolutely necessary to protect the people."[34] I have heard him capture the essence of thirty-five years of continuous effort at acquiring water management on a river system where the extremes are often separated by half a generation. "The world suffers mightily," he says, "from those who don't know what took place beforehand and don't bother to find out or don't give a damn."[35]

In the latter part of the 1970s, residents of the North Dakota portion of the basin began to cast their eyes north to Saskatchewan and the possibility of acquiring flood protection from a structure or structures built in the Souris River headwaters in Canada. The advantage for American interests was that it would be possible to achieve the greatest level of flood protection at the lowest price and without the rancor that would inevitably be attendant on a structure of similar capacity built on American soil. One of the first to recognize that the solution to North Dakota's problems with the Souris lay north of the border was Orlin Hanson.

Residents of the Saskatchewan portion of the Souris basin refused to allow government intransigence to deflect them from their cause. For decades, their calls for water management had fallen on deaf ears in both Regina and Ottawa, but they would not allow that to stop them. For them, the key would be Eric Berntson, member of the Legislative Assembly for the area encompassing the site of the Alameda Dam, future deputy premier of Saskatchewan, and friend and neighbor of Orlin Hanson. As the 1970s came to a close, both hydrologic and political forces were about to coalesce, creating for the first time the right set of circumstances for integrated water management on the Souris River, and the construction of the Rafferty and Alameda dams.

CHAPTER TWO

POLITICIZING A CREEK

At public meetings and hearings related to the Rafferty-Alameda project, I was frequently confronted with the accusation that it was politically motivated. At first I was put off by this, and would attempt to deny it. But my denials fooled no one, and they embarrassed me. After going through the experience a few times, I realized I was not squaring with myself, nor was I being sensitive to the realities of Saskatchewan politics. Eventually I concluded that it was more honest and effective to answer, "Of course the project is political. What did you expect?" At an estimated cost of $120 million in 1985 dollars, and with a $500 million thermal-electric power station hooked up to the end of one of the reservoirs, a political decision was obviously required to proceed. When would an expenditure of this magnitude not involve elected politicians?

On the other hand, many people in Saskatchewan swear to this day that Rafferty-Alameda was predicated entirely on the partisan motivations of the Conservative government. While this is a convenient and, to a certain extent, logical explanation, it is simplistic in the extreme. It ignores the nature of the issue and its historical roots.

Aneurin Bevan, the British Labour Party leader, could have been talking about Saskatchewan when he referred to politics as a "blood sport."[1] For in this province, partisan considerations seem to influence virtually everything. One political scientist has remarked that "it is no exaggeration to say that politics, like wheat, has been a preoccupation of the prairies."[2]

This is a strange phenomenon in some respects, because the Saskatchewan electorate is actually quite conservative, confronting its problems with the pragmatism generally associated with an agrarian economy. But while pragmatic solutions are valued, the debates over the issues are fiercely partisan. Individuals and families are as often labelled by how they vote as by any other criterion.

Among pundits and practitioners alike, the conventional wisdom is that Saskatchewan politics is a contest between the New Democratic Party and the free-enterprise vote. "Saskatchewan has two kinds of political thinkers," one life-long Conservative explains: "those that are left-wing thinkers and those that aren't."[3] The NDP has been the governing party in the province for the majority of the past half-century; it held power from 1944–1964 and 1971–1982, and was returned to power again in the general election of 1991. It is an amalgam of people who call themselves social democrats and other, less ideological, supporters who are simply in favor of good government. Evelyn Eager has noted in *Saskatchewan Government: Politics and Pragmatism* that "the maintenance of at least a basic equilibrium between doctrinaire and moderate has been a consistent factor of CCF-NDP life, and of party-government balance."[4]

It is generally conceded in Saskatchewan politics that the NDP enjoys a fairly solid electoral base of 30 percent of the decided vote. This is not to suggest there is no strong opposition to the NDP; there is, and it generally takes the form of a free enterprise-based vote that has shifted between the Liberals and the Progressive Conservatives. This is evident in the electoral success of the Liberals under Ross Thatcher in the 1960s and that of the Progressive Conservatives in the 1980s.

The strategy for success of the free enterprise parties in Saskatchewan has been to avoid splitting the vote. Often when the Liberals and the PCs have both fielded strong slates, the NDP "runs up the middle" to electoral victory. This was the case in the 1970s when the post-Thatcher Liberals were in a state of decline and the Conservatives were on the rise. Neither party was able to capture a sufficient proportion of the free enterprise vote, and the New Democrats coasted to relatively easy wins in the elections of 1971, 1975, and 1978. This left-right split in Saskatchewan has resulted in bitter election battles. The depths of the division can be seen in the long-time practice of "strategic voting" by Liberal and Conservative supporters, of parking their votes with whatever party seems to have a better chance of defeating the NDP.

It is in this political context that the Rafferty-Alameda project must be examined. Contrary to common perception, the project did not instantly become political when it was announced by Grant Devine in 1986, nor was it even Devine's idea. Its political fate had been sealed almost a decade earlier when the Blakeney government noted that the geographical base of the Conservative Party's increasing strength coincided with the Saskatchewan portion of the Souris River basin. Interestingly, given its ultimate position on the issue, there do not appear to be any documents in the Blakeney government records that question the potential environmental impact of either the Rafferty or the Alameda dams. Rather, the NDP's position was grounded in the increasing popularity of its chief rival.

In 1975 there was significant flood damage in the Souris valley. On September 9 of that year, an organization calling itself the Souris River Flood Prevention Citizens Association called a meeting in Estevan to attempt to deal with the problems created by the flooding. In a briefing note to Premier Blakeney on the outcome of the meeting, the minister of the environment noted that the meeting was attended by 106 members of the public as well as Bob Larter and Eric Berntson, Conservative MLAs representing two of the three provincial constituencies through which the Souris flowed. The note, prepared at Blakeney's request, describes the brief presented by the association:

> Souris River Flood Prevention Citizens Association—presented by Estevan lawyer George Hill. Described by words, slides and song the

flooding problems of the area and criticized the government for lack of remedial action. <u>No copy of this brief was received in advance or since the meeting,</u> though I specifically asked Mr. Hill for a copy before it was presented.[5]

That George Hill was mentioned in the account is not without significance. Hill was prominent in the provincial Conservative Party at the time, and the fact that he had made the presentation would be sufficient to attract the attention of the Blakeney government. Hill maintains there was no political dimension to the issue at that point, that he was acting purely in his capacity as a lawyer on behalf of area interests and as an owner of a business that had been affected by floods on the Souris.[6]

According to the memorandum, no specific mention of the Rafferty Dam was made at the meeting. Area interests were focused more on the removal of obstructions in the river itself, the cessation of organized drainage in the upper reaches of the Souris River basin, and in making the case that the federal-provincial Souris River Basin Study, just undertaken, was "not needed since the valley has been surveyed and studied on many previous occasions."[7] Nevertheless, the memorandum to Blakeney makes it clear that any action from the provincial government would have to await the results of the study three years hence. Given the magnitude of the undertaking, this was not an unreasonable response.

The Souris River Basin Study was completed in 1978, and there is no indication that it was influenced by partisan political considerations. The opposite seems to have been the case; there was a tacit admission that the Rafferty Reservoir had merit or, at a minimum, that it could not be categorically dismissed. This is a far cry from the NDP's later position that the study had totally rejected the project. A summary of its main conclusions noted:

> A general finding of particular local interest was that the proposed Rafferty Reservoir cannot be justified on the basis of flood reduction and foreseeable water demands. That reservoir would, however, be a logical choice if it was decided to build a major reservoir to better utilize existing water supplies and it should be an integral part of any future water importation scheme.[8]

There was acute flooding on the Souris again in the late 1970s, and demands for government action were heard not only from the Estevan area but from the United States and Manitoba as well. In mid-1979, a group calling itself the Souris Basin Action Committee scheduled a meeting in Estevan to discuss the issue of flood control on the Souris and the possibility of building the Rafferty Dam. The list of people invited to the meeting is indicative of how well-organized local interests were, and of the lengths they were willing to go, despite the recalcitrance of the Saskatchewan government. It included the federal secretary of state for external affairs, Flora McDonald; the two local Conservative members of Parliament, Len Gustafson and Alvin Hamilton; the two Conservative members of the Legislative Assembly, Bob Larter from Estevan and Eric Berntson from Souris-Cannington; as well as three provincial cabinet ministers. From North Dakota, the committee had invited the governor and three members of the state senate. From Manitoba, the minister of the environment was also invited.[9]

In addition to federal, provincial, and state politicians, the group had invited representatives from the rural municipal councils along the valley and the leaders of all groups that had concerns about the issue. The increasing internationalization of the water management movement was reflected in the fact that the meeting was co-chaired by Paul Bachorik, an Estevan-area farmer whose land was continually being flooded by the Souris, and a rancher from North Dakota, Orlin "Bill" Hanson.

Government correspondence from this period indicates that ministers in the Blakeney government were keenly aware of the increasing demands for water management on the Souris, and that they were well-briefed on the purpose of the meeting. A memorandum dated June 27, 1979, written by Edgar Kaeding, minister of municipal affairs, noted:

> It is my opinion that it would be unwise for members of Cabinet to be involved in a meeting of this kind. We would not be in a position to stake out a government position; yet, there is no doubt that pressure would be put on us to do so.
>
> You will be aware that the Souris Valley Study Report [sic] recommended strongly against proceeding with the Rafferty Dam flood control project for a number of reasons. We are not likely to quarrel with that recommendation.
>
> Because the Souris is an international waterway, any position or commitment that we could make would be subject to an international agreement and could be misconstrued by U.S. participants and become a matter of international controversy.
>
> I do not believe we should allow Bob Larter to put us in that position for his benefit . . .
>
> I am therefore most reluctant to agree to participate in this meeting. My concerns are shared by Reg Gross and Ted Bowerman [the ministers of tourism and the environment, respectively] who feel as I do that we have nothing to gain by our participation.[10]

The political implications of the meeting were further highlighted a day later when the minister of the environment laid out his concerns in writing to a cabinet colleague:

> It is my opinion that we should avoid official government (Cabinet Ministers) attendance at such a meeting. I would go further to suggest we should rearrange the setting (location and attendance) of same . . .
> . . . Estevan citizens promoted by Mr. Larter have involved North

Dakota politicians and Minot citizens to pressure the Saskatchewan government for the Rafferty dam that was rejected by the Souris Valley Report [*sic*] . . .
. . . The only benefactor appears to be Bob Larter and the PC MLAs in the east and west constituencies.[11]

The meeting scheduled for July 6, 1979, was not held. It is not clear why, but there are indications that the provincial government tried to scuttle it. A letter from Paul Bachorik on behalf of the Souris Basin International Involvement Group to Ted Bowerman, Saskatchewan minister of the environment, requesting his attendance at the meeting, is inscribed with the hand-written notation, "get to boys in Ottawa and turn it off."[12]

The intentions of the government are further confirmed in a September 14 memorandum marked "URGENT" from the executive director of the Intergovernmental Coordination Branch:

> I spoke to Hon. Ted Bowerman, Minister of the Environment, on this matter. He wants the meeting "called off".
> In order to achieve this objective, would you as soon as possible:
> 1. Call Chris Watts, External Affairs . . . [and] tell Chris we want the meeting called off . . . [13]

The memorandum is inscribed with the hand-written notation, "done." Also noteworthy is that the minister of the environment was entangled in the political posturing on the project, despite that in his ministerial capacity he would be involved if the project proceeded. This is important, not only for what it indicates about the partisan dimensions of the project, but it also underscores the highly informal approach given to environmental matters by regulators in the 1970s.

While the province was able to delay the meeting, it couldn't prevent it altogether; on September 27 it went ahead, with approximately 150 people in attendance. A subsequent memorandum to Ted Bowerman, minister of the environment, outlines the province's position at the meeting:

> Mr. [Stan] Blackwell gave Saskatchewan's views. He indicated that the proposal received considerable attention in the Souris River Basin Study and noted that while the reservoir would be effective for flood control or water supply, the cost would greatly exceed the benefits and that it could not be justified without a major industrial demand.
> Considering Saskatchewan's position re: further action Mr. Blackwell noted the Souris is an international stream so the federal government must be involved. He said he was quite sure Saskatchewan is not prepared at this time to promote Rafferty or any other flood control reservoirs on the Souris in Saskatchewan. He suggested that any action in that regard could be most appropriately initiated through the

government of North Dakota. Finally, he said he thought Saskatchewan would probably be prepared to cooperate in any studies into storage possibilities in Saskatchewan provided:

1. the federal governments were involved;
2. there was a clear and formal indication of interest by the North Dakota government;
3. the costs for any further studies were borne by the federal governments; and
4. the studies were under the aegis of the International Joint Commission.[14]

If the provincial government intended to do anything to alleviate water management problems on the Souris River, it did not as a practical matter require another study. It certainly didn't think it needed a study to construct a dam and expand an existing reservoir on the Souris below the city of Weyburn, which at the time was represented by a New Democrat in the provincial legislature. Perhaps the government saw this as a means of placating local interests without doing anything that might politically benefit the Conservative MLAs from the area. This seems to be confirmed in a hand-written memorandum to Grant Mitchell, deputy minister of the environment, from Stan Blackwell, written three months before the September meeting in Estevan:

As requested I discussed this matter at some length with Bob Weese [clerk of the executive council] this p.m. I acquainted him with all the background to the situation that I could . . .
Weese and I also talked about the possibility of some kind of a joint study into water development and flood control in the Souris basin perhaps involving Sask-Man & ND plus two federal governments. Such a study might take place under the aegis of the IJC . . .
Weese concluded his remarks by saying "pray that we don't get into another Poplar R. situation." I concurred, noting the operation related problems with E. Poplar River which is entirely Canadian owned—imagine the situation whereby the Americans had a major say in operation as a result of a substantial financial input to the development of the project![15]

The reference to the Poplar River in the Blackwell memorandum raises an interesting dimension to the position of the Blakeney government on Souris River flood control. In the early 1970s the Saskatchewan Power Corporation (SaskPower) proposed the construction of a coal-fired generating station and dam on the east forks of the Poplar River, which runs adjacent to the international border west of the Souris. Like the Souris, it is an international waterway, and, once again, "creek" would be a more apt description.

In 1973, SaskPower decided to construct the power station immediately north of the forty-ninth parallel, upstream of the state of Montana. In May 1975,

Environment Canada issued an *International Rivers Improvement Act* licence to
SaskPower for the dam. As has been noted, "federal blessing of the project was
given with the knowledge that there could be bilateral problems, but in the be-
lief that none would occur."[16] But downstream jurisdiction, in this case the state
of Montana, expressed serious reservations about the proposal. The entire issue
became more protracted and controversial than anyone had foreseen, and ultimately ended up before the IJC. At issue were the potential environmental effects on Montana from the construction of the dam and the power plant. Not
surprisingly, the issue was marked by a considerable degree of acrimony between Saskatchewan and Montana:

> The Poplar River issues of water apportionment, water quality and air quality
> rank second only to the Garrison Diversion as the most serious bilateral
> environmental disputes on the prairies. These disputes are serious because:
> - there are three separate problems originating from the same power
>   plant, representing all three principal types of transboundary envi-
>   ronmental conflict;
> - there have been two separate references to the IJC;
> - the reaction of the state of Montana has been highly politicized;
> - persistence and stubbornness have characterized Saskatchewan's
>   response.
>
> Poplar is a major prairie environmental issue, and it has left a legacy in
> its wake.[17]

The Blakeney government's position on the Poplar River project was
remarkably similar to the course its successor took on Rafferty-Alameda—
persistence and stubbornness.

During the first days of the Romanow government in 1991 and early
1992—when the NDP was struggling over what to do with a project it had
opposed while in opposition—I was struck by the attitude of the new president
of the agency responsible for constructing Rafferty-Alameda. Jack Messer, himself a former cabinet member in the Blakeney government and anything but a
wild-eyed socialist, was able to bring a rational perspective to the whole issue.
Certain members of the NDP caucus were willing to go to extraordinary lengths
to eviscerate the project once they were in office, but it was Messer's common
sense that prevailed. His position was a pleasant surprise, which only began to
make sense when I learned that, as chairman of the board of SaskPower during
the Poplar River dispute, he had taken just as forthright a position on Poplar
River as had been taken on Rafferty-Alameda:

> The SPC [SaskPower] had informed the commission on a number of
> occasions that the energy needs of Saskatchewan dictated that the util-
> ity move forward with announcement of Unit No. 2. Finally on No-
> vember 22, 1979, Saskatchewan Energy Minister (and SPC board chair-
> man) John Messer wrote that the expansion decision had been post-

poned long enough, SPC could wait no longer, and would proceed with Unit No. 2. Montana was dismayed and turned to the IJC for action.[18]

While the similarities between Poplar River and Rafferty-Alameda are indeed ironical, the reluctance of the NDP administration to get involved in what was potentially another international imbroglio should be recognized. True, partisan considerations were clearly a priority with members of the Blakeney government, but concerns over a possible repetition of Poplar River were also legitimate.

It is also interesting to note how the demands of the locals evolved over the four years they had been pressuring the province to do something about water management on the Souris. At the September 9, 1975, citizens' meeting in Estevan, there was no mention of the Rafferty Dam. At the September 27, 1979 meeting, the principle components of what eventually became the Rafferty-Alameda project were openly proposed. In consultations between officials of the provincial government and the Estevan organizers prior to the meeting, Paul Bachorik's position is detailed:

> Bachorik [co-chair of the meeting] sees Rafferty not simply as a flood control reservoir (he realizes that cannot be justified) but as a multi-purpose reservoir that will serve a number of purposes including another power plant. In this way he is convinced the Project will become very attractive.[19]

This appears to be the first public attention given to the possibility of a thermal-electric power plant in conjunction with the Rafferty-Alameda project. Bachorik's position must be read in conjunction with the conclusion of the Souris River Basin Study that a major industrial use for the water from the Rafferty reservoir was necessary in order to make the structure economically viable.

There is some indication that the Blakeney government's position on the Rafferty Dam might have begun to change during its last days in office. Here, too, partisan politics had their influence. On March 6, 1981, a bipartisan delegation from Saskatchewan travelled to Bismarck, capitol of North Dakota, to meet with state representatives on the issue of water management on the Souris. The delegation from Saskatchewan consisted of three NDP MLAs and Eric Berntson, a Conservative. One of the MLAs on the trip was Jack Chapman of Estevan, who in 1980 had defeated parachute candidate and leader of the Progressive Conservative Party, Grant Devine, in a by-election. By this time local support for the Rafferty Dam had grown to the point that no MLA from Estevan could afford to ignore it. In his own right, Chapman supported the concept of water management on the Souris. In another incarnation, as a SaskPower employee at the Boundary Dam Power Station on Long Creek, he had been responsible for the operation of the dam during floods.

The NDP was cornered in that their MLA was being strongly pressured by his constituents. On the other hand, they were reluctant to do anything in a region where they were not strongly represented and that figured so prominently in the political strategy of the Conservatives. That Chapman had managed to upset a high profile candidate such as Devine placed even greater pressure on him to deliver for his constituents.

Eric Berntson, for his part, had managed to position himself on the issue so that no matter what the NDP did, he couldn't lose. If they went ahead with the project, he would claim it had been at his insistence. If they did as he expected and dragged their heels, he would claim they weren't serious about the issue. Berntson's handiwork can be seen in the outcome of the trip to Bismarck. Statements made by NDP members of the delegation in the North Dakota Senate are not exactly ringing endorsements for the concept of Souris River water management:

> We came down here today at the invitation of Rep. Orlin Hanson and the visit as far as I am concerned has been very worthwhile . . . the problems which exist in the Souris Valley can be resolved if we have proper dialogue rather than get loggerhead [*sic*] so I think the visit today was very worthwhile.

In the House of Representatives, it was much the same:

> We have been here today because of the work of Rep. Orlin Hanson to start a dialogue on a Souris River project. I think it is important that we keep between our two countries that dialogue open so that we better understand each other and keep that understanding strong between us.[20]

The NDP position regarding the overtures from North Dakota is confirmed in a memorandum to Ted Bowerman, minister of the environment:

> The technical staff in Saskatchewan Environment sees no major benefits to Saskatchewan in Rafferty Dam. A joint "study of the studies" or further joint examination would likely up-date the benefits vis-a-vis U.S. residents, especially with reference to Burlington, but would be hard to justify from a purely Saskatchewan perspective unless the intention is to demonstrate on-going interest . . .
>
> I would like to recommend that we send a low-key letter which indicates how the visit was enjoyed and states, gently, that no further moves on Rafferty are contemplated by Saskatchewan . . .
>
> I expect you will wish to talk this over with Mr. Chapman.[21]

While it is not known whether any such letter was sent, the recommendation is a reversal of the position the department took three years earlier, in 1978:

> That reservoir [Rafferty] would, however, be a logical choice if it was decided to build a major reservoir to better utilize existing water supplies . . . [22]

There must be at least two perspectives on an issue to make it political. While much of the responsibility for the politicization of the Rafferty-Alameda project falls to the NDP, the Progressive Conservatives have to shoulder some as well.

Until the 1970s, there wasn't a provincial PC party to speak of. The last Conservative government of Saskatchewan had been elected in 1929 at the height of the Depression and managed to hold onto office for a single term. There had been Conservatives elected to the legislature since then, but they were few in number.

Then came Dick Collver, followed by Grant Devine. But before either of them, there was George Hill, and no history of the modern incarnation of the Progressive Conservative Party in Saskatchewan is complete without documenting his role. He provides a vehicle through which the politics of Rafferty-Alameda can be chronicled.

Born in 1935, George Hill was raised on a farm near Star City in the Melfort-Tisdale area east of Prince Albert. To hear Hill tell it, he knew from birth that he was a Conservative—or, at a minimum, that he wasn't a "socialist," as many in Saskatchewan referred to the CCF government of Tommy Douglas at the time. Likely as a result of his parents' influence—they came to Saskatchewan from conservative Perth County, Ontario, a geographical heritage to which he will admit only with reluctance—Hill became active in partisan politics at an early age. He is mentioned in Peter C. Newman's *Renegade in Power: The Diefenbaker Years* as one of perhaps only two Conservatives in Star City:

> One of [George] Hees' journeys into Saskatchewan won him the dubious distinction of having addressed the smallest public meeting in Canadian history. On a trip through Saskatchewan with Alvin Hamilton, then the Progressive Conservative leader for that province, Hees gave advance copies of his speech to the *Saskatoon Star-Phoenix* marked with dates of delivery. When Hees and Hamilton arrived at Star City, 120 miles northeast of Saskatoon, they were told by Jim Hill the local organizer, that no hall had been hired because no other Conservatives could be found in the district. Hees insisted that he had to make the speech, because the Saskatoon paper might run its report. Hill rounded up his brother George, and the two men sat in the back of Hamilton's car while Hees loudly intoned his address to them.[23]

Hill's commitment to partisan politics continued at the University of Saskatchewan, where he and close friend Bill Lawton (now Mr. Justice William Lawton of the Saskatchewan Court of Queen's Bench) were active in campus politics, although, as Hill admits, "there weren't too many people in PC ranks at the university."[24] The fact was, there weren't many provincial Conservatives anywhere in Saskatchewan in the 1950s.

After he graduated from law school in the mid-1950s, Hill went to Estevan to practice, mostly because he had spent time there as an organizer during the

1956 provincial election. He proceeded over the next twenty years to build what was reputed to be the largest law practice in the province outside Regina and Saskatoon. He also became involved in a number of businesses in the area, one of which was a nursery located in the Souris River valley below the city of Estevan. Throughout this period Hill maintained his loyalty to the Conservatives, at both the provincial and federal levels, and he relied on his legion of friendships in developing the party within the Estevan constituency. It was through his political activity in Estevan that Hill and Eric Berntson became friends. It was Berntson who convinced Hill to run for the presidency of the party. They both understood that if the Conservatives were to gain office, the Liberal vote would have to be minimized. Accordingly, he and Berntson devoted much of their time to attracting the best possible candidates across the province. It was during Hill's tenure as president of the provincial party that the first electoral breakthrough was made:

> The surprise of the 1975 election was the resurrection of the provincial Conservative party. The Conservatives captured seven seats, their best showing since 1929, and received nearly 28 percent of the popular vote, only 4 percent less than that received by the Liberals. After the election, the Conservative resurgence continued, spearheaded by leader Dick Collver. By 1978, by-election wins and Liberal defections, including that of the son of the late Ross Thatcher, had given the Conservatives 11 seats, the same number held by the Liberals.[25]

In politics, events are driven as much by chance and circumstance as they are by design and forethought. So it was that George Hill met a young agricultural economics professor named Grant Devine at one of the party's annual meetings. As a result of this encounter, Devine joined the Conservative Party and ran, albeit unsuccessfully, in a Saskatoon constituency in the 1978 election.

As events in the latter part of the 1970s unfolded, a significant number of Conservatives in Saskatchewan were becoming dissatisfied with their leader. Dick Collver's continued inability to take advantage of the weaknesses of the Blakeney government, and his failure to live up to his guarantee that the Conservatives would win the 1978 election, sealed his fate. Discontent within Conservative ranks was of sufficient magnitude that Eric Berntson was being pressured to run for the leadership. Berntson had spent much of his time since being elected trying to find suitable candidates, but he had no aspirations to run for the leadership himself. Within the Tory caucus, however, Berntson saw no one, himself included, who could lead the party to electoral victory against the NDP and Allan Blakeney.

With a good mind for political strategy, Berntson recognized in Grant Devine a number of attributes essential to keeping the free enterprise coalition together. Devine was young; with four university degrees, he was well-educated; he was Saskatchewan-born, and he was, by marriage, Catholic. This latter factor should not be underestimated; it was part of the Conservative strategy to make inroads into the Liberals' base of support. As Evelyn Eager has noted, the Liberals in Saskatchewan have had a higher proportion of Roman Catholics in legislative membership than any other party.[26]

These characteristics were attractive to the liberal, urban middle-class whose support Berntson accurately identified as necessary for the Tories to get elected. The result was that Dick Collver was essentially forced out of office by the party, and Grant Devine won the ensuing leadership contest on November 10, 1979, on the first ballot. Interestingly, George Hill did not support Devine's bid for the leadership.

Devine was now confronted with the problem of where to run as a candidate. He was originally from the Moose Jaw area, but the Devine family farm was in a constituency that was held for the Conservatives at the time by Colin Thatcher. Devine was taunted and dared by the NDP to run in two constituencies he had little hope of winning: North Battleford and Melfort-Tisdale. Eventually, the Tories were forced to open up one of their own seats; Berntson and Hill prevailed upon the sitting member for Estevan, Bob Larter, to resign for health reasons. Devine became a parachute candidate in what the Tories considered one of their safest seats. They ended up losing the 1980 by-election, however, principally because Devine brought in a number of outside advisors who managed to alienate the rank and file of the party within the constituency. Hill, who was on vacation until the middle of the campaign, later commented, "I knew within five minutes of walking down the main drag of Estevan after I got home, that Devine had lost the by-election to Chapman."[27]

The by-election defeat of Devine is an example of a phenomenon that would occur again—his advisors getting him into political trouble. As will be apparent in the Rafferty-Alameda example, neither Berntson nor Hill were comfortable with the political advisors immediately surrounding Devine. The resulting schism would have major consequences for the dams and the government.

It was during this period that George Hill personally experienced the effects of flooding on the Souris River. In the mid-1970s, he and Estevan businessman Darwin Sawyer had purchased Prairie Nursery, which supplied tree stock to the western Canadian market. Neither had any experience in the operation of a commercial tree nursery, and their timing could not have been worse.

In 1975 and 1976 the Souris overflowed in some of the worst flooding the valley had experienced in this century. Hill and Sawyer had no sooner purchased the nursery than they suffered significant losses as their crop was destroyed two years in a row by the flooding Souris. Hill perceived an opportunity in his adversity, and it was then that he agreed to represent a local group—the Souris River Flood Prevention Citizens Association—that was attempting to pressure the provincial government into action to solve the water management problems on the Souris.

The landslide victory of the Progressive Conservatives in the provincial general election of 1982 provided an essential part of the equation that permitted Rafferty-Alameda to proceed. Philosophically, the project fit into the partisan political agenda of the government, and into its policy agenda as well. In political terms, the Devine government relied heavily on the rural vote. As Devine's mandate progressed, the number of Conservative members representing urban constituencies decreased significantly. This rural-urban split exacerbated an already polarized political situation in the province. The electoral reality was that the government's support disproportionately came from rural areas. From this political imperative flowed the policy agenda of the Conservatives in office.

Also, being a parachute candidate—he won his seat in 1982 in Estevan—Devine was particularly sensitive to the "needs" of his own constituency. Throughout his tenure as premier, road construction, a new airport, a new hospital, a $500 million thermal-electric generating station, and a major water project were all delivered to the Estevan constituency—and at a time when the provincial government was racking up record deficits.

Much of the rhetoric surrounding the Rafferty-Alameda project would lead one to believe that Berntson, Devine, and Hill had created the need for it, which was clearly not the case. Given that the Rafferty Dam was first proposed as early as 1932, and the Alameda in 1907, it is safe to say that none of these individuals was behind the concept. They all acknowledge that the project was given a political spin it might not have had initially if the dams had been situated elsewhere in the province, or if the constituencies had been represented by Liberal or NDP MLAs. In the context of Saskatchewan politics, the location of the Rafferty and Alameda dams was more than sufficient to guarantee that the project would be attacked on partisan grounds. The written records from the NDP years in the 1970s cited above underscore this. On the other hand, had Devine, Berntson, and Hill not been so intimately involved in the project, and had they not had such a large personal stake in its development, it is doubtful whether it would have been started in the first place, let alone completed. With the two main parties so clearly aligned on the issue, the politicization of the Rafferty-Alameda project was assured.

CHAPTER THREE

UNDERCURRENTS

While the positions of the two major political parties in Saskatchewan on the Rafferty-Alameda issue had been determined in the 1970s, other factors also contributed to the controversy. Even before the project was announced, significant substantive and procedural problems related to the dams had developed within the Saskatchewan government. Without question, during 1985 and 1986, many people working on the venture simply didn't understand it. We didn't understand the technical, jurisdictional, or regulatory complexity of what we were involved in. The uneasy relationship that always existed between the Devine government and the Saskatchewan civil service also had a major impact on how the project evolved. Some of these problems could not have been avoided. Most of them could.

By the spring of 1986 I was working on the project full-time, and it began to dawn on me that the whole thing was considerably more complicated than anyone had realized at the outset. Remembering that first meeting in the basement of the Minot airport, I was struck by the fact that the Saskatchewan engineers had acted as if the Rafferty and Alameda dams were a *fait accompli,* although it was obvious six months after this North Dakota session that fundamental questions remained unanswered. It was also abundantly clear that all parties were under intense political pressure to reach an agreement. Frequent references were made to Senator Burdick, the senior senator from North Dakota, for whom the issue of Minot flood protection was a priority, and Governor George Sinner, who was also committed to finding a solution to Minot's flooding problems. And from my perspective, there was no question of where the Rafferty Dam stood on Grant Devine's agenda, nor the Alameda Dam on Eric Berntson's.

In the early 1980s, SaskPower had begun to consider various options for the next source of power for the province after the Nipawin hydroelectric dam and generating station, then under construction, had been completed. In a report released in August 1985, the corporation concluded that it should "select Shand [near Estevan] as the site of Saskatchewan's next major electric power development and take the necessary steps required for a 1991 target in-service date of the first unit of the Shand thermal generating station."[1] The Shand site was desirable for several reasons: it would not require scrubbers, it would have greater diversity in terms of its sources of cooling water, and coal prices would likely be lower there than at other available options. Not coincidentally, it would also be the major industrial use identified in the Souris River Basin Study as necessary for the Rafferty Dam to be economically viable.

From the government's point of view, SaskPower was the only agency it could rely on to develop the Rafferty-Alameda project. It was the only provincial entity that had ever been involved in the construction of dams, and the only one with the resources to attempt a project of this scale. But SaskPower was a single-purpose utility; as such, it was driven by concerns related to the construction of the generating station and meeting its forecast in-service date of 1991. It therefore had an understandable desire to focus its efforts on the Rafferty Dam, which would create the impoundment that would provide the cooling water for the Shand Generating Station. But interest from American agencies in acquiring hundred-year flood protection for the city of Minot was not formally addressed until after the planning for the Rafferty Dam was well under way, and Rafferty alone would not afford this level of flood protection; the only Saskatchewan-based method of acquiring comprehensive water management in the Saskatchewan portion of the Souris and providing hundred-year flood protection to the United States was to construct the Alameda Dam.[2]

The effect of all these variables was that SaskPower found itself "telescoping" everything—completing pre-feasibility and feasibility analyses at the same time it was undertaking the baseline studies required for an environmental assessment of the project. Concurrently, it was also leading the negotiations with the United States to determine if that country would participate. All this activity, occurring at the same time, ignored the simple reality that, unless it was known whether the United States would contribute to the project, it would not be possible to determine how the Souris River system would operate. Without an answer to this fundamental question, it was impossible to answer other fundamental questions, such as where the dams should be located, how high they should be, what their environmental effects would be, or if the Alameda Dam would even be built.

The situation was, in part, a result of the developer's traditional approach to large projects. Organizations such as SaskPower frequently have exhibited biases in favor of large project development, and they have a natural tendency to allow that desire to overwhelm the need for careful planning. (The Poplar River project, discussed in the previous chapter, is a case in point.)[3] This is an inherent tendency in most major project developers, and the Canadian landscape is strewn with examples, from the James Bay II hydroelectric development to the Oldman River Dam in southern Alberta. The more complex the project, the more red tape it will encounter, the greater the potential for opposition, and the greater the pressure on those responsible to expedite matters.[4]

Despite the irreconcilability of the situation, work on the Rafferty-Alameda environmental impact statement (EIS) continued throughout 1985 and early 1986. The consultant preparing the EIS was severely constrained by the number of unresolved issues associated with the project, issues that made it impossible to conduct credible water quality or quantity studies, let alone determine the impact on wildlife, fisheries, and archeological resources. Given sufficient time, many of these difficulties could have been resolved. Unfortunately, time was short and getting shorter as Rafferty-Alameda became an issue in the run-up to the next provincial election.[5]

In a memorandum dated late 1985, I wrote:

> While it may be possible for the premier to initial an agreement-in-principle on the Rafferty project, the signed document would have no legal status. Moreover, the technical aspects of the process are not far enough along to allow their inclusion in an agreement at this time. Announcing the project at this time *without* this information leaves the government vulnerable to questions from the press regarding issues such as expropriation, oil mitigation and impact on pasture lands in the area for which we do not have answers at the present time.[6]

Within a month of that memorandum, the probability of the government going ahead with the project had become one of the most poorly kept secrets in the province. A litany of leaks from the Premier's Office placed the project irrevocably in the vice of partisan politics. The government's tenuous position was obvious to at least one member of the Saskatchewan media. Ron Petrie of the *Regina Leader-Post* commented:

> He [Devine] will most certainly want to go into that election with a firm commitment from the Americans on financing for the dams, and he will want to be able to extol the benefits to all of Saskatchewan from the construction of the dams and power plant. He most certainly will not want to go into the election with the whole thing still hanging fire.[7]

The high political risks Devine was taking were also apparent to those close to him. His advisors on the issue were uncertain about the project and were reluctant to become personally involved in it. In hindsight, this should have come as no surprise, given all the problems that plagued the Executive Council. In the nine years Devine was in office, there were five deputy ministers to the premier. The continuous turnover in this most critical of positions made any continuity or administrative stability within the government impossible. The Devine Executive Council was rife with internecine political battles, and the absence of any widely agreed-upon set of rules on how the government should function in an administrative sense only exacerbated matters. Over the course of my own tenure in the Executive Council, 1984–85, I observed the functions of government taking on a kind of hideous logic: the closer one came to the locus of power, the higher the political stakes, the more time wasted on procedural matters, the more insidious the political games.

Soon enough, it became obvious that "hanging fire" was exactly where the project stood. No agreement had been signed or initialled between the parties. There was nothing on paper to indicate that a deal had been reached. All that was certain on the international negotiations at the beginning of 1986 was that hundred-year flood protection from the Saskatchewan dams was possible and that if the American federal government was to participate, the financial contribution would be in the order of $41 million (U.S.).

The political fate of the project was sealed on February 12, 1986, when, before a hand-picked audience of over 150 in Estevan—including United States Senator Quentin Burdick, North Dakota Governor George Sinner, as well as Len Gustafson, MP for Souris-Moose Mountain and parliamentary secretary to the prime minister—and with province-wide media coverage befitting the preelection hype, Devine announced that, subject to environmental approval and the participation of American interests, the government of Saskatchewan would be constructing the Rafferty and Alameda dams and the Shand Generating Station. At the same time he announced that an Estevan-based special purpose crown corporation, the Souris Basin Development Authority (SBDA), would be established to coordinate the project, and that George Hill had agreed to become its president.

There were both political and policy motivations behind the establishment of the SBDA and the appointment of Hill. Since the earliest days of Rafferty-Alameda, the major aspects of its development had been carried out by SaskPower. As the province's electrical utility, SaskPower was accountable to the Public Utilities Review Commission (PURC), which had a mandate to review virtually all the operations of the crown corporations that fell under its purview. This it did on a regular basis, in disturbing detail for those operating SaskPower.

SaskPower was of the view that it would eventually be called to task by PURC for its participation in a project that had the generation of electricity as only one of its objectives. The Souris Basin Development Authority, as originally conceived, was intended to act as an arm of SaskPower that would allow it to control the project yet at the same time avoid the regulatory strictures imposed by PURC.

The selection of George Hill as president proved to be an essential marriage of political weight and administrative capability. In policy terms, the decision made sense, given that Hill had served as vice-chair and then chair of the Board of Directors of SaskPower from 1982 until his appointment by the federal government to the Court of Queen's Bench in 1984. In 1985, Hill resigned from the bench, citing boredom as the reason. The Hill appointment as president of the SBDA ensured that there would be strong political control over the project. From the outset, both Devine and Berntson were aware that it would be attacked on political grounds, and that it would be necessary for the government to defend itself. George Hill would be able to do this, as well as provide the project with a degree of protection from political interference from contrary influences in the Devine government. Hill was arguably the only individual in the government at either a political or a bureaucratic level with the weight to tell almost any member of the Cabinet to keep his or her hands off the project. This would prove to be critical.

In May 1986 I accepted an offer from George Hill to work full-time for the Souris Basin Development Authority, initially as the director of planning and operations and then as its vice-president. Hill's decision to hire me was one he would be forced to defend to many people, including Eric Berntson who, given my previous position in the Executive Council, coupled with the fact that I was hired during the Blakeney administration, feared I was a plant either for Devine's advisors or for the NDP. This speaks volumes about the factional infighting within the Devine government. Neither Hill nor I—"The Two Georges," as we were often referred to—were engineers. Neither of us knew much about dams, nor had we been previously involved in any environmental assessment. Strangely enough, given what was to follow, all these things would prove to be assets.

As originally conceived, the SBDA was to function as a special-purpose crown corporation with only three or four permanent staff. It would enter into contractual arrangements with SaskPower and SaskWater, permitting the former to work on the project without incurring the wrath of PURC, and the latter, as the ultimate owner of the facilities, to control the flow of funds to the SBDA, participate in international negotiations, and manage the hydrology-related aspects of the environmental impact statement. The intent was for the SBDA to second personnel and resources from existing agencies in order to build the dams, and then dissolve itself after construction was complete. It made sense in the abstract because it anticipated utilizing existing expertise within the government. Personnel from the Department of Energy and Mines, for example, would assist the Authority in carrying out mitigation activities related to oil field facilities affected by the project. SaskPower

"The Two Georges," or as George Hill liked to remark, "He's George the Hood and I'm George the Good." Courtesy Camera One, Regina, Sask.

would continue to occupy a central role, working on a fee-for-service contract to the Authority. Involving half a dozen government agencies, the concept was not only administratively efficient, but it would also allow the offloading of costs for the project onto other departments.[8]

Bureaucratically, however, it was naive in the extreme. Line agencies of the Saskatchewan government were vigorously opposed to devoting resources to a new initiative in which they had no stake. Even departments that were willing to cooperate were unwilling to devote their best people to the project. As early as April 1986, it was apparent that the SBDA would not work.[9] It was also a harbinger of things to come, as it was apparent that officials in many of the line agencies who were being asked to participate were not favorably disposed toward Rafferty-Alameda, as they perceived that it would draw scarce resources from their departments.

Because of the government's decision to announce Rafferty-Alameda in such an obviously political manner, work on the project had to proceed with even greater haste. The first major task in the summer of 1986 was to ensure that SaskPower complete the Environmental Impact Statement and submit it to Saskatchewan Environment and Public Safety (SEPS). But Rafferty-Alameda created two major problems for SEPS, one that is endemic to governments in general and one that was unique to this project. First, the agency reviewing Rafferty-Alameda was an agency of the very government proposing to build the project. Although an independent board of inquiry would be appointed in 1987–88 to review the proposal, the board itself had a mandate only to make recommendations, and the ultimate authority on whether the project was to proceed was vested in the provincial minister of environment and public safety. Understandably, accusations were made about a potential conflict of interest. The situation was exacerbated by the fact that the minister of environment and public safety at the time the Rafferty-Alameda EIS was under review was also the minister responsible for the Saskatchewan Water Corporation. SaskWater was actively involved in the development of the project and would ultimately assume its ownership. This gave the critics not only another argument against the environmental assessment process, but against the project as well.

A second problem for SEPS was that, as part of its process of reviewing environmental impact statements, the department had relied on the expertise of the line departments of the government of Saskatchewan. Under this procedure, a proponent would submit an environmental impact statement to SEPS that would be completed in accordance with a set of general guidelines SEPS had prepared to assist developers, as well as a set of project-specific guidelines. Once an EIS had been submitted, it would be reviewed internally by the staff of the Coordination and Assessment Branch, then forwarded to the relevant agencies within the government for comment. (For example, the portion of the EIS dealing with the impact on oil field facilities would be forwarded by SEPS to the Saskatchewan Department of Energy and Mines; the portion dealing with wildlife to the Wildlife Branch of the Department of Parks and Renewable Resources, and so on, for their comments.)

The SEPS staff would assemble these comments, which would then form the basis of the department's technical response to the EIS. With a skeleton staff of less than twelve at the time of the Shand-Rafferty-Alameda EIS, SEPS had neither the resources nor the expertise to evaluate the proposal adequately on its own. As if that weren't bad enough, a leaked memorandum from SaskPower acknowledged that the agencies helping to prepare the EIS for the Souris Basin Development Authority were the same agencies that would be evaluating it. This was factually correct since Energy and Mines had assisted the SBDA in the preparation of the EIS, and was also being asked to comment upon the EIS as part of the assessment process. In essence these agencies were being asked to participate as both developers *and* regulators; clearly an unacceptable situation. Without question, the way the Rafferty-Alameda project was handled stretched the credibility of the whole environmental assessment process in Saskatchewan— a process that was devised by the Blakeney government, although this was never raised by the public nor the NDP during the ensuing controversy.

In light of the fundamental uncertainties surrounding the project in the first half of 1986, it came as no surprise when the response from SEPS to the combined Shand-Rafferty-Alameda Environmental Impact Statement was less than favorable. On August 8, 1986, officials of the Authority and SaskPower met with SEPS officials to discuss the statement that had been filed. This became known to those of us working on the project at the time as "The Woodshed Meeting." Some of the more critical comments from SEPS included:

• lacks basic information relative to the assessment of Alameda;
• fails to identify and evaluate the cost-effectiveness of specific mitigative measures;
• fails to provide cost-benefit analyses of proposed development;
• fails to present operational plans or scenarios which are critical to impact assessment;
• lacks substantiation for many statements made and conclusions drawn;
• presents biased arguments, largely through omission.[10]

We were told in no uncertain terms that, if the EIS we had filed was the basis on which the project was to be evaluated, we might as well forget it. The dams would never be approved. It took three hours for the SEPS officials just to list the deficiencies of the statement.[11]

After the Woodshed Meeting, Hill and I took stock: we were sitting on the premier's pet project; we had just got started and we found there was significant opposition within the civil service, and its cooperation could not be counted on; the EIS apparently wasn't worth the paper it was written on; negotiations with the Americans were far from finalized; a provincial election was looming on the horizon; and, almost certainly, the project would be shelved if the NDP were elected. I recall sitting in the meagre surroundings of our one-room office in the SaskPower building in Regina (we called it "The Dam Room") trying to figure how we were going to get ourselves out of the mess. "Hood," Hill said in his nasally drawl, "the only thing we can do is plough a straight furrow. We'll worry about the things that we can control and hope for the best, because we can't do anything about the stuff outside our control. Do as much as you can as fast as you can. Hell, the way things are going right now, Devine will likely lose the election and you and I will be out of a job."[12]

The first substantive issue dealt with was the lack of cooperation we were getting from other agencies in the provincial government. This had implications that went far beyond the Rafferty-Alameda project or, indeed, the government of Saskatchewan. Bureaucracies have their own interests apart from those of their political masters and the governments they serve. When there is a divergence between the interests of a government and its bureaucracy, it can result in intransigence, if not outright opposition.

A good example of this was the reaction of the civil service to the Fair Share Saskatchewan Program proposed in the last days of the Devine government. The plan was to decentralize many government agencies to small centers around the province as a means of stimulating the economy of rural Saskatchewan. That the government derived virtually all its seats from the communities that would benefit from this proposal was, of course, not coincidental. Enormously costly, poorly prepared, and blatantly transparent, Fair Share Saskatchewan immediately aroused the fury of the civil servants who would be forced to move. This became obvious on June 13, 1991, when 1,500 government employees forsook their bureaucratic anonymity and demonstrated on the steps of the Legislative Assembly.[13]

To a lesser extent, the same type of intransigence met Rafferty-Alameda. The Souris River project did not emanate from the civil service, nor was it ever formally vetted through the conventional bureaucratic processes, such as they were, before it was announced. No government agency wants to see itself by-passed on an issue within its jurisdiction, yet a number of them were by-passed on Rafferty-Alameda. The Department of Finance, arguably the most powerful central agency of the Saskatchewan government, was not fully included in the analysis of the project. Ironically, neither was the Policy Secretariat of the premier's own department, the Executive Council. Both these agencies have traditionally occupied major policy-making roles in the Saskatchewan government, and throughout Devine's tenure they fought continually for the preeminent role in policy review. While some structural conflict among central agencies is inevitable, and, within limits, healthy, in this case it bordered on outright hostility. This battle reflected the perception held by parts of the Devine government that the Department of Finance was political in a partisan sense, a suspicion resulting from the key role Finance played in the Blakeney government.

The Policy Secretariat was formed from the remnants of the old Planning Bureau of the Blakeney government, and acted as a countervailing force for the Department of Finance. But with the constant turnover in the senior administration of the Executive Council, it was impossible to attract the quality of personnel into the Policy Secretariat that would allow it to act as such. Given the absence of any clear administrative procedures and the perpetual in-fighting, it was inevitable that tension existed between these two central agencies as they fought for control of the government's policy imperative. In such a situation, it is probable that many issues did not receive detailed consideration by either agency. Certainly this was the case with Rafferty-Alameda.

The following incident illustrates how far and high this lack of cooperation went. In June 1989 I received a heated phone call from the deputy minister to the premier prompted by our publication of a brochure entitled "Rafferty-Alameda: An Informed Perspective." Keeping in mind that the project had been announced over three years earlier and that the Rafferty Dam was situated in Grant Devine's own riding, I found myself answering the most basic questions about the project from the most senior public servant in the government, and he was decidedly unsympathetic. I responded to his call with a letter:

> I am writing in response to our conversation of earlier today regarding the brochure that has been prepared by the Souris Basin Development Authority entitled "Rafferty-Alameda: An Informed Perspective" . . .
>
> To deal specifically with the concerns you raised in our discussion, I offer the following comments. With respect to your question of why we are building the dam, the answer is, "to store water." You cannot cool a thermal electric power plant with water from a river such as the Souris without trapping it. To impound water you must build a dam, hence Rafferty . . .
>
> One final comment regarding your cryptic remark dealing with the situation this Project is currently in. In virtually every conversation you and I have had over the last six months on Rafferty-Alameda, you have deemed it appropriate to take verbal potshots at either George Hill, me or both. If you have problems about the personnel in charge of Rafferty-Alameda, I suggest it would be more appropriate to raise the issue with my Minister. These comments place me in an awkward position and cannot, in any way that I can think of, be construed as being in the best interests of the Project.[14]

It was clear that if this was the type of cooperation we were getting from the premier's own staff, there was little doubt there would be opposition from the rank and file of the civil service.

Another reason for the tension between the Devine government and its bureaucracy relates to the overall relationship between the two. When the Conservatives were elected, two factors combined to create problems between the government and the bureaucracy. Few of the members elected in 1982 had had any experience running a provincial government. Several had been members of the Opposition, but there was a dearth of government experience among the newly elected Tory caucus, and it showed. As Eric Berntson once said to me, with a tidal wave, you get drift wood.

After three consecutive mandates, the NDP had succeeded in placing its own partisan stamp on the government. Upon comparing the Blakeney government to the previous administration of Ross Thatcher, one columnist noted:

> The NDP presence ran much deeper through the civil service, a situation that evolved over the eleven years the Blakeney Government was in power. By the end, it reached a point where individuals with direct political links to the party in power were slotted into middle management positions throughout the civil service and crown corporations.[15]

Other observers have noted that "the Blakeney Government had made a large number (some twelve hundred) of order in council appointments during its years in office, largely, though not entirely, at the senior and middle ranks of the hierarchy."[16]

The problem this practice created was that it made it difficult, and in some instances impossible, to differentiate between people who had been hired by Order-in-Council for administrative convenience and people who had been appointed for political purposes. The mere perception among Tory supporters that the civil service was politicized was sufficient to put pressure on the Devine government to make changes. There was a strong desire to "root out the reds," as the process was referred to among zealous Tories who incorrectly perceived that the entire civil service was made up of NDP patronage appointments.

For at least a year after the election of the Devine government, the Saskatchewan civil service experienced what seemed like an ever-cresting tide of dismissals following the weekly Cabinet meeting where such decisions were made. That it was occurring was bad enough, but in a number of cases, the people fingered were not political and were "victims of rumor and guilt by association."[17] It was the arbitrary nature of the firings, more than anything, that created hostility among the civil service toward the Conservatives. Many professional public servants would not have minded a "depoliticization" of the government, but the perception that partisan NDP supporters survived while career civil servants were being dismissed fuelled the paranoia and hostility throughout the whole system, and the only place they could lay the blame was at the feet of the Devine government. Journalist Dale Eisler has written:

> No one seemed secure as the Tories tried to root out anyone in government who was in any way tied to the NDP. The extent of the purge was so great, and the subsequent politicization of government ranks by Tory partisans so pervasive, that the civil service was deeply traumatized.
>
> What happened was that almost immediately the Devine government became alienated from its public service. The relationship was so poisoned it eventually weakened the administration to the point the relationship became part of the Tories' downfall.[18]

The hostility of the civil service toward the government spread naturally to what was widely perceived as the government's pet project, or at least the pet project of the two most powerful and senior members of the government. After the Woodshed Meeting, as we attempted to salvage what we could from the first EIS, we discovered that we had not been provided with critical information that would have assisted in the preparation of the document. We repeatedly ran up against intransigence, if not outright opposition, from within the ranks of the public service. Leaks and the withholding of information were common.

While opposition from within the government was significant, it was a minor irritation compared to the damage done by two government employees who were associated in different ways with the development of the project. In the latter part of 1986, as we were attempting to repair the EIS, we began to sense that there were leaks. Technical information that had not been released to the public was somehow finding its way into the public domain, and it was being used by those opposed to the dams.

Opposition to the Rafferty-Alameda project had until this point not been significant—certainly not disproportional for a development of this size and complexity. Then, during the summer and fall of 1986, a few individuals within the impact area of the Rafferty Reservoir began to cite anonymous "environmental engineers with the government" who had told them the Rafferty-Alameda project would not work. This was obviously of concern to us, and we set about trying to find out what was going on. We soon discovered that two government employees had taken it upon themselves to travel to the valley prior to the October 1986 general election and speak in less-than-glowing terms about the project. This was not a matter of a government employee "blowing the whistle" on the government. The environmental assessment process had hardly begun, and while there obviously had been some problems on the project, few of them could have led to the conclusion that Rafferty-Alameda was environmentally unsound. Yet this was the "spin" that was being placed on it by these two employees.

It is difficult to describe the damage this did. On the public relations side, opposition to the project began to increase—although, interestingly, it didn't really grow in the impact area. Rather, it was outside interests that began to get involved.[19] More important, perhaps, is that we didn't know who we could trust any more. Nothing about the situation was certain. The project had been announced, but we didn't know how many dams were going to be built. We didn't know where they would be situated. We had no idea what the operating rules for the river would be because there was no assurance that the U.S. government was going to participate. Our Environmental Impact Statement was seriously flawed. A significant portion of the Saskatchewan bureaucracy was overtly hostile. There had been a major breach of security, and it was more than likely that all these problems were now known to interests opposed to the project. "If something is not in control," someone remarked at the time, "then, by definition, it is out of control, and this thing is definitely out of control."

The question was, how do we get ourselves out of this situation and bring it under control? The first thing we did was try to repair the EIS. We decided first to separate the much more technically complex Shand Generating Station portion from the part dealing with the Rafferty and Alameda dams. This would give SaskPower the chance to develop the Shand facility, using ground water as a coolant, if we were unable to turn Rafferty-Alameda around.

In our discussions with SEPS officials, it was obvious that not only was the EIS in a state of disarray, but so was the review process. For the first EIS, there had been no project-specific guidelines as required under the *Saskatchewan Environmental Assessment Act*. For reasons unknown, someone from the Premier's Office, perhaps in the name of "helping things along," had ordered that a set of specific guidelines not be prepared. But without a set of questions, as a matter of logic, it is impossible to give any answers. The intent of project-specific guidelines is to ensure that project-specific concerns are addressed. This interference had the effect of undermining the assessment process even further, and is an excellent example of why the process and those administering it must be protected from political interference. It is also an example of what happened all too frequently in the Premier's Office, when people working there, with disturbing frequency and often disastrous results, would invoke the name of the premier in order to get something done.

A set of specific guidelines was drafted by SEPS and eventually finalized. While this helped rectify the procedural problems, there were still substantive deficiencies to be overcome. More than anything else, what we needed was time: time to revamp the EIS, time to get a new team in place to prepare the document, time to reach at least a tentative agreement with the Americans.

Frequently, through adversity one discovers opportunity. That was certainly the case in late 1986 and early 1987, when negotiations with the American interests were not going well. Discussions had bogged down over the issue of evaporation losses from the Rafferty and Alameda reservoirs and whether these were to be considered part of the Saskatchewan or the North Dakota apportionments. We needed time to get a new EIS ready, and these negotiations gave us the opportunity. In January 1987, I wrote to the director of the Coordination and Assessment Branch of SEPS:

> As you are aware, the Souris Basin Development Authority is in the process of completing the Environmental Impact Statement for the Rafferty Dam Project. This report is being completed by the Authority as per the Guidelines issued by the Department of the Environment. It has been brought to my attention that various sections of the Environmental Impact Statement which has been prepared in draft form [the first EIS] are currently in circulation in government departments.
>
> In the interests of ensuring that the project is not pre-judged and in an attempt to provide you and your officials with an adequate response if questioned as to the contents of these drafts, I am hereby informing you that the Souris Basin Development Authority withdrew these aforementioned drafts as a result of on-going negotia-

tions with various American interests, the outcome of which would demonstrably influence the content of the Statement. To this end, any draft copies should be disregarded pending the conclusion of these negotiations and the formal submission of the Statement.[20]

Given the procedural difficulties we had encountered within the bureaucracy and the substantive deficiencies of the EIS as enumerated by SEPS, we now had little alternative but to start over with a new team on the preparation of a new EIS. Unable to rely on government departments for help, Hill and I decided to insulate ourselves as much as we could from the government and the recalcitrant bureaucracy. We consulted widely about the best private sector consultants to help us complete the studies necessary to comply with the project-specific guidelines. Ignorance, in this case, was truly bliss. That neither Hill nor I had any experience in this field meant we were later able to state unequivocally that the independent consultants we used had written the terms of reference for the various studies that comprised the EIS, and were given a free hand to complete the work as they saw fit. Throughout the Byzantine course of events that would follow, opponents of Rafferty-Alameda would make the accusation that the studies were rigged, that we had somehow fixed the results. With complete confidence we would offer to produce the consultants and their terms of reference to prove such claims were groundless. As for the consultants themselves, the mounting controversy did not dissuade them from being involved and, in the latter part of 1986 and the first half of 1987, work on a new EIS continued at fever pitch.

Prior to the filing of the new EIS in the summer of 1987, we consulted with the government to make sure it still wanted to go ahead with the project. It was obvious by this time that there was going to be organized opposition from interests outside the impact area. This was further confirmed when we learned of a joint meeting of the Canadian Wildlife Federation and the (U.S.-based) National Wildlife Federation on March 19, 1987, in Quebec City. At this meeting the two bodies passed a resolution containing information that almost certainly came from the first EIS, which had never been made public. The tone of the resolution was critical, even though the new EIS had not yet been released. It was at this point that Hill and I began to realize what we were really up against, and we needed to know if the government wanted to see it through. This was the last chance, at least politically, to turn back.

They told us to proceed.[21]

After a sixteen-week blitz in the summer of 1987 to get the Environmental Impact Statement completed, the document was filed with SEPS. The project proposed in the eighteen-volume, 1700-page document bore little resemblance to the one described a year earlier in the first EIS. Among ourselves, though, we acknowledged that there were gaps, particularly on the Alameda portion. The site of the Alameda Dam, for example, had still not been finalized. Where there were gaps, we committed the SBDA to fill them, and we started the studies before being told to do so by SEPS. If nothing else, we hoped it would be an indication of our good faith.

The project involved the construction of four main structures—the Rafferty and Alameda dams and two channels—and a broad array of development and mitigative components. The Rafferty Dam, we determined, should be situated six kilometers upstream from the city of Estevan on the Souris River. A twenty-meter-high earth-fill embankment, approximately one kilometer in length and with a fill volume in excess of two million cubic meters, the Rafferty Dam at full supply level would create a reservoir fifty-seven kilometers long. Downstream of the dam site, the river channel was poorly defined and flat—so much so that when in flood, the waters entering the Souris from Long Creek immediately below Estevan would cause the Souris to back up past the site of the Rafferty Dam. The channel capacity in this reach of the river was so limited that virtually any releases from the Rafferty Dam would overtop the banks of the river. It made little sense to construct the dam and not excavate a channel in this reach of the river. The SBDA therefore proposed the excavation of a new channel, along with the removal of a number of obstructions and the cutting off of a number of meander loops, all aimed at increasing the channel capacity in this reach of the river.

The largest impoundment in the Souris basin in Saskatchewan prior to the construction of the Rafferty and Alameda dams was Boundary Dam on Long Creek, constructed in the late 1950s to provide cooling water for the Boundary

The author leans on a stack of papers that comprises the Rafferty-Alameda Environmental Impact Statement. The document eventually grew to over 4,000 pages.
Author photo

Dam Power Station. A single-purpose structure, there was no flood storage integrated into its design. During the floods of the 1970s, flows on Long Creek on a number of occasions caused the reservoir to exceed its capacity, resulting in significant flood damage.

The hydrology of the Souris basin in Saskatchewan is such that its three main water courses—the main stem, Long Creek, and Moose Mountain Creek—each contribute roughly one-third of the basin's flows. The single-purpose reservoir on Long Creek provided a graphic illustration of the water management challenges here. In the 1970s, Boundary Dam didn't have the capacity to store the large volume of water flowing down Long Creek. In the 1980s, acute shortages forced SaskPower to drill wells and pump ground water to augment the surface water supply. To redress these two problems—the water shortages and the flooding on Long Creek—a ten-kilometer channel connecting the Rafferty Reservoir to the Boundary Reservoir was proposed as part of the Rafferty-Alameda project. This would result in a more rapid filling of the Rafferty Reservoir, a reduction of flooding in the immediate vicinity of Estevan, and a greater certainty of supply for the Boundary Reservoir.

The fourth structure proposed was the Alameda Dam on Moose Mountain Creek, some sixty kilometers east of Estevan. The original site selected was thirteen kilometers north of the creek's confluence with the Souris. Late in the summer of 1987, in the middle of hearings on the project, we selected a new site for the dam, based on environmental considerations, ten kilometers downstream and three kilometers east of the town of Alameda. The earth-fill dam would have a height of forty-one meters and a length of 1,000 meters, requiring 2.3 million cubic meters of fill. The reservoir at full supply level would stretch twenty-three kilometers behind the Alameda Dam.

At the project-specific level, environmental assessment has three main phases: the assessment of the baseline or pre-project conditions, a prediction of the project's impact on the biophysical and human environment, and a program to mitigate the project's environmental effects. The EIS filed with SEPS in 1987 reached a number of important conclusions with respect to its impact on the environment. The water quality within the Souris River at the time was very poor. As a result of low flow in the 1980s, a significant proportion of the water in the Souris River between Weyburn and Estevan was effluent from the Weyburn sewage lagoons. Consultants for the SBDA forecast that post-project water quality would, on balance, be better than pre-project water quality.

As for wildlife, we committed ourselves to the principle of no net loss as a result of Rafferty-Alameda. This commitment was made for two reasons, one environmental and one political. The nature of the wildlife habitat in the area made it possible to create sufficient replacement habitat so that the effects on wildlife could be completely mitigated. In our view this was not only the environmentally responsible thing to do, but it would increase the probability of the project receiving environmental approval. To the best of our knowledge, never before had such a commitment been made on a major Canadian water project. If we completely mitigated the project's effects on wildlife, it would neutralize the opposition—or so the argument went.

Fisheries and wildlife biologists used a new technique to determine the project's impact on fauna. Instead of conducting population studies of target species, which involved attempting to count the actual number of animals potentially affected by the development, the SBDA, on the recommendation of its consultants, decided to utilize Habitat Evaluation Procedure (HEP), a methodology developed by the United States Fish and Wildlife Service. HEP involved analyzing the animal-carrying capacity of the habitat and the population it could support, allowing one to predict with greater precision the effects of the project on various species of wildlife, and the possibilities for mitigation. As it turned out, we found it was possible to produce a net *gain* of 31 percent in wildlife habitat after the project was completed.[22]

To achieve this, the Souris Basin Development Authority was proposing to acquire sixty-one quarter sections of marginal, cultivated land adjacent to the two reservoirs, thirty-one contiguous to the Rafferty Reservoir and thirty at Alameda,[23] with white-tailed deer, sharp-tailed grouse, blue-winged teal, Baird's sparrow, red-tailed hawk, and mink as our target species. Two-thirds of each quarter section would be planted to permanent grass, the remaining third with trees. In addition, the SBDA committed itself to establishing an ecological reserve downstream of the Rafferty Dam site as a means of protecting rare native grasses that were indigenous to the area but threatened by agriculture. This illustrates the trade-offs that have to be made on these kinds of projects, for often what is valued by naturalists is condemned by farmers. One of the species of grass we were attempting to protect in Saskatchewan, we were told, was classified as a noxious weed in Manitoba.

There were also three community pastures affected by the Rafferty Reservoir—two federal and one provincial. Governments issue cattle grazing rights on these pastures to area farmers; the leases are highly valued, and treated virtually as fee simple rights by the farmers who hold them. Given the importance of the farm sector to Saskatchewan, there was no question but that we would have to ensure the community pastures were kept in their entirety. To this end, we made the commitment to completely mitigate the project's impact on the three pastures affected; the area would support the same number of cattle after the project was completed. Thousands of acres adjacent to the existing pastures would be acquired to replace the land lost to inundation, and it would be seeded and fenced, and corrals would be built.

Other aspects to the project involved the mitigation of its effects on oil field facilities, archeological resources, and recreational facilities. The total of all the mitigation efforts being proposed exceeded 30 percent of the initial estimated cost for the whole enterprise.[24] A fierce debate over the add-ons raged among those of us working on the project, particularly the financial commitment to mitigate the environmental effects of the project. Some who had been involved in setting the first cost estimate at $120 million argued that what we were proposing was far in excess of what was necessary for a project of this type. Hill and I, however, were in favor of a more aggressive environmental protection program. If a legitimate issue was identified, we attempted to address it, and we depended on the advice of groups such as the Estevan Branch of the Saskatchewan Wildlife Federation. If the people directly affected by the development could support it, we reasoned, it would make it more difficult for others to launch an effective campaign against it.

Rafferty-Alameda signalled the dawning of a new era in major project development. Given the increased prominence of the environment as an issue of concern for Canadians, and the nebulous standards that existed (and continue to exist) with respect to the requirements a developer must meet, a substantial commitment above past practices was a necessity.

With all these efforts to protect the environment, a not unreasonable question is, Why the controversy? A critical distinction must be made here between the substantive impact a project may have on the environment and the procedural aspects of how it was reviewed. Setting aside the political rhetoric, the majority of the controversy associated with Rafferty-Alameda was related to matters of process, not substance. Of the fourteen challenges that eventually reached the courts, the principle justiciable issues in all of them were related to the procedural aspects of the environmental assessment.

From the outset, we were aware that there were a large number of approvals, licenses, and permits—some twenty-five in all—that would have to be obtained. We knew that individual licenses to construct the dams as well as separate licenses to operate them were required under the *Saskatchewan Water Corporation Act*. We were also aware that a permit from Environment Canada was required under the *International River Improvements Act*.[25] As well, a ministerial permit under the *Saskatchewan Environmental Assessment Act* was required.

Saskatchewan Environment and Public Safety followed a double-track process in dealing with its public review of the Rafferty-Alameda EIS. First, it doubled the period in which members of the public could express their views on the contents of the documents, from thirty to sixty days. This provided a direct conduit to the department. The second track was created in the summer of 1987 when the Saskatchewan minister of environment and public safety appointed a three-member board of inquiry with a mandate to review the EIS filed by the SBDA, to hold public meetings, and to make a recommendation to the minister as to whether the project should proceed, not proceed, or proceed with conditions.[26]

The board of inquiry, the first ever appointed pursuant to the *Saskatchewan Environmental Assessment Act,* consisted of John Brennan, dean of the College of Commerce at the University of Saskatchewan; Regina lawyer Darla Hunter, now Madam Justice Hunter of the Saskatchewan Court of Queen's Bench; and Clarence Fleck, a municipal politician and farmer from the Souris River basin. The composition of the board is illustrative of the state of the environmental assessment process in Saskatchewan at the time. Composed of people with minimal technical expertise, it depended on the technical review of the proposal conducted by SEPS, on the briefing of the staff, and on consultants of the SBDA. From these sources and from what the public had to say, it was supposed to come up with opinions based on the voluminous and highly technical material before it.

At the direction of the board, the SBDA held a series of public meetings throughout the basin in mid-August 1987 to explain the proposal to the public. Within a month, the board convened its own informal public meetings. If I didn't know I was involved in something extraordinary before the board of inquiry, I certainly did once the meetings began. At a meeting in Weyburn on August 17, 1987, I was told by a vocal opponent of the project that there was nothing wrong with me that a good horse-whipping wouldn't fix. At the September 9 meeting in Carlyle, I was confronted by an angry farmer who informed me that because I was from the government, I didn't have to tell the truth about the project. Still naive enough to rise to the bait, I told him that his statement was about as useful as if I had said that, because he was a farmer, he therefore must be receiving government largesse. Within a day I was hauled onto the carpet by my minister, Eric Berntson, who explained to me what my role was. I was there to take the heat for the government. All this flack was political, explained Berntson, and it was aimed at Devine and him. None of it was directed at me personally. He went on to explain that, if this process was going to work, I had to take the abuse. The only interests served by my intemperate responses were those opposing the project.

My skin became thicker, my mouth smaller.

Attendance at the meetings was heavy. There were times of great emotion as people on both sides of the issue spoke either of the destruction of the valley or of the toll that had already been paid as a result of the frequent and unpredictable flooding. At the end of the process approximately two-thirds of those expressing their views to the board supported the project.[27] This was perhaps the best indication to this point of how much the people of the area supported the project.

On January 25, 1988, the board issued its report recommending that the project be allowed to proceed subject to thirty-four conditions. On February 23 the Minister of Environment and Public Safety issued a ministerial approval, with twenty-three conditions, to permit construction of the Rafferty Dam, the Rafferty Dam to Boundary Dam diversion channel, and the channelization of the Souris River channel below the Rafferty Dam through the city of Estevan. Ministerial approval for the Alameda Dam, with twenty-three conditions, was conditional on receipt of funding from the United States government.

It is worth examining the ministerial approval issued for the project because it reflects the *laissez-faire* attitude that existed at the time among environmental regulators. Some of the conditions are so vague as to be impossible to implement. Condition #5, for example, states that "The proponent shall encourage the implementation of land use controls in areas surrounding the development to minimize erosion, farm chemical drainage and effluent discharge into the reservoirs." What does "encourage" mean? Which areas surrounding the reservoirs does this apply to? What does "minimize" mean?

The most significant deficiencies of the ministerial approval, however, can be found in the provisions that deal with oil field facilities. In its final incarnation, the Rafferty-Alameda project would effect over 100 oil field facilities— oil wells, salt water disposal wells, flow lines, trunk lines, injection lines, pipe lines, and lease access roads. Dealing with these facilities was an enormously complicated task, estimated to cost $23 million in 1989 dollars. As Gregg Trout, director of oil field mitigation for the SBDA, has noted, "Not a lot was known about how we should approach the oil field mitigation. There were no precedents of the magnitude of the Rafferty-Alameda project. Therefore policy and procedures had to be developed for the approval by the Board of Directors of the SBDA."[28]

What is interesting is the manner in which the issue was handled by Saskatchewan Environment and Public Safety. Condition #12 of the Rafferty-Alameda ministerial approval states:

> The proponent shall meet, and if possible exceed, the existing regulatory standards set by Saskatchewan Energy and Mines with respect to all aspects of oil well mitigation.

Condition #13 of the same approval states:

> Except where otherwise approved by Saskatchewan Energy and Mines and by the Minister [of Environment and Public Safety presumably], the proponent shall remove, and where necessary replace, all active pipelines and flow lines of any type, regardless of the substance they carry, from areas to be inundated by the reservoirs.[29]

If one ignores that the drilling of oil wells and the construction of pipelines were allowed in the flood plain in the first place by Saskatchewan Energy and Mines—a questionable practice from an environmental point of view—there seems nothing unreasonable about these provisions. There was one problem, however: the regulator was imposing a requirement on a proponent who did not have the legal authority to carry it out. All the facilities potentially affected by the Rafferty and Alameda reservoirs were owned by private oil companies. The SBDA, as constituted, had no authority to carry out the terms of the ministerial approval with respect to the mitigation of oil field facilities. If a regulatory permit is to have any effect, it has, in the first instance, to be enforceable, and then it has to be enforced. Not only were the many terms of the ministerial approval not enforceable, but Environment and Public Safety at the time did not appear to have the legal authority to enforce the approval.[30]

Equally troubling, as noted earlier, was the competence of SEPS to evaluate project proposals that were submitted to it. With fewer than ten project officers in the Coordination and Assessment Branch at the time Rafferty-Alameda was under review, there were clearly constraints on the available expertise within the department. When the SBDA decided to use Habitat Evaluation Procedure as the means of determining the project's impact on wildlife, for example, we found there was not sufficient expertise within the government to evaluate HEP-based analysis. Consequently, we found ourselves sponsoring a training workshop for the provincial regulatory agencies so that they could evaluate the reports we would be submitting.

There were problems on other fronts for SEPS. Section 9 of the *Saskatchewan Environmental Assessment Act* stipulates:

> 9(1) The proponent of a development shall, in accordance with the regulations:
>> (a) conduct an environmental impact assessment of the development; and
>> (b) prepare and submit to the minister an environmental impact statement relating to the development.[31]

There was one problem: no regulations to the act had ever been passed. As one law professor has noted,

> The *Environmental Assessment Act* when passed in 1980 was quite appropriately heralded nationally as a significant piece of environmental protection legislation. Drawing on the Ontario legislative experience, or perhaps more appropriately learning from the Ontario mistakes, the legislation was at first blush one of the more strongly drafted EIA Acts in the country. Unfortunately eight years later the shortcomings of the process have become evident. For example, although the legislation is broadly drafted so that all major projects of significant environmental impact should be subject to the process, the interpretation of the criteria which establish the need for environmental impact assessment has been most narrowly construed.
>
> Even if an environmental impact assessment is deemed necessary, there are no regulations in place to flesh out the legislation. Instead, the province has published a series of guidelines for particular activities as well as a general guideline for the process and pursuant to these less-formal avenues the process continues ...
>
> Admittedly, in most cases the actual mechanics of the legislation do not cause problems, however, the recent controversy regarding the Rafferty-Alameda dam project illustrates that pitfalls in the legislation can lead to serious difficulty.[32]

It came as no surprise when this procedural shortcoming was brought before the courts by a group opposed to the project.[33]

An examination of the regulatory process within the Saskatchewan government reveals the absence of any real effort to harmonize or coordinate related responsibilities on an intragovernmental basis.[34] For example, two separate licenses were required from SaskWater for each of the water control facilities we were proposing: one for approval to construct the Rafferty Dam, and another for approval to operate it.

There are two problems here. The first is that SaskWater was acting as both a developer and a regulator, a clear conflict of interest. As a regulator it was, in effect, granting licenses to itself, as the SBDA was acting as its agent and SaskWater would eventually end up owning the structures. The second problem was that the licensing requirements of the Saskatchewan Water Corporation could not be coordinated with those of Saskatchewan Environment and Public Safety. While the latter had an interest in assessing the environmental impacts of the proposal, the former was concerned with the technical aspects and structural integrity of the project. A public hearing procedure was specified in the *Saskatchewan Water Corporation Act,* and in February 1988 formal complaints were filed against the license to construct the Rafferty Dam. The complaints varied from loss of irrigated land to reduced land access, and from the loss of a tax base to reduced cattle access to the river. While these complaints were eventually dismissed by SaskWater after the complaint hearings, that they were allowed to be heard underscores the nature of the problem—the absence of any harmonization of regulatory processes. At least three of the complainants had already made their views known at the public meetings held by the board of inquiry. This process redundancy arose because when the *Saskatchewan Water Corporation Act* was drafted, no one considered the possibility that a license would ever be issued for a project that would also be reviewed pursuant to the *Saskatchewan Environmental Assessment Act.*

When we spelled this out to officials from SaskWater, their response was that it would take an amendment to the legislation to rectify the situation and, given that this involved the controversial Rafferty-Alameda project, SaskWater officials didn't want to take the heat for it. This meant that the project proponent (the SBDA) was confronted with an additional set of public meetings with few new issues being raised.

Yet another procedural problem occurred with fisheries permits. At the outset of the Rafferty-Alameda project, an inventory was taken of all the permits, licenses, and approvals that would be required. No fisheries-related permits were identified. In early September 1988, officials of the Saskatchewan Department of Parks and Renewable Resources notified us that a permit under the federal *Fisheries Act* was required, and that the Department of Fisheries and Oceans in Winnipeg had been contacted by a representative of the Environmental Law Center in Edmonton, Alberta who was working on contract to the Canadian Wildlife Federation. The center was inquiring whether or not it "had issued any authorization under the Fish Habitat provisions of the Federal *Fisheries Act* to allow Rafferty-Alameda to proceed."[35]

The inquiry came as a surprise, because on at least two previous occasions we had asked our legal counsel if a fisheries permit might be required, and their answer was no. I contacted our lawyers immediately and requested a written opinion on the issue. Tom Gauley and Bob Kennedy, from the firm of Gauley and Company in Saskatoon, outlined the ambiguity of the fisheries issue in jurisdictional terms. Fisheries are a federal responsibility. The decision to give the federal government jurisdiction in this area was made, presumably, on the basis that the major fisheries in Canada were located in the coastal waters, which also fell under the jurisdiction of the federal government. Inland fisheries were another matter. Evidently not a priority with the federal government, responsibility for the fresh water fishery was turned over to the provinces. In Saskatchewan, responsibility devolved to the province when the federal government passed the Saskatchewan Fisheries Regulations in 1954. These regulations provided that "the Saskatchewan Minister of Natural Resources is the appropriate minister for the purposes of construction of fishways."[36] The 1954 regulations were repealed by federal Order-in-Council in June 1979, removing Saskatchewan's authority under a number of sections of the act. The Order-in-Council passed in 1979 did contain a section that Saskatchewan treated as giving it authority to effect or approve changes in fish habitat:

> Section 42: No person shall, except as authorized by a license . . .
> i. Alter or cause to be altered the configuration of the bed, bank or boundary of any water frequented by fish; or
> j. Remove gravel from or displace gravel in waters frequented by fish.[37]

Gauley and Kennedy informed us that there were apparently no equivalent provisions made with any other province, and that "the Saskatchewan Department's activities pursuant to the Section [42] have apparently received at least tacit approval by the Federal Government pursuant to a policy paper for the Western provinces promulgated two or three years ago."[38]

I contacted the Department of Parks and Renewable Resources to ascertain what the status of the permits was. The actual impact of the project on the fishery was never in question, given that there would be up to a thousand-fold increase in the amount of fish habitat after it was completed.[39] I was informed that, even though the Department of Fisheries and Oceans had participated in the Saskatchewan environmental assessment process through the federal Department of the Environment, and given its approval, "a legal question may be raised over the lack of a federal Fisheries approval."[40] For over a decade, Saskatchewan had knowingly been issuing Fish Habitat Alteration Permits of questionable legality. An internal memorandum noted:

> If push comes to shove we may have an out under Section 42 (i)(j) [sic] of the Sask (federal) Fishery Regulations that allows the Provincial Minister to authorize the alteration of the bed or branch of the river to create better fisheries habitat. We've used this on other similar (but less high profile) projects. Although I should warn you that the feds question the legality of this section that they passed on our behalf.[41]

In our view, there were only two practical options open to the SBDA. The first was to do nothing and wait to see if we were sued by either the federal government or a member of the public. I made a cryptic note on my copy of the Gauley legal opinion: "note activity of the Canadian Wildlife Federation & Environmental Law Group—can't bet that won't happen." The second option was to apply to the Saskatchewan minister for a license, taking the position that it was valid and that dozens of others like it had been passed. We took the second option; we applied for and were granted a license from the Saskatchewan minister. The minister who signed the permit was Colin Maxwell, now executive vice-president of the Canadian Wildlife Federation.

That there were procedural problems with the way the Saskatchewan government handled Rafferty-Alameda is obvious. Some were political and should have been avoided: two striking examples were the absence of project-specific guidelines (due to interference from someone in the Premier's Office) and the minister of the environment also holding the SaskWater portfolio.

Other problems arose as a result of administrative practices of the SBDA and the Saskatchewan government. The SBDA, as the proponent, should have realized from the outset how complicated the project was—we didn't and it hurt. Conducting feasibility analyses and environmental studies without knowing the scale of the project and whether the Alameda Dam would even be built was not a good idea. But the provincial bureaucracy has to take its share of the blame as well. Even though the *Saskatchewan Environmental Assessment Act* had been passed a half-decade prior to Rafferty-Alameda, the absence of regulations to the act invited litigation and controversy. And, from a regulatory point of view, it is highly questionable to have agencies imposing regulatory requirements that were so vague as to be unenforceable, or conditions that the SBDA did not have the ability, in a legal sense, to carry out.

Another obstacle was that there had been no attempt to harmonize or coordinate regulatory processes on an intragovernmental basis, resulting in a form of procedural musical chairs among those opposed to the project. As well, the provincial government had been issuing fish habitat permits that were of questionable legal status. These irregularities made the project more vulnerable to attack than would otherwise have been the case.

Despite all of this, though, as the Saskatchewan environmental assessment of Rafferty-Alameda was nearing completion, I recall thinking that the worst of these procedural difficulties were behind us.

I was overly optimistic.

CHAPTER FOUR

SUBSTANCE AND PROCEDURE

In many ways, Rafferty-Alameda is like a political inkblot test. Considering the emotional nature of the issue, the style of Saskatchewan politics, and the sheer complexity of the project, everyone who looks at it will come away with a different image. For me, the image that lingers is the way the project was handled by the federal government, specifically Environment Canada.

The actual environmental effects of the project were never really at issue; they merely provided the backdrop. From the Saskatchewan perspective, the issues were drought and that time-honored Western lament, treatment equal with the rest of Canada. From the Ottawa perspective, what was at issue, seemingly, were matters of jurisdiction, process definition, and bureaucratic turf protection. It started with the Environment Assessment Review Process—the EARP Guidelines, as they are commonly known. These guidelines and how they were created are at the root of much of the controversy surrounding Rafferty-Alameda and a litany of other major projects across Canada.

Environmental assessment is both a planning tool for a developer and a regulatory mechanism for the state. In the latter context, it is a process administered by governments to ensure that certain types of economic activities are developed in ways sensitive to the environment. It is a graduated process; ideally, economic activities that will have little environmental impact are subjected to a cursory review and then allowed to proceed, while activities whose potential impact will be greater are subjected to more stringent requirements. The challenge for government is to develop a regulatory framework that applies to a widely divergent set of circumstances, and to administer it uniformly.[1]

Clearly, this is not an easy task. In the first place, it isn't possible to set rules that will be applicable to every circumstance. Second, the division of responsibilities between the federal government and the provinces at the time the constitution was drafted did not recognize the environment as an issue, let alone one falling into the exclusive jurisdiction of either order of government. As a result, we have a policy field shared among the provinces, the federal government, and, frequently, municipalities—with great potential for duplication, inefficiency, and confusion.

A third difficulty is politics. Politics enters the picture by virtue of what environmental assessment generally does *not* apply to. Agriculture is a good example here because of its obvious relevance to Saskatchewan. There is arguably no activity that has a greater impact on the environment than farming. The use of herbicides, pesticides, and fertilizers, the location of cattle feedlots—all have major biophysical effects. Changes in agricultural policy have a tremendous impact on the use of chemicals, yet these decisions have, in large part, escaped environmental scrutiny. The family farm, it seems, in both environmental and political terms, is the home of sacred cows.

Should activities such as farming be subjected to environmental reviews? In principle, the answer has to be yes. In political terms, the answer is more often something else. Certainly in Saskatchewan, the government has been extremely reluctant to make any attempt to regulate the impact of agricultural activities on the environment. For these reasons, among others, the task of developing environmental assessment processes in Canada has met with a mixed degree of success. In the Canadian context, what the environmental assessment process applies to, particularly at the federal level, has been determined as much by how it evolved as anything else.

The EARP Guidelines originated in the early 1970s and have as their historical antecedent the *National Environmental Policy Act* (NEPA), which was implemented in the United States in 1969. The principle effect of NEPA was to require that environmental impact statements be included "in every recommendation or report on proposals for legislation or other major Federal actions significantly affecting the quality of the human environment."[2] Its intent was to ensure that nonenvironmental agencies of the American federal government took environmental values into account when making decisions. "Formulators of NEPA," according to U.S. political scientist L.M. Wenner, "hoped to achieve this result at two levels: through internal reform by forcing agencies to incorporate environmental values into their thinking, and through external oversight, by informing the public and other agencies about projects under consideration and eliciting comments from them."[3]

While the procedural objectives at the federal level in Canada were similar, the results were much different. Whereas in the United States NEPA was enacted as legislation, environmental assessment in Canada did not enjoy such power. NEPA lays out in detail how the process is intended to function, and where responsibility for enforcement lies. In Canada, the EARP Guidelines are neither as detailed nor as coherent.

In 1973, the federal Cabinet issued a directive creating the assessment process. According to federal officials currently involved in this area, the fact that formal legislation was not passed was deliberate. The rationale was that a process would be created that would allow for flexibility and, hence, discretion. The actors could grow from the experience.[4]

While the NEPA influence can be seen in the inward-looking nature of the EARP Guidelines and their reliance on self-assessment, that they have been treated as a discretionary instrument by other agencies of the Canadian government underscores a critical difference. " 'If the various federal departments were as rational and environmentally conscientious as is implied by such discretion,' one observer has noted, 'then EARP [would be] unnecessary.' They weren't and it wasn't. Most departments and agencies to which EARP applied treated the process as entirely discretionary; it thus could not provide the impetus for administrative reform provided by NEPA."[5]

In 1977, a second Cabinet directive was issued, making provision for appointees to assessment panels from outside the federal government. The legal status of the guidelines was not affected. That did not occur until 1984, by which time they had been under review for a considerable period. The federal government recognized the need to redress some of the deficiencies. It was, in part, a political imperative. An election was in view, and the Liberal government of the time anticipated that the environment would be an issue in the campaign. Revising the guidelines would be an expedient move; it would appeal to the environmental policy community.

As a rule, in Canada, laws are created by the federal Parliament and the provincial and territorial legislatures. But there are other ways for governments to create legally binding mechanisms. Three options were open to the federal government with respect to amending the EARP Guidelines in 1984: retain them in their current state as policy, implement them as legislation, or give them enhanced status by passing an Order-in-Council.

Maintaining the *status quo* would not provide the desired political benefit. Legislation was not feasible, either, given the time constraints and the status of Environment Canada as, at best, a middle power in the federal bureaucracy. Almost certainly, legislation would have infringed on the bureaucratic territory of other federal agencies, and such an event would not occur without a struggle. In 1984, this was a bureaucratic battle that FEARO—the Federal Environmental Assessment Review Office—could not have won. Consequently, the decision was taken to issue an Order-in-Council.

FEARO, as defined in the 1984 guidelines, was virtually toothless. To be effective, the agency responsible for the administration of the assessment process should be at arm's length from other government agencies. As we have already seen, this was not the case in Saskatchewan, and it appears not to have been the case with FEARO; in fact, the executive chairman of FEARO reported, in bureaucratic terms, through the deputy minister of the environment to the minister of the environment.[6] FEARO, it seemed, was functioning as an arm of Environment Canada.

Political scientist Bruce Doern has written of the problems Environment Canada was experiencing during this period:

> Environment Canada's inherent capacity was blunted from 1975 until the late 1980s by four dynamics. The first was an inability to establish and carry out rigorous compliance procedures. The second was a weakening through budget cuts of an already overtaxed scientific and investigation capacity. The third was the federal government's insecurity in its relations to the provinces and among its own departments. And finally Environment Canada was itself mainly a technical department, possessing only limited economic and to some extent legal literacy and

analytical capacity. Directly or indirectly, all of these elements were indicators of the low position that environmental policy and implementation occupied on the political and economic agenda.[7]

Prior to Rafferty-Alameda, there was considerable variation across the agencies of the federal government in their administration of the EARP Guidelines. "The principle weakness of EARP in this context," as Professor Paul Brown has noted, "was that it left the power of initiative for conducting assessments squarely in the hands of sectoral departments, rather than Environment Canada. Attempts to correct this weakness, as in 1977 and 1984, foundered in the face of fear by other departments that a vigorous EARP under the sway of the environment minister would give Environment Canada considerable power over their activities."[8]

As for the guidelines themselves, their deficiencies will become quite apparent as the story of the litigation on Rafferty-Alameda unfolds. For now, it will suffice to note what others have said:

> The EARP Guidelines consist of a complicated web of inter-related definitions, mandatory requirements and permissive guidelines that do not yield easily to interpretation. Prior to the now famous rulings of the Federal Court in respect of the Rafferty-Alameda Project, they were largely ignored by federal officials and agencies. They were seen, at best, as being in the nature of administrative directives that carried no legal consequence.[9]

The weaknesses inherent in the EARP Guidelines have also been acknowledged in the academic literature. Vanderzwaag and Duncan have noted that there were "numerous cracks latent in the Guidelines. These allowed for further interdepartmental and federal-provincial political maneuvering and opened the door for environmental lip service to be paid in the name of economic progress."[10]

Just how many cracks there were in the guidelines became apparent in the mid-1980s, when Rafferty-Alameda was still on the drawing board. There were a number of consultations between Saskatchewan and the federal government on regulatory matters. That Saskatchewan initiated these contacts to determine which federal regulations applied to the project is not insignificant in terms of how the issue played out. The principle concern of the federal government at the time was not with environmental assessment but with the negotiations then just getting under way with the U.S. Army Corps of Engineers. Ottawa was disinclined to become involved in what at the time were preliminary and highly technical discussions. In March 1985, as planning for the project was beginning, Saskatchewan was given a copy of a letter from the director general of the Inland Waters Directorate of Environment Canada to the Department of External Affairs. "The following environmental or legislative considerations have been identified with regard to the Rafferty Dam project," the letter noted, and went on to list, among other things, a "federal environmental assessment and review process if federal funding is involved."[11]

There was no federal funding at the time, but we still had cause for concern. On October 29, 1986, I received a letter from Bob Walker, director of the Coordination and Assessment Branch of Saskatchewan Environment and Public Safety. It was a portent of things to come:

> As you are aware, I am becoming increasingly concerned that Saskatchewan Environment has, as directed, not yet involved either federal or Manitoba environmental interests in the review of the proposed Rafferty/Alameda project. By not having done so Saskatchewan risks having these projects unnecessarily referred to the Federal Environmental Assessment Review Process and, therefore, to a federally administered public hearing. Such a hearing would duplicate Saskatchewan Environment's responsibility, would undoubtedly impose significant project delays and would shift the ultimate environmental decision for these projects outside the province.[12]

The issue of the federal government's role in the environmental assessment of Rafferty-Alameda was of sufficient concern that we sought a legal opinion from the Saskatchewan Department of Justice. The opinion was far from clear. "EARP is established pursuant to a cabinet directive and is not based on any legislative authority," it stated. "It therefore lacks any binding force in law."

On the other hand, the opinion noted that "although the EARP Guidelines largely seem to be directed to federal[ly] initiated projects or projects involving federal funds or federal property, it certainly is possible to interpret them more widely to include projects where less federal involvement is present." The opinion continued:

> As the process has no statutory basis and lacks binding force in law, the ultimate determination of how a project is dealt with in the event that the minister of the initiating department and the Minister of the Environment cannot agree could be a reference to Cabinet . . . [I]t is doubtful whether outside parties could successfully take legal action to require an assessment under EARP if the federal government decided it was not necessary.[13]

Different interpretations of the responsibilities of the federal government are further illustrated in a letter sent to me in March 1987 by the deputy minister of Environment Canada. In words that would come back to haunt the federal government, the letter stated:

> Your letter to Mr. R.M. Robinson [Raymond Robinson, executive chairman of the Federal Environmental Assessment Review Office] of January 9, was recently forwarded for my attention. You are commended for

having started consultations with parties having a direct interest in the proposal.

Although, as Mr. Robinson has pointed out, the Federal Environmental Assessment and Review Process does not apply to the proposed Alameda and Rafferty dams proposals, Environment Canada will have both specific and program interests in the project.[14]

The head of the federal agency responsible for the EARP Guidelines and the deputy minister of the federal department responsible for licensing the project were both of the view that Ottawa did not have a responsibility to review Rafferty-Alameda. On the other hand, the agency responsible for the provincial environmental review of the project (SEPS) was clearly of the opinion that the federal process *did* apply. Saskatchewan Justice, for its part, felt that the guidelines lacked the force of law.

Given the obviously conflicting views, the question was, What should we, as the project proponents, do? I laid out the rationale for our strategy in a letter to Bob Walker at SEPS that was correct in substance but should never have been written. Given the controversy it aroused, a substantial portion of it is included here:

I am writing in response to your letter of October 27 in which you raised a number of concerns regarding federal involvement in the Rafferty-Alameda Environmental Impact Statement. At the outset I want to point out that it is the intention of the Souris Basin Development Authority to comply fully and completely with all environmental requirements associated with the project.

As you are aware, the multiple objective project we are undertaking is fairly complex involving a number of jurisdictions on either side of the Canada–U.S. border. The prolonged gotiations we have been engaged in with the Americans is probably the best example of the problems associated with this multiple agency involvement. Having noted the problems inherent in the process, the complexity question is further compounded by the fact that the Souris River and the possibility of constructing flood control reservoirs on it has long been the subject of considerable public debate and attention from both supporters and detractors alike. The undeniable fact is that the Rafferty Dam is a *very* controversial project with the potential, if not managed carefully, to attract significant opposition on both sides of the 49th parallel.

The principals involved in this project have deliberately attempted to keep the *initial* number of agencies involved on both sides of the border to as few as possible. The rationale is simply this: the project given its complexity both in terms of hydrology and jurisdictional interdependence will have a far greater chance of success if the principals (that is, those most directly involved, in this case Saskatchewan, North Dakota, the Army Corps of Engineers, and the City of Minot) have the chance of building a consensus on the most difficult aspects of the project. It will come as no surprise to you, I am sure, that a number of federal officials have in the past, expressed their aversion to this particular project. Given that a number of these individuals are still working in related areas the distinct possibility exists that if given the opportunity, they would deliberately attempt to scuttle the project. Our strategy has been and will continue to be, to take the project as far as we possibly can on our own and build up as much momentum behind it before we open the process to other governments.

I now want to refer to the current state of the project. There are, as you know, a number of key issues regarding the project and how it will operate, that are currently outstanding. My personal preference would have been to have had these concerns addressed some considerable time ago, however, such is not the case. I am reasonably confident that the bulk of these concerns will be cleared up within the next few months. Once these issues have been cleared up, it will be much easier for us to talk in definitive terms about such items as the operating regimes of the reservoirs, their impact on the environment, and the various items of agreement between ourselves and the principals on the American side of the border. At this current point in time, given the number of unresolved issues currently before us, I do not think it advisable for us to initiate an "open-ended" consultation process with either the Canadian federal government or the government of the Province of Manitoba.

Now having said this, I am not unsympathetic to the realities of the environmental review process which we must comply with. My understanding is that the federal Environmental Review Process was established pursuant to a federal Cabinet directive and is not based on any legislative authority. It, therefore, lacks any binding force in law and, as a result, does not bind the provincial government on any purely provincial project. I think it is clear that the Rafferty and Alameda Project is not a "purely provincial project" in that the federal government will have some involvement as defined in the EARP Guidelines as federal "decision-making responsibilities." In particular section 6 b of the Guidelines would appear to likely apply in this case. Moreover, I am supportive of the position you expressed in your letter that FEARO not duplicate provincial review processes.

Recognizing the sensitive stage the project is currently at as well as the interest of the federal government in what we are doing, I would suggest the following course of action. The Government of Saskatchewan should provide the federal government with a copy of the specific Environmental Assessment Guidelines stating that our review process is proceeding on the basis that all probable federal concerns will be addressed if these guidelines are adhered to. I do not think it advisable to directly involve the Province of Manitoba in our environmental review process. Given the fact that the Souris River flows from Saskatch-

ewan through North Dakota into Manitoba, we in Saskatchewan cannot provide definitive information to Manitoba. I would point out in
this regard that the Army Corps of Engineers are conducting their
own NEPA review and that they are better situated to address the
concerns of Manitoba.[15]

There is little, if anything, in the letter that is not factually correct, but the
way it was received when it eventually leaked was proof that there are certain
things better left unsaid. In March 1989, representatives of SCRAP (Stop Construction of the Rafferty-Alameda Project) held a press conference, calling for a
police investigation and citing alleged criminal wrong-doing by officials of
SaskPower, the Souris Basin Development Authority, and Saskatchewan Environment and Public Safety under Section 122 of the Criminal Code—breach of
public trust. My letter had done nothing to dispel the perception that there was
a politically manipulative tenor to the project, although I was at a loss to see
how there was anything criminal about it. The letter also provided predictable
fodder for Question Period in the Saskatchewan Legislature. If complaints to
the RCMP under the Criminal Code were not enough, one of the conclusive
indications of Rafferty-Alameda's profile across the province was that we had
our own opposition critic, the NDP MLA for Regina-Rosemont, Bob Lyons. Lyons was indefatigable. He proposed alternatives to Rafferty-Alameda without
detailed analysis of their environmental effects. He tried to rake us over the
coals during the review of the SBDA Annual Report before the Crown Corporations Committee of the Legislature. He wrote to President-elect George Bush in
an attempt to derail the American component of the project. While one must
give Lyons full marks for his efforts, he never created a serious impediment to
the project's development.

Lyons had a great time with my letter, but far more significant are the issues
the letter raises in terms of the assessment process and the problems Rafferty-
Alameda was experiencing at the time. It was apparently standard practice on
Saskatchewan environmental assessments to give other government agencies,
provincial and federal, an opportunity to participate on those aspects that affected them. This was never given any formal legal status in the *Saskatchewan
Environmental Assessment Act,* rather, it was an administrative practice. On most
projects, it would probably not have mattered, but Rafferty-Alameda was not
just any other project. Its jurisdictional complexity alone meant that these were
extraordinary circumstances. On Rafferty-Alameda, the practice had the potential to injuriously affect the whole project.

Regulatory agencies have a real conflict any time they engage in
nonregulatory activities, and this became quite apparent on Rafferty-Alameda,
particularly when Manitoba became involved. In this case, the agency representing the Manitoba government at the international negotiating table likely
would have already staked out its position as part of the Saskatchewan environmental assessment. If this was allowed to occur as a matter of process, it was our
view that it could undermine the negotiations and the assessment of the project.

This, coupled with the increasing sensitivity of the environment as a policy area, and that the project was taking away water that downstream jurisdictions—Manitoba particularly—had enjoyed for decades, placed a considerable strain on the assessment process.

Procedure aside, we had political concerns about Ottawa and Manitoba even at the earliest stages of the project. We were aware that, in two previous apportionments on the Souris River, the federal government had not given priority to Saskatchewan interests, and there was no reason to believe the same thing would not occur again. As for Manitoba, it is, almost without exception, a downstream jurisdiction. The Churchill, Saskatchewan, and Qu'Appelle rivers flow out of Saskatchewan; the Red flows out of North Dakota; the city of Winnipeg draws its municipal water supply from Shoal Lake, which is bisected by the Ontario border. The Souris, too, flows in from somewhere else. Through this quirk of geography, Manitoba has been forced to defend its rights on every river system crossing its borders, if for no other reason than the precedent that might be set if it didn't.

The Souris has been a particular challenge for Manitoba since the 1970s because of the Garrison Diversion, an irrigation project in North Dakota that involved the inter-basin transfer of water from the Missouri River, which flows south into the Mississippi, into the Souris, which flows north, eventually ending up in James Bay. Manitoba was concerned about the potential for the introduction of foreign biota and the effects it could have on the commercial fishery in Lake Winnipeg. When the State of North Dakota and the American government formally proposed the Garrison Diversion, Manitoba opposed the project and, after considerable lobbying on the part of the province, the Canadian government did as well. As a result of its efforts on Garrison, the government of Manitoba had well-established contacts among American environmental groups and government agencies. All of this had major significance for Rafferty-Alameda. We were concerned that the issue would get blown out of proportion in Manitoba, that it could reach the scale of another Garrison Diversion. If this occurred one of the first steps the Manitoba government would take would be to call on Ottawa to protect its interests. The federal government might then have little choice but to get directly involved in the environmental review as well as the negotiations of the international agreement, and to oppose the project.

For all these reasons, the SBDA wanted to limit the involvement of the federal and Manitoba governments. In May 1987, two months after the letter from the federal deputy minister of the environment stating that the EARP Guidelines did not apply to Rafferty-Alameda, Deputy Premier Eric Berntson wrote to Tom McMillan, then federal environment minister:

> The Province of Saskatchewan is the only agency from this side of the border with any financial involvement in the Rafferty-Alameda Project. There is no federal money involved nor have we asked for any, and this has been a deliberate move on our part. Given the multiple objective

nature of the project and the very stringent timelines we are facing, if we are to meet future electrical demands of Saskatchewan, we have sought to restrict the number of agencies involved. This has proven to be a successful strategy on our part, as we have progressed rapidly in our negotiations with the U.S.

It was therefore, with considerable concern that I discovered that a number of federal bureaucrats were attempting to inject themselves into the Rafferty-Alameda project. I say concern, because quite frankly, public servants from both the provincial and federal governments have attempted to frustrate our efforts on this project.[16]

McMillan did not deny Berntson's accusation. His response, which was almost certainly drafted by his officials, confirmed our apprehensions about Manitoba:

I read your comments with keen interest, particularly the section where you describe the depth of your political commitment to the plan. I want to ensure, however, that transboundary environmental effects are adequately considered and that the appropriate licensing requirements are followed. In addition, I am concerned that the project might have a negative impact on wildlife habitat and undesirable consequences downstream in Manitoba.[17]

There was a handwritten postscript:

Eric, I am extremely sensitive to your concerns, and to those of the Premier and you can be assured of my full cooperation, consistent with my obligations as Minister of the Environment. I am confident that all outstanding issues can be resolved. Don't hesitate to call me should you encounter obstacles, bureaucratic or otherwise.[18]

A briefing note to Devine and Berntson from George Hill outlined the extent of the opposition to the project within the federal Department of the Environment:

The following are my sources of concern:
1. As you are both aware, the Board of Inquiry has been holding informal public meetings around the province on the Rafferty-Alameda Project.
      During these meetings, a letter from Environment Canada to the Saskatchewan Department of the Environment, which was critical of the project, was leaked to the NDP here in Saskatchewan. There can be no question that:
(a) this letter came from the federal government because the blind copy list of civil servants is included on the bottom of the letter and,

(b) that the leaking of the letter was inspired by partisan motives to hurt the project given that it was released just before the Regina hearing, in my view, to attract maximum media attention.

2. In October of this year, officials of the Souris Basin Development Authority met with officials of the North Dakota State Health Department to discuss water quality on the Souris River. During this meeting, officials from North Dakota informed Saskatchewan officials that they had been contacted by an Environment Canada official who was raising concerns that North Dakota should have about the Rafferty-Alameda Project.

3. Last week, Saskatchewan officials met with officials of both External Affairs and Environment Canada to outline our desire to wrap up all transboundary issues as close to the end of the year as possible so as to enable a 1988 start of construction.

The response from federal officials was one of skepticism as to whether such a schedule *should* be met, non-commitment in even *attempting* to meet our deadlines, the need to receive the *total* concurrence from the Province of Manitoba because of possible downstream impacts before any formal negotiations begin with the United States, the need for a *different* agreement with the United States instead of an exchange of diplomatic notes as was previously agreed to and *the probable reference to the International Joint Commission* because of a revised Operating Plan, which we believe is totally unnecessary.[19]

From the inception of the project, we had known that a license from Environment Canada under the *International River Improvements Act* (IRIA) was necessary. The IRIA, a federal statute put in place in 1955 largely in response to the Columbia River Project in British Columbia, provides the legislative base for the federal government to assert its jurisdiction over projects on rivers that traverse the border between Canada and the United States. A license issued pursuant to the act is required before water projects can go ahead, and there are stiff penalties for violations.[20]

On January 7, 1988, the Saskatchewan Water Corporation applied to the Department of the Environment for an IRIA license. On June 17, 1988, the federal environment minister issued one. In environmental terms, the license issued for the Rafferty-Alameda project was the most stringent ever issued up to then. While some preparatory work at the site had taken place beforehand, with the issuance of the license, construction on the Rafferty Dam began in earnest. In the June 18 *Regina Leader-Post*, I was quoted as stating that "this is the last regulatory improvement on the Canadian side so it means that we can proceed full-speed."[21] It was not the last time I would be wrong on this front.

As early as 1987, we had heard that the Canadian Wildlife Federation (CWF) was concerned about the Rafferty-Alameda project. In the fall of 1988, the CWF passed a resolution:

> Whereas the decisions by the federal and Saskatchewan governments to authorize construction of the Rafferty Dam create a dangerous precedent for the future exercise of federal authority over international waterways;
> Therefore be it resolved that the Canadian Wildlife Federation institute legal action against the federal government for failing to comply with the federal Environmental Assessment Review Process . . . [22]

We thought at the time that there was more to it than anxiety over process, that there must also be a substantive basis for the CWF's concern. I was convinced that it was merely a misunderstanding, that if all our efforts to protect the environment were explained to them, their concerns would be satisfied. This was not a completely erroneous conclusion. It was based, in part, on an editorial written by CWF Executive Vice-President Ken Brynaert entitled "CWF Viewpoint" in the May-June 1988 edition of *International Wildlife*. The editorial not only questioned the process, it also questioned the environmental effects of Rafferty-Alameda and, in so doing, made a number of factual errors.[23]

On November 7, 1988, I issued instructions to our wildlife consultants directing them to prepare a briefing paper that would address what we thought were the CWF's substantive concerns. The paper dealt specifically with the wildlife and fisheries components of the project, and outlined in detail the program we had proposed to ameliorate the effects on fish and game. We might as well have been speaking Greek. The issue was about process, not substance.[24]

On January 19, 1989, the Canadian Wildlife Federation filed suit against the federal minister of the environment, the Saskatchewan Water Corporation, and the Souris Basin Development Authority in the Federal Court of Canada (the case is hereafter referred to as CWF I). Notwithstanding the weaknesses and ambiguities of the EARP Guidelines, we went into the CWF I case fully expecting to win. Counsel for the federal government arguing the case was also confident. As the court date approached, however, we began to see signs that gave us cause for concern. We had written assurances from the deputy minister of the environment that the EARP Guidelines did not apply to Rafferty-Alameda, so it came as a bit of a surprise when the director general of the Inland Waters Directorate of Environment Canada, stated in a sworn affidavit previous to the trial that he didn't regard those assurances as a statement of policy: "It is an opinion being expressed as it relates to the specific project at that point in time, but had not been fully evaluated."[25]

At a minimum, the assurances of the deputy minister of the environment and the above statement by the director general of the Inland Waters Directorate would seem difficult to reconcile. When the case was argued before Mr. Justice Bud Cullen on March 30, 1989, the precise nature of the federal government's role in the administration of the EARP Guidelines became even more ambiguous. Counsel for the federal government indicated that Environment Canada had complied with the spirit of the EARP Guidelines, even though "the paper trail . . . may not be crystal clear. The absence of that evidence is not necessarily conclusive the [review] process was not followed by spirit or intent."[26] This was, to say the least, a weak defence. It was also a sign of things to come. Within a fortnight, Mr. Justice Cullen had issued his decision:

> ... it is my opinion that the Minister of the Environment is re-
> quired, before issuing a license under the *International River Im-
> provements Act,* to comply with the EARP Guidelines Order. By not
> applying the provisions of the Order, the Minister has failed to com-
> ply with a statutory duty, has exceeded his jurisdiction and there-
> fore the applicants are entitled to their order for *certiorari.* Further
> the EARP Guidelines Order indicates that certain procedures, namely
> the preparation of an environmental assessment and review, must be
> carried out when dealing with a proposal that may have an effect on
> an area of federal responsibility. The Project being such a proposal,
> and the Minister being a participant (in that he issued the license
> under the *International River Improvements Act*) and by not com-
> plying with the Order, has in my opinion not performed his duty and
> therefore the applicants are also entitled to an order for *mandamus,*
> and costs forthwith after taxation thereof.[27]

What the decision meant was the federal government had a legal responsibility to administer the guidelines as a mandatory instrument. Given that it had
not fulfilled that responsibility in its review of Rafferty-Alameda, the license it
had issued for the project was invalid and was, in effect, cancelled.

The various reactions to it reflected the nature of the issue and the perspective of the interests involved. For those of us working on the project, the
decision came as an unbelievable blow. There was a media feeding frenzy as
my office took over 150 calls on the day the CWF I decision was issued. But
even then, the significance of the decision and the loss of the license was not
immediately apparent. We had to get a legal opinion from our lawyers on the
significance of CWF I and what options were open to us. Considering that
we were not at fault, that it was the federal government that had got us into
this mess, it seemed logical that they would assume some responsibility for
getting us out of it.

The Canadian Wildlife Federation was ecstatic. "It goes beyond our expec-
tations," Ken Brynaert confided to a *Globe and Mail* reporter. "This is exactly
what we petitioned for. We're delighted."[28] The CWF indicated that any on-going construction on the Rafferty Dam would be met by an application for an
injunction to stop the work.

Within a week of the decision, Saskatchewan launched an appeal. Naively,
we expected that the federal government would follow suit. After reviewing the
situation, we realized that we had no option but to halt construction. It was both
logistically and politically difficult to do. Getting these projects started is hard
enough. Shutting them down is even harder, particularly when you don't know
how long the shut-down will last. Contracts had been let, specialized equipment

had been purchased. While there were cancellation clauses in all our contracts, we still had hopes of getting back to work in the 1989 construction season. To this end, we set out to negotiate stand-by arrangements.

The workers had to be told of the decision. This unenviable task fell to Berntson. One day after the Cullen decision, in a highly emotional speech to a standing-room-only crowd in Estevan, Berntson was at his best. The *Moose Jaw Times-Herald* recorded the event:

> "We're madder than hell that we are caught at the end of the day in a matter of process," Berntson said as he waved a microphone in one hand and slammed his fist on a podium. To loud applause, he vowed to do everything possible to get the Rafferty-Alameda project started again, including appealing the court ruling and asking for a stay of the judgement to allow work to continue pending the appeal. "I am totally angered and frustrated with this whole exercise," he said.[29]

The other thing Berntson did when he addressed the workers in Estevan was follow the time-honored Saskatchewan practice of blaming the NDP. On the face of it, this might seem unfair, but everything in Saskatchewan is

Eric Berntson at the Elk's Lodge in Estevan on April 11, 1989—the day after the first Canadian Wildlife Federation decision of the federal court. An emotional Berntson announced to those assembled that the government was suspending all construction activities on the Rafferty Dam. Courtesy Regina Leader-Post

political, and by this time the Rafferty-Alameda project had politics tat-
tooed onto it. The legislature was in session when we made the decision to
halt construction. Again, Berntson was at his best, this time recorded by
Dale Eisler:

> "They are no more interested in the environment than they are in flying
> to the moon. What they want to do is stop the project," Berntson said,
> his booming voice almost drowned out by the background roar from
> agitated government and opposition members.
>
> Since the federal court revoked the license, Berntson and the To-
> ries have sought to blame the NDP for the loss of jobs. The argument
> Berntson makes is that the NDP's goal is to scuttle the entire project.
>
> Curiously, when Berntson accused the NDP of wanting to stop the
> project, the Opposition benches erupted into spontaneous applause as
> if to punctuate and endorse the claim.[30]

For our opponents, the halt to construction meant that they could now focus
their energies on trying to stop the project in the United States. Accordingly,
one of the first steps we took was to ensure that all cooperating government
agencies in the United States—collectively known as "The Family"—were aware
of the decision and its implications. While there is no question that the group
would have preferred to avoid the halt, no one was surprised by it. We had
assumed from the outset that there would be litigation on the project, only we
had assumed it would be in the United States, not Canada.

We had pledged to our American counterparts that we would not let American lawsuits tear the deal apart. Having made this commitment eased our own
position somewhat when we explained our predicament to them. The U.S. Army
Corps of Engineers is nothing if not patient; it has a long-range perspective and
considerable experience in dealing with project delays resulting from litigation.
We were told it could wait. Then on April 14, a representative of the U.S. National Wildlife Federation was quoted as saying that his group would "lobby the
American federal government to reconsider its involvement in the $125 million
project."[31] While these were uncharted waters for us in Canada, we had as good
a guarantee as we could get. We held our breath and hoped.

It became apparent early on in our dealings with the federal government
after the CWF I decision that, as a chain is only as strong as its weakest link, a
project is only as good as the agency regulating it. In this case it was Environment Canada, and it wasn't very good. Having decided to appeal the decision,
we wrote to Environment Canada and offered to cooperate fully in its Initial
Environmental Assessment of the project. In a telephone conversation with the
director general of the Inland Waters Directorate, he indicated that Environment
Canada was considering getting some form of motion before the courts that
would allow construction to continue while the Initial Environmental Assessment was being completed.[32] For various reasons, however, this option was ruled
out, and the decision was taken instead to duck as much flack as possible. From

the point of view of the federal government, which had a well-known propensity for watching the polls, Rafferty-Alameda could not have come along at a better time. Concern for the environment was at an all-time high among Canadians. The CWF I decision gave Ottawa the opportunity to appear to be taking a tough stand. The decision of the Federal Court had given the environmental bureaucracy in Ottawa something that it had been unable to achieve on its own—influence and credibility.

That elements within the federal public service were happy with CWF I quickly became obvious. In an article entitled "Ruling on dam cheers environment official," *The Globe and Mail* reported:

> The Chairman of the federal environmental watchdog agency is enthusiastic about a court ruling last week that found the federal Environment Ministry guilty of neglect.
>
> "It is enormously significant," said Raymond Robinson of the Federal Environmental Assessment Review Office, which theoretically oversees all federal projects laden with environmental implications.
>
> The decision on the Rafferty-Alameda Dam project in Saskatchewan and the government's response may finally "turn us into a proactive agency instead of a passive agency," he said.[33]

What made this more difficult for us to accept was that this was the same Raymond Robinson quoted in the letter from the deputy minister of the environment to me indicating that the EARP Guidelines did not apply to the project.

As is evident from the discussion to this point, Environment Canada was no bureaucratic powerhouse in the federal government. The federal environment ministry was not unique in this regard, as similar situations existed within provincial governments. There were, however, close relationships between environmental ministries and their officials on the one hand and environmental interest groups on the other. Throughout the controversy on Rafferty-Alameda, even when things weren't going as the national environmental interest groups would have liked, they were extremely careful about criticizing Environment Canada. The reason for this is simple: they had too much at stake to risk alienating federal officials. Other issues would develop in the future, and burning the bridges on this one made no sense. What criticism there was from environmental interest groups was generally levelled at the politicians rather than the bureaucrats, even when the bureaucrats were obviously to blame. And it usually came from Saskatchewan-based issue-specific groups that were substantively opposed to the project. As one researcher has noted, such groups have little to lose and are rarely well-organized.[34]

With the federal decision not to appeal CWF I, officials from Environment Canada set out to comply with the terms of the EARP Guidelines Order. On April 28 I was speaking with the North Dakota State Water Commission, and I learned from them that Environment Canada was proposing to establish a

Canada-U.S. task force similar to one established to review the Burlington Dam proposal for the Souris a half-decade earlier. It is an unwritten rule of the bureaucracy that if you want to put a stop to something, establish a committee or a task force. Accountability becomes diffuse, the issue gets buried, and it's never heard from again. This is one of the oldest tricks in the book, and we were not about to be fooled by it. While the Saskatchewan government would have found it difficult, if not impossible, to stop the federal government on its own, the Americans could do it at once. Within two weeks, a meeting of the Family was convened in Denver and all parties agreed that the United States would not participate in the proposed task force.

In early May 1989, Environment Canada announced that it would be holding meetings throughout the Souris River basin, that they would be chaired by an external moderator, Vern Millard, past chairman of the Alberta Energy Resources Conservation Board, and that a report was being prepared with the assistance of a consultant and would be distributed in advance of the public meetings. The venues of the meetings during the week of June 22–29 were Regina, Estevan, and Oxbow in Saskatchewan; Souris, Melita, and Brandon in Manitoba; and Minot, North Dakota, in the United States. That an agency of the Canadian government was proposing to hold a public meeting in another country was, to say the least, unusual. Not completely insensitive to the international implications, Environment Canada officials contacted the City of Minot and inquired whether it would agree to invite them to a public meeting. Minot City Manager Bob Schempp called me and asked how we wanted to handle the situation. It presented an interesting problem. In his decision, Mr. Justice Cullen had stated:

> I agree that unwarranted duplication should be avoided but it seems to me that a number of federal concerns were not dealt with by the provincial Environmental Impact Statement, including a review of the impact of the Project in North Dakota and Manitoba. As such, I do not think that applying the EARP Guidelines Order would result in unwarranted duplication but would fill in necessary information gaps.[35]

It is not difficult to predict how the Canadian federal government would react if the U.S. Army Corps of Engineers arbitrarily decided to hold a public meeting in Canada. Canadian nationalists would go crazy, and with justification. Taking the high level of support for the project into consideration, the Family decided that the benefits of having the meeting and complying with the CWF I decision outweighed the liabilities, including potential opposition from the U.S. State Department. Minot extended the invitation and the meeting was held, with only two of some thirty presenters opposing the project.

Since the CWF I decision, we had recognized that we were not in a strong bargaining position, as Environment Canada literally controlled the project's future. A week after the decision, George Hill had written to the regional director general and offered the full cooperation of the staff and consultants of the

Souris Basin Development Authority. The response from Environment Canada was that it would appreciate it if a representative of the SBDA could be present at each of the meetings. Little was said about the report that was being prepared, and requests for clarification concerning the voluminous information we had made available to them—copies of the EIS along with studies that had subsequently been completed as per the terms of ministerial approval, in all some 3,000 pages—were few.

Prior to the public meetings, Environment Canada issued a document it called a "Draft Initial Environmental Evaluation (IEE)," in which it and other agencies of the federal government identified several potential negative impacts from the project; also enumerated were ten areas where more information was required. Among the issues identified were post-project water quality at the Manitoba–North Dakota border, the need for establishment of water quality objectives, and impacts on waterfowl, fish in the United States, and rare flora and fauna.

I convened a meeting of the consultants working on the project to see how best to respond. Some of the comments made by Environment Canada were, no doubt, correct. But there were numerous errors in the document. Information contained in many of the studies we had completed subsequent to the filing of our Environmental Impact Statement with Saskatchewan Environment and Public Safety, and which we had provided to Environment Canada, had been ignored. When I drew this to the attention of Environment Canada officials, they acknowledged that some information the SBDA had provided had been omitted.

The draft IEE was released early in June. The public meetings were scheduled for the last week of the month. The staff and the consultants of the SBDA decided that we had to respond to the shortcomings in the draft IEE before the public meetings. To do otherwise was, in effect, sanctioning them by our silence. We set out to respond to every concern and deficiency Environment Canada had identified. By the middle of June we had prepared a 330-page response.

On the first day of the public meetings, we held a media conference to present our response. It was a painstaking process, and took almost three hours. Considering that Environment Canada controlled the future of the project, we were careful not to engage in commentary critical of the department. In my remarks to the reporters in attendance, I was careful not to criticize the draft IEE. "We present this document not in a confrontational mode," I said, "but in a cooperative mode." These were the last civil words anyone from the project would utter about the federal government for a long time.[36]

Reporters in attendance were not impressed. Kathleen Petty, then of the CTV affiliate in Regina and now with *CBC Newsworld*, asked me why we were providing the media with all this technical information. The implication seemed to be that this was just as bad as trying to hide information. It was then I realized that most journalists were members of that large and growing constituency that had no interest in the actual environmental impacts of the project.

Our appeal of CWF I was heard the same day, and our lawyers were given short shift by the Federal Court of Appeal. The court issued an oral decision from the Bench, an infrequent occurrence and not something any lawyer looks forward to. When the telephone message from Tom Gauley was delivered to me at the press conference, it was a simple one: "Blood on the floor."

The level of public support for the project during the Saskatchewan Board of Inquiry in 1987 had been significant. By our count, fully 66 percent of those appearing in front of the provincial panel were in favor of the project. Going into the second set of hearings, we weren't sure what had happened in the intervening two years. As far as we could tell, there was still strong support in the Souris basin. But given the increased attention now focused on the project, the stakes were considerably higher. The question facing the government of Saskatchewan was what profile to give the issue. There were those in the Premier's Office who wanted Devine to distance himself from an issue they perceived as an increasing political liability. Given the media coverage and the draft IEE, this was not an entirely unreasonable position to take.

To his credit, the premier would have none of it. He seemed to relish the notion of putting his reputation on the line, and he agreed with Berntson,

Premier Grant Devine at the June 1989 Environment Canada meeting held in response to the decision of Justice Cullen in the first Canadian Wildlife Federation case. Devine's advisors disagreed on whether he should appear at these meetings or not. To the premier's left are Environment Canada official Bev Burns and Vern Millard, chair of the proceedings. Courtesy Regina Leader-Post

Hill, and me that he should appear at the IEE meetings. Certainly, he should appear at the first meeting, which was in Regina and would receive the most media attention. This would send a clear message to Ottawa that the project was of the highest priority to Saskatchewan.

In addition to Grant Devine, North Dakota Governor George Sinner also appeared at the Initial Environmental Evaluation meeting in Regina in support of the project, as did the majority of those giving presentations. The main critics of Rafferty-Alameda were also there.[37] However, one of the intriguing aspects of the whole controversy was, for all the opposition, the most vocal critics chose to appear only at the public meetings of the IEE; they managed to avoid the actual formal hearings into the project.

Attendance at these meetings throughout the basin was high and, while there were pockets of opposition, particularly in Manitoba, overall public support actually increased to about 75 percent of those expressing their views.[38] This increase was owing, perhaps, to disaffection over Ottawa's handling of the issue.

The meetings were completed in the last week of June 1989. In early July, the government of Saskatchewan submitted its formal brief as part of the IEE. Given the jurisdictional and hydrological complexity of the issue, the regulatory problems that had been imposed on the project by Ottawa, not to mention the controversy and the misunderstanding that existed within the federal government, we felt it necessary to get our position on record—over and above the voluminous documentation contained in our Environmental Impact Statement—which we did, in a seven-volume submission. On July 4, I learned that federal officials were working on the terms of a new IRIA license. Among the provisions under consideration were fish by-passes in irrigation weirs, no net loss in waterfowl productivity, the establishment of ecological reserves, and mitigation provisions for the Ferruginous hawk and Baird's sparrow. While in substance, these provisions would not be difficult for us to live with, and in a number of instances were activities we had already committed ourselves to, that they were being considered for inclusion in the IRIA license bothered us.

The *International River Improvements Act* is a federal statute that concerns itself with water flows on rivers that cross the international border from Canada into the United States. While the regulations to the act provide for a somewhat broader interpretation, this is the primary intent of the IRIA. Environment Canada's inclusion of nonhydrology provisions in our license was of concern simply because many of them were not within the jurisdiction of the federal government. Protecting Ferruginous hawks is important, to be sure, but it would seem to be equally important that before a government imposes a regulatory requirement it ought to have the legal authority to do so. When we drew our concerns to the attention of Environment Canada, we were told basically to take it or leave it. From the Saskatchewan perspective, the choice was obvious.

On August 31, Environment Minister Lucien Bouchard held a press conference in the Hotel Saskatchewan in Regina to announce that he was issuing a new IRIA license for the Rafferty-Alameda project, this one with twenty-two conditions as opposed to the thirteen of the original. The federal government came to the press conference armed with documents to show how rigorous the new license was and how extensively Manitoba's interests and the environment were going to be protected. Bouchard also released a copy of the Moderator's Report and the final version of the Initial Environmental Evaluation. From Saskatchewan's point of view, Moderator Vern Millard could not have drafted a better report. It stated, in part:

> ... the basic issue is the relative importance of the residents' needs for flood control and assured water supply versus the possible loss of some populations of endangered or rare species and the loss of a portion of the river. If the project is not approved the only alternatives for valley residents are to either continue to suffer from floods and inadequate water supplies or leave the valley. While the environmental impacts are significant and serious, they do not appear to be of such magnitude as to justify such harsh treatment of residents of the valley.
>
> ... This is a unique case that does not fit into the normal categories. Unlike the normal case, the Project has already been subjected to review by the Saskatchewan Board of Inquiry in 1987 as well as the recent public meetings respecting the IEE. The same arguments were presented at both reviews by mostly the same people or organizations. Therefore, the views of the public are known.
>
> ... In my view the information necessary to make a fair and informed decision is available today and nothing would be gained by another round of hearings and argument. Indeed further hearings would likely increase the dissension between the parties and make final resolution more difficult.[39]

Bouchard provided his own justification for the reissuance of a license for the project:

> ... the Initial Environmental Evaluation, coupled with previous environmental impact studies and hearings conducted by Saskatchewan and American authorities, provide entirely sufficient information on which to base a fair and informed decision regarding the Rafferty-Alameda decision. The Court found that the federal government did not completely assume its responsibility. Now we did it and we can tell the people that at the end of the process we are now sure that we can go along with the project provided the new conditions be implemented and be respected ...
>
> ... in light of all the studies completed and the extensive public discussions on the project to date, it is unlikely that a panel review would produce significant additional information. The objectives of a panel review have in fact been achieved.
>
> The Rafferty-Alameda Project is a living example of the sustainable development challenge: maintaining environmental qual-

ity while fostering economic development. I am persuaded that the project, governed by some twenty-two conditions, will leave present and future generations better positioned to meet their needs—for food, water, electricity and security from floods that have so devastated this part of the North American plain.[40]

The response from all sides was predictable. Grant Devine claimed that it was "a victory for the people of Saskatchewan."[41] For those opposed to the project it was another story. Interest groups were openly disdainful. Lorne Scott of the Saskatchewan Wildlife Federation (SWF) said it was "a very disappointing decision. We are back to square one, where it's build now, study later. Really, it's basically a sell-out from an environmental perspective . . . as far as I can see right now, we have far more evidence for a successful court case than we did the first time, because the federal environment staff indicated major problems."[42]

Another outspoken opponent of the project, referring to Lucien Bouchard, stated, "I think he declared war on the environment movement in Canada. I think he sold us out."[43]

The NDP waded into the fray with their environment critic, Ed Tchorzewski, saying that the Devine government couldn't be trusted to live up to the commitments in the license: "It makes absolutely no sense to tell this government to go ahead and build the dam and then afterwards we will determine if it is legal."[44]

(Left to right) *Estevan Mayor John Empey, Premier Grant Devine, Jack Muirhead (head of the Souris Basin Support Association), Joyce Muirhead, and Deputy Premier Eric Berntson pictured at a street dance held when residents of Estevan celebrated the issuance of a second* International Improvements Act *license in August 1989.* Courtesy Estevan Mercury

The people of the Souris basin in Saskatchewan were euphoric. The residents of Estevan responded by holding their first street dance since 1945. A third of the population of the city of 10,000 came out to celebrate.[45] For those of us working on the project, there was relief coupled with a sense of foreboding. The bulldozers were moving again, and it was nice to see the politicians and the local people in a spirit to celebrate. But George Hill and I shared with complete certainty the expectation that this thing was going back to court. The "Final" Initial Environmental Evaluation issued when Bouchard made his announcement was not all that different from the draft document that had been issued for the public meetings. Environment Canada had screwed up again, and only those of us who were most familiar with the issue knew it. The first federal mistake, we estimated, had cost Saskatchewan over $5 million. We both knew that this next one was going to cost more—a lot more. The only question was, Who would pay for it? Standing on the main street of Estevan while provincial politicians crowed and the residents of the Souris basin danced in the street, Hill and I were adamant it wouldn't be us this time.

CHAPTER FIVE

GETTING THE BETTER OF THEM

The instructions were explicit: once I had a signed copy of the new IRIA license in hand, I was to call Hill. Leaving in the middle of Bouchard's press conference, I placed the call from the second-floor foyer in the Hotel Saskatchewan. Hill immediately called the main contractor on Rafferty, Walter "Jumbo" Panteluk in Estevan, and the bulldozers and scrapers that had sat dormant all summer began to roll. Panteluk's machines didn't stop for the street dance, weekends, darkness, or anything else until the weather made them. Beginning on August 31, work continued twenty-four hours a day, seven days a week, through Labour Day and past Thanksgiving. We had our window of opportunity and we made the most of it. Over those seventy-five days, more than a million cubic meters of fill were placed. When freeze-up finally came on November 14, the dam was 80 percent complete. More important, river closure had been effected. We were past the point of no return.

It didn't take opponents of the project long to reach the same conclusion we had—that the way Environment Canada had conducted the IEE left the project vulnerable to further litigation. By that time, we knew the federal department leaked like a sieve. The more the issue evolved, the more apparent it became that officials in Environment Canada were closer to the interest groups within their own policy community than they were to the rest of the government.

A close association between a government department and various interest groups is not uncommon, for ongoing relationships develop between agencies and client groups all the time. What makes environment ministries unique is that they have been staffed by committed environmentalists who maintain a close association with institutionalized interest groups. Governments and projects come and go, but the relationships between departments and vested interests continue.[1]

For some time we had been aware that factions within Environment Canada were pressing for a referral of the project to a panel. We also knew that, if we knew it, the Ottawa-based environmental interest groups knew it as well. It didn't take a legal expert to see that the federal environmental assessment process was inadequate, or that any project being reviewed pursuant to it was vulnerable to litigation. Neither did it take a legal expert to determine that the Environment Canada Initial Environmental Evaluation report on Rafferty-Alameda seemed to be written without any consideration for the provisions of the EARP Guidelines.

While our primary concern was the Rafferty Dam, as the timing of its completion was related to the completion of the Shand Generating Station, we were also working on other aspects of the project. The reissuing of the federal license meant that we were able to proceed with everything but the Alameda Dam. Under the terms of the ministerial approval issued by the Saskatchewan minister of the environment, we could not begin that until the agreement with the United States had been finalized.

Within a week of my phone call to Hill from the foyer of the Hotel Saskatchewan, I received a call from one of the consultants working on the project. He had learned that three groups, led by the Canadian Wildlife Federation, were about to contest Bouchard's decision to reissue the IRIA license. The only surprise in this was the speed with which it occurred. There was nothing we could do about it but keep the pressure on the construction crews and work as quickly as possible to finalize negotiations with the Americans.

On October 3 the project was dealt another blow by a shuffle of the provincial Cabinet. Berntson was no longer deputy premier or our minister. His contribution to the project had been inestimable. He was the only elected politician at either the federal or the provincial level who truly understood Rafferty-Alameda in all its complexities and nuances. His departure was an omen for the government. He had acted as a counterbalance to some of the political advisors to Devine. Without Berntson to rein them in, the crazies

When the second IRIA license was issued by Lucien Bouchard, work on the Rafferty Dam rumbled on into the night, unabated, twenty-four hours a day, seven days a week until freeze-up. Local residents, with lawn chairs and picnic hampers, congregated daily at the site to observe the Panteluk Construction company workers and machinery. Courtesy Estevan Mercury

would have a field day. It was tantamount to putting the lunatics in charge of the asylum.

With the shuffle, Harold Martens became our minister. A former municipal politician from the Morse area west of Moose Jaw, Martens was a nice enough fellow, but he had no Cabinet experience and he was certainly no Berntson. If Devine had known that the project was almost certainly going back to court, he would never have filled this portfolio with someone with no Cabinet experience. The appointment placed an additional burden on the project, and also demonstrated how far we had fallen out of favor with those in the Legislative Building.

On numerous occasions Berntson had defended both Hill and me to the Cabinet and the caucus. He had defended us through all the internecine squabbles that characterized the Devine government. Berntson let you know where you stood. He felt you had a right to know who your friends and enemies were. One of his first statements to me when I started working full-time on Rafferty-Alameda was, "Hood, I'll stand behind you all the way until it begins to hurt me, then you're on your own." With Berntson, you never forgot who you were working for, or what his interest was on any given issue.

It was no secret that Hill and I had made enemies in the Cabinet. With the project situated in Devine's and Berntson's constituencies, it was difficult for ministers to criticize it without criticizing either the premier or the deputy premier. And with Rafferty-Alameda eating up the government's rapidly declining political and financial capital—as it was perceived by some—we became the only targets that Cabinet ministers could aim at.

Hill was arguably more powerful than any elected politician in Saskatchewan other than Berntson and Devine. This alone made him the target of attacks from within the party. Without Eric Berntson around, I knew it would not be long before the knives were drawn.

Within days of the Cabinet shuffle the Canadian Wildlife Federation announced that it was taking the federal minister back to court. Their argument was a simple one. Lucien Bouchard, in his capacity as minister of the environment, had attempted to comply with the EARP Guidelines. That much was accepted. The point the CWF sought to make in Federal Court was that he had applied the guidelines incorrectly. Since the IEE had concluded that the project would have "significant" impacts on the environment under the terms of the EARP Guidelines, the minister was legally obliged to refer it to a review by an independent panel.

The CWF was joined in the litigation by two brothers from the Alameda area, Ed and Harold Tetzlaff, who had been involved indirectly in CWF I. The Tetzlaffs, who operated a seven-quarter section farm adjacent to the site of the Alameda Dam, provide a human dimension to the story.

When the Souris Basin Development Authority was first formed, we had questioned many of the assumptions about the project, including the sites that had been selected for the two dams. We learned that the identification of the dam sites at both Rafferty and Alameda had been made in the 1960s by the Prairie Farm Rehabilitation Administration (PFRA) as part of the Saskatchewan-

Nelson Basin Study. Not surprisingly, the criteria for the site selections had a great deal to do with hydrology and geology and very little to do with environmental effects. The formation of the SBDA provided the opportunity to implement integrated resource planning techniques, and the criteria for dam site selection were expanded to include environmental and socioeconomic considerations. Consequently, alternative sites for both dams were chosen. The original site for the Alameda Dam had been ten kilometers further north, or upstream, of the site that was ultimately selected.

The decision to move the site was made for all the right environmental reasons. The new site—what became known as Site C—would create a reservoir in a deeper part of the valley where more water could be stored, less land would be inundated, and losses from evaporation would be lower. Fewer roads, granular resources, wildlife habitat, and oil field facilities would be affected at the new site, which would also provide greater recreation benefits than had the original site. All of this could be done for the same cost, or so we thought. But the reservoir at the new site would inundate land owned by Ed and Harold Tetzlaff.

Shortly after we had made the decision to move the Alameda Dam, I got a call from Berntson. "Hood," he said, "I hear that you've moved the Alameda Dam. What's going on?" I summarized the analysis, told him the results, and explained why it was the logical decision. Berntson then asked if we had con-

Harold (left) and Ed Tetzlaff at the Alameda Dam site. The land belonging to the two bachelor brothers became a battleground in the fight over Rafferty-Alameda. Courtesy Regina Leader-Post

sidered who would be affected at the new site who wouldn't have been affected at the old site, and if we had taken that into account. I remember actually scoffing, saying that the matter had not been considered because it was inherently illogical. This was a project that would last hundreds of years; it made no sense to premise such a fundamental decision on which landowners might be affected.

"Why do you ask?" I inquired, finally.

"Well," he said, "I hear that Ed and Harold Tetzlaff are mighty pissed at the decision to move the dam, and you might be opening up a real can of worms by doing this. I just wanted to be sure that you smart guys were certain you had it in the right place, or if you might want to consider moving the thing slightly upstream so that it doesn't affect them."

"No need to worry, Eric," I said. "We've got it all cased. We've made this decision for all the right reasons. We've got a good land policy that pays about two-and-a-half times the going market value for land. Nobody can be that unreasonable."[2]

I remember going into Hill's office and telling him about the conversation I'd just had with Berntson. "Can you believe it? He was actually suggesting that we move the dam again, only slightly upstream this time in order to avoid the Tetzlaffs!" It wasn't a moveable dam. We couldn't just relocate the thing every time someone didn't like what we were doing.

As I learned, when Berntson called you a "smart guy," you checked your wallet. It usually meant that he was right. If we had paid attention to the landowners who were affected at the new site, we would have found two bachelor brothers who were to become what a developer least wants—a martyr, or in this case, martyrs.

Ed and Harold Tetzlaff, as local rumor had it, were the bachelor sons of immigrants who had come to Canada because their land had been confiscated by the state after the Bolshevik Revolution. The brothers had farmed all their lives and knew no other lifestyle. They lived by themselves in a two-story fieldstone house across the highway from the town of Alameda. Another local rumor suggested the brothers had money buried on their land, and that was why they were so opposed to the project.

Ed and Harold Tetzlaff were featured in the national media determinedly heading into court with their farm caps on. They provided a powerful television image of two defenceless brothers having their way of life attacked by a cold-hearted government willing to dam Moose Mountain Creek at any cost. They joined SCRAP, and were willing to oppose both the federal and the provincial governments at every turn. They were willing to litigate even when the CWF was not. They proved to be a powerful opposition simply because of what they represented. If I had known then what I know now, I would have moved the dam.

Imagery aside, the Tetzlaff case provides an important lesson for those developing environmentally sensitive projects. It used to be that the primary considerations for dam building could be expressed in three basic questions: How high should the dam be, given the amount of water to be stored? What are the foundation conditions at the site where you want to put the dam? Where will the

material to build the dam come from? With the increase in environmental awareness in the 1970s, other considerations were taken into account, including the
impact of the development on the biophysical environment as well as its socioeconomic effects. While we analyzed all of the biophysical factors at Site C, we
did not analyze the perceptions of the people who would be affected by the
move. Obviously, this was a mistake. Environmental assessment has become
sufficiently sensitive to public opinion that a major project developer can ill
afford not to do this.

The response from Saskatchewan supporters of the project to the decision
by the Canadian Wildlife Federation and the Tetzlaffs to contest Bouchard's
reissuing of the license ranged from anger to disbelief. The Saskatchewan Wildlife Federation, a federated member of the CWF, had experienced dissension
among its members because of CWF I and the decision to support the litigation.
A number of SWF branches had expressed reservations about the position of the
CWF on the Rafferty-Alameda issue for a variety of reasons, not the least being
that two past presidents of the SWF resided in the area and were strongly in
support of the dams. In an effort to allay internal dissension, the SWF had gone
to the trouble of announcing that its concerns about the Rafferty-Alameda project
had been satisfied by the additional conditions placed in the new IRIA license.[3]

The response from residents of the Estevan area was one of disbelief. John
Empey, mayor of Estevan, expressed his frustration: "It's absolutely absurd!
The damn thing has been studied to death—what more do they want?"[4] What

*Estevan Mayor John Empey being interviewed by Minot television reporter Rae
Schoebinger. Unlike many major projects, Rafferty-Alameda was overwhelmingly supported by those most affected by it, on both sides of the border.* Courtesy Estevan Mercury

Empey and others from the area didn't realize was that, from the CWF's perspective, the argument was now about process and precedent. The federation was openly acknowledging the fact. The dam had never been the issue, as CWF Executive Vice-President Ken Brynaert told the *Regina Leader-Post*: "The issue is whether the federal minister has complied with the environmental guidelines— we believe he hasn't." In the *Saskatoon Star-Phoenix* he was quoted as saying, "We have never said, nor do we say now, that we are opposed to the Rafferty-Alameda dam. What we take exception to is the method in which the license was issued.[5]

The CWF case (hereafter referred to as CWF II) was heard in Winnipeg at the end of November before Mr. Justice Francis Muldoon of the Federal Court–Trial Division. Justice Muldoon conducts himself in court in an open, congenial manner, and is easily liked. Going into court, we were hopeful that he might harbor some latent sympathy for Saskatchewan because of the clearly awkward position the federal government had put us in. Counsel for the CWF, Brian Crane of the Ottawa law firm of Gowling, Strathy, and Henderson, stated that the federation was not out to stop the project. Counsel for the federal minister, Brian Saunders, urged that, if the minister had erred, the license be left intact. Federal Justice lawyers had indicated to us their concerns that there could be problems because of the absence of a "paper trail"—there was little on paper to record if or on what basis Lucien Bouchard had made the decision to reissue the IRIA license for the project. From the way things were going, I sensed we were in trouble.[6]

I went to Ontario for Christmas. It wasn't much of a surprise when I got a call from Tom Gauley on December 28 (I hadn't had an uninterrupted holiday since I started working on the project), but his salutation—"Are you sitting down?"—threw me. Muldoon, Gauley told me, had rendered a scathing decision critical of the federal government, and in terms rarely encountered in legal decisions:

> It is perhaps unfortunate that the IEE does not, in its terminology, conform with or adhere to the very descriptions expressed in the EARP Guidelines Order, which surely must have been known to the IEE's authors. After all, it was the Minister's failure to follow the EARP in the first place which persuaded the court to set aside the first license.

Muldoon went on to deal with Environment Canada officials:

> . . . The authors of the IEE, Volume I, p. 12–2 under "Summary of Adverse Environment Impacts Caused by Altered Flows and Lake Levels," for example, speak of "*Significant* Impacts" to be sure, but also of "*Moderate* Impacts." How inattentive, or silly, of those authors. What did they expect the Minister to make of that? The EARP Guidelines do not refer to "moderate" adverse environmental effects. Whatever the Minister understood, the court must also understand what it means. It

seems clear that as between significant and insignificant effects, "moderate impacts" must be taken clearly to mean "not insignificant." Effects which are not insignificant ("minimes") must obviously be significant ("importants") effects, in second place of importance among the significant adverse effects . . . So, the court must take it to be the authors' meaning that moderate impacts are significant adverse environmental effects.

Lucien Bouchard did not escape Muldoon's indignation:

> . . . the Minister ought lawfully to have subjected the proposals to such public review, as it is clearly mandated by this binding, authoritative legislation. The Minister's advisers ought to have advised him to embrace the EARP Guidelines warmly, instead of seeking ways to abridge or avoid the process.
>
> The respondent Minister's counsel urge that, if the court finds that the Minister did not comply with the EARP, then the court should nevertheless exercise a discretion to excuse that lawbreaking. It is notionally easier to excuse an individual tangled in regulations and bureaucracy than it is to excuse a Minister of the Crown from noncompliance with relevant, binding legislation, whether regulatory or not. If there be anyone who ought scrupulously to conform to the official duties which the law casts upon him or her in the rôle of a high State official, it is a Minister of the Crown. That is just plainly obvious.[7]

It was a stinging rebuke for any minister of the Crown. For Bouchard, a lawyer, it must have been especially harsh. The question for Muldoon, as he phrased it in the decision, was, "What is the best way to unscramble the omelette which has been made of the EARP Guidelines in this case?"

His solution was to order that the IRIA license be quashed and set aside at the close of business on Tuesday January 30, 1990, unless in the meantime the minister of the environment appointed a panel pursuant to the EARP Guidelines Order to conduct a public review of those aspects of the Rafferty-Alameda project that were identified in the IEE as having adverse environmental effects.

After reviewing the decision, we were convinced that Muldoon was right in his analysis—Bouchard and his officials had erred—but wrong in his remedy. If the federal minister was under a legal obligation to appoint a panel prior to issuing a license, then Muldoon had no option but to quash the license in the same manner that Mr. Justice Cullen had done in CWF I. The opinion we were getting from Gauley and Kennedy was that the Muldoon decision likely would not stand if there was an appeal or at least the remedy portion of it wouldn't. We would lose the appeal, and the license with it.

Room to maneuver was limited. River closure had been effected on the Rafferty Dam and the dam itself was 80 percent complete. The Shand Generating Station, which was to be cooled with water from the Rafferty Reservoir, was past the point where other cooling options could be economically considered. The hydrology of the Souris River is precarious at the best of times; we felt we could ill-afford to lose the 1990 runoff.

Individually, we were also becoming worried about our own legal positions. If the IRIA license was revoked, the Rafferty Dam would be illegal. If things turned nasty, and there already had been signs that the opponents of the project were playing hard-ball, the federal government might be forced to invoke the penalty provisions of the act—a major consideration, as the act contains provisions for fines and imprisonment for violations. The way things were going, the possibility that we could all end up in jail was no laughing matter.

Many opponents of the project got a great deal of mileage from Saskatchewan Premier Grant Devine's close relationship to the prime minister. Devine himself had made much of the fact that, during the 1986 provincial election, he was able to cajole $1 billion from the federal government in drought assistance for western Canadian farmers. Given Devine's narrow margin of victory in that election, the cash from Ottawa might well have been the deciding factor. In Canadian politics, however, there is a limit even to what your friends can do for you. Because of the nature of the Muldoon decision, Saskatchewan and Grant Devine were about to learn that they had reached the end of the line.

CWF II had placed the federal government in general, and Lucien Bouchard in particular, in an extremely awkward position. Bouchard had been appointed minister of the environment with considerable fanfare. Much had been made of his longtime friendship with Brian Mulroney. He had been given a mandate to bring the full weight of his position to Environment Canada and elevate it to a position of prominence within the federal government.[8]

CWF II must have been embarrassing to Bouchard not only in political terms, but in professional terms, given its condemnation of ministerial efforts to circumvent the law. Environment Canada and Bouchard were under pressure from the environmental policy community to allow the IRIA license to lapse. Environmental lobby groups were primarily concerned about precedent and process definition through the decisions that were then winding their way through the Federal Court. For them, it was not a question of the specifics of Rafferty-Alameda, although this was an issue, it was a matter of ensuring under which set of circumstances a federal panel review would occur. Lingering in the background was the position the federal government would take on James Bay II and how Lucien Bouchard, an ardent Quebec nationalist, would respond. For issue-specific anti-project groups whose sole *raison d'être* was to stop the project, attempting to convince the federal minister that the license should be allowed to lapse before a panel was appointed was another way of trying to stop the project.

Public pronouncements to the contrary, no one on either side of the issue could have been under any illusions about what the EARP Guidelines were or were not. Their flaws were obvious. As McGill University's Thomas Meredith has noted:

Public workshops have been held to consider reform of EARP itself. Concerns regarded the use of "self-regulation," noting that assessment has been "carried out inconsistently and in some cases is not being implemented" (FEARO, 1988), and noting also that there is a general lack of accountability.[9]

Almost everyone agreed that, if one set out to draft a new federal environmental assessment law, the odds were it would not look anything like the EARP Guidelines. If environmental assessment was to be meaningful, how could a panel review be carried out while construction on the project continued?

On the other hand, Rafferty-Alameda was no ordinary project, and the guidelines were no ordinary regulatory instrument. There was nothing in the EARP Guidelines that expressly forbade construction during a panel review. While this didn't make sense, it is what happens when a regulatory instrument that was not written with the intention of its being interpreted as law is deemed by the courts to be mandatory.

Interests substantively opposed to the project felt if they managed to halt construction a second time, they might be able to kill that portion of it that had not yet begun—namely, the Alameda Dam. A review by a federally appointed panel would take at least a year, perhaps longer. Grant Devine's mandate ran out in 1992, and it was already apparent that he was going to have difficulty getting reelected. If the Alameda Dam was not far enough along by then, it was a sure bet that an NDP government wouldn't build it.

The dynamics of the situation were not good, and we knew it. We wanted to avoid an appeal of CWF II at all costs, for we felt that Muldoon's remedy was wrong, that he was in fact obligated to quash the license. If that happened, both the project and the people working on it would be in big trouble.

In the first week of January, we contacted Bouchard's office and set up a meeting for January 12. The impact of the provincial Cabinet shuffle became immediately apparent, as we didn't have Berntson to carry the political ball for us. Indeed, so confused were things in Regina that our newly appointed minister, Harold Martens, either backed out or was pushed aside, and the task of representing Saskatchewan at the meeting with Bouchard was inexplicably assumed by George McLeod, minister responsible for SaskPower. During the meeting with Bouchard, McLeod was nervous, obviously not in command of the complex technical issues. Despite our proposal to allow construction to continue during the panel review, Bouchard's reaction was what we expected: Ottawa was abandoning us. The realities of the federal system had finally asserted themselves. Bouchard faced two options: allow the IRIA license to lapse and upset Saskatchewan with its fourteen seats in the House of Commons, only two of which were held by the federal Conservatives, or appoint the panel by the specified date and undermine his own credibility as minister of the environment.

Bouchard spoke in bitter terms, in front of his department officials, of being betrayed by the lawyers, and, indeed, his own bureaucrats.[10] When he uttered those words, I knew we'd had it. Blaming one's bureaucrats is the last refuge of a weak and desperate politician.

It was clear that the minister was not going to appoint the panel by the time Muldoon had ordered, and thus the license would lapse. As an alternative, we proposed that he appoint a panel by the date prescribed and allow construction to continue in the meantime, as was clearly intended by the CWF II decision. Bouchard's response was that "no government could live with your proposal."[11] He did indicate, however, that if we could reach some form of accord with the CWF and the Tetzlaffs, he would be willing to appoint the panel. It had all the appearances of political expedience.

We began to prepare for the worst. The officers and directors of the SBDA, including Hill and me, were indemnified in order to protect ourselves, as much as possible, should the license be quashed and charges laid. We instructed our lawyers to initiate discussions with counsel for the CWF and the Tetzlaffs to determine whether there was a will among the parties to reach a settlement. Saskatchewan would agree to delay the initiation of construction and land acquisition at the Alameda site in return for an agreement that the parties would not appeal CWF II. Early in the third week of January, our lawyers informed us that no multilateral deal was possible. We were left with the prospect of dealing bilaterally with the federal government and running the risk that one of the other parties would litigate anyway.

Environment Canada was faced with a public that had become increasingly concerned about the quality of the environment and, not unreasonably, was looking to it to protect their interests. It was dealing with a number of major projects that were either in the process of being developed or were on the drawing board, and questions about how they would be handled by the federal government were not clear. The Oldman River Dam and the Alpac Pulp Mill in Alberta, the Kemano hydroelectric project in northwestern British Columbia, and the James Bay II hydroelectric project were all putting demands on the ministry. And in one way or another, at the center of the debate was how the federal government would respond to Rafferty-Alameda—a project that it did not understand, that had caused it acute embarrassment, and that was fundamentally misunderstood by much of the Canadian public.

One might have thought that people at the political and senior levels of Environment Canada would have anticipated how Saskatchewan would respond to the move to allow the license to lapse. Perhaps they thought it was an affordable risk as they attempted to placate the forces calling for greater federal intervention in this area. Or perhaps, as Hill and I suspected, it was a reflection of the lack of respect in Ottawa for the current Saskatchewan government. Whatever the case, there was something Ottawa did not factor into the equation: in Saskatchewan, the issue was no longer about federal environmental assessment or saving the federal government embarrassment. It was now pure politics.

Confrontation was not Grant Devine's nature. Throughout his tenure in office, arguably to the point of sycophancy, he steadfastly supported the Mulroney government. It is difficult to argue with his success in obtaining federal support for agriculture. That having been said, the growing animosity between the federal and provincial governments over Rafferty-Alameda created major difficulties for Devine. Beginning in late 1989, a faction within the Saskatchewan government wanted to start taking a hard line with Ottawa on Rafferty-Alameda.

Berntson and Hill were convinced that the government would have to draw a line in the sand and play some tough politics with Ottawa in order to get a settlement. Both men had as much riding on the project as anyone, including Devine. The problem was that Berntson was no longer directly involved, and Hill wasn't in the Cabinet. It was also painfully clear that Devine, despite his support for the project, was not prepared to fight with Ottawa on any issue, let alone this one.

Devine's reluctance to take a stand in support of Rafferty-Alameda and the loss of Berntson had begun to affect relations between Hill and the premier.[12] Leaving the Legislative Building one day, after a briefing with Devine, I asked Hill what he would do if he were in Devine's shoes. Stopping abruptly, he said, "Hood, if I were in his shoes, we wouldn't be in this fucking mess." As for Berntson, he indicated that he was willing to resign from the legislature and wage the battle against the federal government from the outside; indeed, so strong were his convictions on the matter that he offered to start an interest group called the Coalition for Environmental Justice that would initiate a litany of lawsuits against projects and activities across the country, including the Sky Dome in Toronto (then under construction on federal land), the issuing of defence contracts in Quebec, and the advance payment to grain farmers. From our reading of the EARP Guidelines, they were so nebulous that all these activities were vulnerable to litigation.

By January 22 we were within a week of the deadline Mr. Justice Muldoon had set in the CWF II decision. The only options Bouchard was willing to consider were the voluntary cessation of construction or the loss of the license. Losing the license was out of the question for us, so it became an issue of negotiating the terms under which we would bring a halt to construction.

On January 22, 1990, during a telephone conversation between Hill and the federal deputy minister of the environment, Len Good, Hill put forward the Saskatchewan position. Saskatchewan would be willing to:

1) cease construction of the Rafferty Dam after safety and stability matters were taken care of;
2) not start construction of the diversion channel between Rafferty Reservoir and Boundary Reservoir; and,
3) not acquire land or start construction of the Alameda Dam.[13]

In return, Saskatchewan would receive financial compensation, to be negotiated, and a mutually agreed upon statement from the federal government that the delays in construction were not the fault of Saskatchewan.

Throughout the week of January 22, numerous phone conversations took place between Hill and Good on the terms of the agreement. It became obvious that federal officials were treating these negotiations as a matter with no down-side risk; they were merely playing out the string, and the license would be allowed to lapse. Environment Canada had made it clear that, if the license did lapse and Saskatchewan continued construction, Bouchard would seek an injunction to restrain us, and this would actually leave him in a better political position.[14]

To strengthen our position we needed leverage, and we found it in three areas. First, stopping the construction of a dam involves the resolution of a number of serious technical concerns, such as the routing of next spring's runoff and limiting damage to the structure from a delay of unknown duration. It was clear that some work would be required in order to leave the Rafferty Dam in a safe and stable condition. We took the position that the decision to stop construction on Rafferty would have to pass the scrutiny of existing standards in the engineering profession. The federal government started negotiating in a very aggressive manner, insisting that only a limited amount of work should be allowed. They altered their position significantly when we insisted that, if this was to be the case, we would insist that the seals of Environment Canada engineers be placed on anything that was done.

While Environment Canada had little experience in the environmental assessment field, it had even less in the dam design business. The engineers in Environment Canada wanted nothing to do with putting their necks on the line on a project as sensitive as the Rafferty Dam. Eventually, we convinced Environment Canada that the Engineering Review Board should be allowed to decide what work was necessary. The board, made up of preeminent members of the engineering profession, had been advising us on the adequacy of the plans submitted by our dam designers. As a result, the board members were far more familiar with the design details of the Rafferty Dam than Environment Canada could ever hope to be. We were fairly confident that the inherent conservatism of the engineering profession, the fact that river closure had already been effected, and the latent sympathy of the Engineering Review Board with our plight would ensure that as much of the Rafferty Dam as possible would be completed. We were betting the board would recommend our virtually completing the structure in order to stabilize it.

The second factor in gaining leverage in the negotiations to halt construction was that, because the federal government had insisted on the IRIA license being drafted in the form of a contract and signed by both parties, it could not be amended without the consent of the Saskatchewan government. This meant that, if the license were kept in place, the federal government would need the cooperation of Saskatchewan if the recommendations of the panel were to have any effect. If the license were allowed to lapse, then Ottawa ran the risk that, after the federal panel had reported, its minister would find himself in the position of being able to issue a license dealing only with federal jurisdiction, for there was no guarantee that Saskatchewan would agree to any incursion into provincial jurisdiction in a third IRIA license. This would mean the third IRIA license for the project could actually be weaker than the one currently in effect.

Negotiations between Saskatchewan and Environment Canada continued via telephone and fax throughout the week of January 22. They were held at all hours of the day and night. As the time remaining to Muldoon's deadline diminished, the tension increased. As Hill noted, it appeared " . . . that the major stumbling block would be the payment of money by the federal government for compensation and an acknowledgement that the federal government were to blame for the delays."[15]

The third factor that increased our leverage with Environment Canada was, in reality, a combination of factors. In the CWF II decision, Mr. Justice Muldoon had been extremely critical of both the federal minister of the environment and Environment Canada. It was apparent from the wording of his decision and the nature of the order that he held no sympathy for the federal government on this matter. Clearly, in writing the order the way he did, Muldoon anticipated that Bouchard would appoint the panel by January 30. By the midpoint of the week of January 22, we knew that, left to his own instincts, Bouchard would do no such thing.

Another factor was the addition to our legal team of David Wilson of the law firm Osler, Hoskin, and Harcourt in Ottawa. To this point, we had relied on Osler, Hoskin, and Harcourt to act as our agents in Ottawa, in which capacity they merely expedited the filing of material and the acquisition of court dates, as well as fulfilling other administrative functions. In January, Gauley and Kennedy suggested that David Wilson be added to the team. Wilson, in his mid-thirties, had articled at the Supreme Court and had considerable experience appearing before the Federal Court of Canada.

Enormously capable, Wilson came up with a strategy that allowed us to put pressure on the federal minister to reach some form of accommodation and allow the license to remain in place. Wilson suggested that we make an application to Mr. Justice Muldoon to have his order in CWF II varied, that we apply for an extension in time to have the panel appointed and an even longer period of time for the license to be quashed in the event that the minister did not appoint the panel. It was a sound strategy, for if we were successful, and if the minister did not appoint the panel by the new date, we would have sufficient cause to go back before Muldoon and apply to have the federal minister cited for contempt of court.

On Wednesday, January 24, Hill told Len Good of our intentions to apply to Muldoon for a variance of the order. In the bland language of his sworn affidavit, Hill recounted: "the speed of negotiations did not seem to increase as a result of such information being given to Dr. Good."[16] What this meant was that the deputy minister of the environment either did not understand the potential significance of the action or he was underestimating our willingness to go through with it, or perhaps both.

The discussions continued through Thursday, January 25, with little result. The range for the financial compensation was broad, from a few million dollars to more than $50 million. Hill was also pushing for a time limit, with a target date of late spring or early summer for the panel review. But according to Hill,

Dr. Good implored me not to insist on a final reporting date for the proposed Panel, as they, the federal government, wanted to leave the impression that the Panel was genuinely independent. Dr. Good advised me and I verily believed that, he, Dr. Good, could and would control the Panel. He explained that the Chairman of the Panel would be an employee of the Federal Environmental Assessment Review Office and would report to Ray Robinson who headed up that office and that, he, Ray Robinson, reported to Dr. Good. He gave me his personal assurance that he would see that the Panel expeditiously dealt with all matters before it. That while Dr. Good did not indicate a final date that the Panel would report he left me with the clear impression that late spring or early summer was not only reasonable but achievable because the Project had already been reviewed twice before and both times had received the go-ahead . . . [17]

By Thursday afternoon we had run out of time. We were convinced that the negotiations were going nowhere. As late as Thursday evening, Good told Hill that he "can't go anywhere on the money" and that he had "no mandate to put more money on the table."[18]

If we were to appear before Muldoon within the time prescribed by Federal Court rules, Friday, January 26, was the last possible day. With a resolution from the SBDA Board of Directors authorizing the action—Don Stankov, also chairman of the SaskPower Board, made the motion "with deep pleasure"—I headed to Ottawa to rendezvous with the lawyers.[19] In his discussion with Good, Hill made it clear what Saskatchewan was proposing to do. It was a question of who would blink first. The flight to Ottawa involved stops at Winnipeg and Toronto. At each stop I disembarked and phoned Hill to find out whether we had a deal or not. Each time he said no.

Friday, January 26, 1990, was one of the most fascinating days I experienced on the project. Early in the morning, we met at the offices of Osler, Hoskin, and Harcourt in Ottawa to review the documents to be filed with the Federal Court and served on the federal minister. Meanwhile, in Regina, Hill was still trying to reach a settlement with Len Good. Around 10:30 AM Hill was told that Good had no more to offer. Within fifteen minutes, Good was back on the phone to Hill, expressing disbelief. He had just learned that the federal government had been served with our court documents indicating that we would be making a motion to amend the CWF II order, and that we were asking Mr. Justice Muldoon to hear the case that afternoon at 2 o'clock. They thought we were bluffing.

"We told you that Wednesday," Hill responded. "I don't know how many times I have to tell you."[20]

Good phoned Hill back at about 11 AM Regina time, still expressing disbelief. He asked what Saskatchewan was asking for from the court. Hill told him that we were asking Muldoon to extend the date for appointing the panel from January 30, 1990, to February 27, as well as the date for quashing of the IRIA license from January 30 to March 20. Good asked why the difference in the two dates, and Hill said that if our request was granted by the court, then if the minister did not appoint the panel by February 27, 1990, he would be in contempt of court. Good asked what would happen if the judge decided that the federal minister was in contempt. Hill told him that he wasn't a judge (and it wasn't clear if Good knew that Hill had once been a judge), but he understood that it was not uncommon for a person who is found in contempt to be put in jail until the situation was rectified—that is, until the person did what the court had told him to do.

Good said that he could offer us $1 million for every month that construction on the project was shut down, to a maximum of $10 million. Hill had no political authorization to accept any offer, but somebody had to make the decision. So Hill told Good that, while he had no authority to accept, he would.

Good then said that the statement Saskatchewan was demanding, which called for Environment Canada to accept responsibility for the halt to construction, was no problem, so we should call off the lawyers. Hill replied that he would do no such thing, that unless we were in agreement on the text of the statement and who was going to make it, the lawyers were going to court. Good responded that he only had an hour-and-a-half until the 2 PM deadline. Hill replied that was Good's problem. Good said that he had to consult people in the Prime Minister's Office. Hill told him that he'd better hurry.[21]

David Wilson, who was seeing the political and legal machinations for the first time close up, asked in amazement, "Is it always like this?" Gauley, Kennedy, and I had to acknowledge that what was happening was extraordinary, even for Rafferty-Alameda. At half past one, the lawyers left the Osler offices for the Federal Court, which is housed in the Supreme Court Building. I stayed behind on the phone with Hill, who was waiting on Good to come up with an acceptable text for the statement of responsibility Saskatchewan was demanding. At quarter to two I could wait no longer, and told Hill that I would call him from the court house. Once there and once again on the telephone, Hill told me he thought he had a deal, but that he wouldn't know for another twenty minutes or so, and I was to stall. I remember saying, "You've been a judge, George. How the hell do you stall when we were the ones who requested the hearing?" Hill told me I would think of something, and that I was to call him in fifteen minutes, and with that, he hung up on me.

I hurried into the courtroom and told the lawyers that we were very close to a deal, but we needed at least another half-hour. They asked the clerk to let Muldoon know, and the judge agreed to grant a one-hour delay. Within the hour, Hill told me that he was as close to a deal as he could get, but the final details had not been resolved and he didn't trust the feds not to try and wiggle out of it. We should make arrangements with Muldoon to get back in front of him the following Tuesday in case the deal fell through. This meant that the lawyers needed to address the court.

In his remarks, Muldoon expressed that, just as the judiciary should not be interfered with by members of the legislative branch, it followed that the judiciary should not interfere in political matters. He reminded federal Justice lawyer

Brian Saunders that he had argued that, even if the minister had erred in granting the license, the license should be allowed to stand. From his affidavit, it now appeared that the minister was going to allow the license to lapse. Muldoon told Saunders if this was an argument he was going to make on Tuesday, he should anticipate being challenged.[22]

When I caught up with Hill late that night back in Regina, he was euphoric. The deal had been agreed upon, and under the circumstances it was better than what we had started out with a month earlier. The federal government had agreed to pay Saskatchewan $1 million per month up to a maximum of $10 million as compensation caused by the delays. In a press release, Bouchard issued a statement that confirmed our suspicions about Environment Canada:

> "As responsible Minister, I took the steps necessary to maintain the integrity of the Environmental Assessment and Review Process," said Mr. Bouchard. The minister noted, however, that the circumstances in this case are unique.
>
> The Minister welcomed the full cooperation of the Saskatchewan government and its support for his efforts to protect the environmental review process.
>
> . . . Mr. Bouchard also committed the federal government to assist Saskatchewan in offsetting the cost incurred by the work stoppage, which he acknowledged to have resulted not through any fault of the provincial government but from ambiguities associated with judicial interpretation of the 1984 Guidelines Order.[23]

In return, Saskatchewan agreed to:

1. . . . not acquire land for the Alameda Dam nor to start construction thereof . . . ;
2. . . . cease construction of the Rafferty Dam and the Boundary-Rafferty Diversion Channel until the Minister has had the opportunity to amend the license . . . but may do such work as to assure the safety of the public and the safety of the works in accordance with instructions to be received from the independent Rafferty/Alameda Engineering Review Board;
3. . . . that the license granted to the Corporation on August 31, 1989, may be amended by the Minister to incorporate additional or modified mitigation measures . . . which fall within areas of federal jurisdiction;
4. . . . give favorable consideration to the amendment of the license of August 31, 1989 to incorporate additional or modified mitigation measures . . . which fall within areas of provincial jurisdiction.[24]

To those of us directly involved, the actions of the federal government and the Bouchard press release were nothing short of hypocritical. Saskatchewan had every right to feel victimized, and we did, but we also had reason for hope. We had managed to put enough pressure on Environment Canada to negotiate an agreement, and we had observed the senior people in that department in a situation that had allowed us to judge their capabilities. There was no question we would have preferred not to have been in this situation. But now, at least, we knew who we were dealing with. Bouchard and his officials had underestimated us. It was clear: if Environment Canada officials were incompetent enough to get themselves (and us) into this mess, when push came to shove we should be able to get the better of them.

CHAPTER SIX

STRADDLING THE LINE

On October 1989, amid all the chaos over Rafferty-Alameda, the *Agreement Between the Government of Canada and the Government of the United States of America for Water Supply and Flood Control in the Souris River Basin* was signed by representatives of the respective federal governments in Washington, DC.[1] The result of protracted discussions over a five-year period, the negotiations involved no less than eighteen government agencies from both sides of the border. There are three reasons we were able to sign the agreement with the United States. There was a balance to the negotiations. There was a strong political commitment among key politicians in both Canada and the United States. And, because of the political weight behind the project, it was possible to circumvent government strictures in both countries and build a strong coalition of key officials who were capable of forging an agreement.

In any successful negotiations there must be a degree of symmetry between the parties: there has to be a mutual desire to reach some accommodation. This was certainly the case in the negotiations with the United States on the Rafferty-Alameda project. In Saskatchewan, there was a desire among senior members of the Devine government to lay claim to the waters of the Souris River, to which the province was entitled according to the terms of the 1959 interim apportionment. In North Dakota, the city of Minot sought to alleviate the flooding that had plagued it since its founding. In particular, Minot wanted protection against a catastrophic event such as the 1969 flood, which had a probability of reoccurring once every 100 years (commonly referred to as 100-year flood protection). There was only one site in North Dakota where this level of flood protection might be acquired, and that was at Burlington, a village less than sixteen kilometers upstream of Minot. The only other sites where this degree of flood protection could be assured were in the headwaters of the Souris in Saskatchewan.

Among the interested parties, these circumstances were as close to being in perfect balance as one was likely to find. The foundation for the agreement, then, is seen first in the overwhelming desire among basin residents on both sides of the forty-ninth parallel to manage the Souris River. Saskatchewan had a legal right to a share of the waters of the Souris; North Dakota wanted, in essence, to get rid of the water, and it was willing to pay a premium to do so.

The second reason the negotiations with the United States were successfully concluded amid all the problems north of the border was the political weight behind the project. Domestically, the fact that high-profile politicians were closely identified with Rafferty-Alameda was detrimental to it. On the international side, however, the involvement of senior politicians was a definite asset. Without Eric Berntson and Orlin Hanson, it would have been impossible to marshall the necessary political weight in either country. They were the ones who established the political foundations for the international negotiations.

For Orlin Hanson, the acquisition of flood protection for North Dakota had occupied a major portion of his adult life. Since the 1950s, he had campaigned for water management on the Souris. To him, the viability of storing water was never in question; it was only a matter of the means. It was in this spirit that he was instrumental in putting a stop to the Burlington Dam, a $250-million dry dam: a structure that was designed to store water only when extraordinarily large floods occurred. Hanson opposed the project because of the adverse environmental impact of the intermittent inundation of a valley. He also opposed the first alternative to the Burlington Dam proposed by the Army Corps of Engineers: a 1.2-meter increase in the elevation of the existing Lake Darling Dam upstream of Burlington. The problem with this alternative, Hanson saw, was that it would only produce a fraction of the flood protection the city of Minot was seeking. He was convinced that, if real flood protection for North Dakota was to be realized, the solution lay north of the border in the headwaters of the Souris.

When the Blakeney government was unwilling to participate in a joint water management project with American interests in the early 1980s, Hanson began to work with other Saskatchewan interests who were in favor of water management on the Souris. These interests included Eric Berntson. From his perspective in Opposition, Berntson saw a political opportunity. With strong support for such a project among his constituents, and with a government that could not afford, politically, to respond to the issue, Berntson positioned himself for maximum political advantage.

Shortly after the 1982 election of the Conservatives in Saskatchewan, Orlin Hanson approached the newly appointed deputy premier, his old friend Eric Berntson, about a number of bilateral issues, including possible American participation in a Saskatchewan flood control project.[2] George Hill recalls that Berntson first raised the matter with him and Grant Devine at a social occasion in Regina in 1983. Hill, at the time, was vice-chairman of the board of the Saskatchewan Power Corporation. On the basis of that casual discussion—which, if nothing else, speaks volumes about the management style of the Devine government—the decision was made to go ahead with the Rafferty-Alameda project. With Devine and Hill on board, Berntson had all the political capital he would need.

Eric Berntson, a native of Carievale, a village in the heart of the Souris basin, was the government's deal-maker. Throughout the tenure of the Devine administration, no project of any size or with any provincial involvement was developed without first passing Berntson's scrutiny. Irrigation projects, pulp mills, boiler and turbine manufacturing facilities, heavy oil upgraders, even automated

language translation programs—despite the celebrated failures, no other politician in the Devine government, including Devine himself, could claim such
accomplishments. And no project had a higher priority for Eric Berntson than
Rafferty-Alameda.

The political coalition Berntson and Hanson were able to build is a graphic
illustration of the steps necessary to develop a transboundary water project.
This is particularly the case given the stringent contemporary environmental
requirements and the internationalization of environmental interest groups.
Hanson knew all the American actors whose support would be necessary to
make the deal work. Although he was a Republican, he knew from his involvement in the Burlington Dam that flood control did not divide cleanly along
party lines. In August 1981 Hanson and Democratic State Representative Dick
Backes cosigned a letter to the deputy director of civil works in the U.S. Department of the Army. The letter reflects Hanson's bipartisan approach, and shows
how organized he was as early as 1981:

> We have been debating, arguing and yes, fighting over this project [the
> Burlington Dam] for over 26 years in the Souris Basin. As Mayor Reiten
> [Chester Reiten, then mayor of Minot] stated, "it has pitted brother
> against brother, friends against friends, community against community
> and rural against city" until it is about to destroy a good portion of
> North Dakota as we know it today. Something had to be done to resolve
> this situation before it generated problems that would be unresolvable.
> The feelings over this project were highly volatile on both sides as you
> very well know...
>
> It is very important that every effort possible be expedited to work
> with the Canadians in developing a total water management program
> that would benefit the entire Souris River Drainage Basin. Specifically
> to investigate the possibilities of a dam above Estevan known as Rafferty
> Dam, a Diversion Channel from Boundary Dam on Long Creek and
> Alameda Dam on Moose Mountain Creek as a possible means of con-
> trolling the water coming from the upper regions of the Souris Drain-
> age Basin.[3]

As the first step in building the political coalition, Hanson and Berntson
arranged a meeting between Grant Devine and North Dakota's senior senator,
Quentin Burdick. The two established a rapport that continued throughout the
life of the project. Burdick's involvement was a key factor in the equation, as he
was able to ensure that the project received high priority from the relevant agencies of the United States federal government.

At the time of the Rafferty-Alameda project, Quentin Burdick was the third-
ranking senator in the United States Senate in terms of seniority. Although he
represented a small state and was not a major power broker, Burdick brought to
the issue the full weight of his tenure—a factor of considerable significance in
the Senate. In the most critical days of the negotiations, he was a member of

both the Senate Environment and Public Works Committee and the powerful Senate Appropriations Committee. The Environment and Public Works Committee has a mandate to review the operations and policy proposals of various departments and agencies of the United States federal government, including the Army Corps of Engineers and the Environmental Protection Agency. These assignments proved to be crucial to the Rafferty-Alameda negotiations.

Even in the days of the Republican-controlled Senate in 1985, Burdick, a moderate, had sufficient influence to ensure that Rafferty-Alameda received Senate support. This is apparent in a letter he received from the Senate floor leaders on December 13, 1985:

> The four-foot [1.2 m] raise of the existing Lake Darling Dam would be dropped in exchange for a $41.1 million maximum United States contribution towards construction of two dams in Canada. Flood protection to the Souris River Basin would increase from 25-year to 100-year flood protection cycle . . .
>
> In closing, we are in agreement that your amendment will be included as part of the floor manager's package when S. 1567 comes to the floor. We appreciate North Dakota's efforts to develop a more favorable flood protection plan which reduces federal obligations by $170 million under the original 1970 Burlington Dam authorization.[4]

It is not insignificant that, in the first major water bill to make it into law in the United States in over half a decade, Burdick was able to ensure not only that his state's interests were secure on a major water project, but that federal financing would be available for a project whose major components weren't even

Senior North Dakota Senator Quentin Burdick. As a young man, Burdick summered at a camp on the Souris River near Estevan. Burdick took full advantage of his senior position in the U.S. Senate to marshall Administrative support for Rafferty-Alameda.
Courtesy Minot Daily News

situated in the United States. Another significant aspect of the letter is that it was written in response to a request from Saskatchewan that the United States provide some written commitment to the project that would allow it to be announced prior to the 1986 provincial election.

Devine's decision to announce the project on the basis of the Senate floor leaders' letter to Burdick reflects the state of the project in early 1986—"hanging fire," as Ron Petrie of the *Regina Leader-Post* had described it at the time. It also reflects the trust that existed between Devine and Burdick and between Orlin Hanson and Eric Berntson. This was not the last time that fundamental decisions about the project would be made on the basis of implicit understandings and unwritten agreements. No one knew at the time that it would be a year-and-a-half before an agreement in principle would be reached between the two countries, and almost four years before a formal agreement would be signed. In the interim, all that kept the process moving was the understanding and trust among the politicians involved. The informality of it all never seemed to be an issue with either Devine or Burdick. Both were supremely confident that an agreement would eventually be reached.

Burdick had a political stake in Rafferty-Alameda as well. The strong local support for the project meant that he was being lobbied by Republicans and Democrats alike, and he certainly remembered how divisive the debate over the Burlington Dam had been. And he had more than a passing familiarity with this area in Saskatchewan. In his youth, he had spent portions of his summers at a park in the Souris River valley near Estevan.

When the Democrats regained control of the Senate after the mid-term elections in 1986, Quentin Burdick was appointed to the Senate Appropriations Committee, where he sat on the Interior and Related Agencies Subcommittee. This was fortuitous, for it was this subcommittee that was responsible for reviewing the expenditure proposals of the Department of the Interior, including the Fish and Wildlife Service, which held the second-oldest license on the Souris River within the state of North Dakota. It operated three national wildlife refuges and twenty-one of the forty dams that existed in the Souris basin prior to the construction of Rafferty-Alameda, so its operations there would obviously be affected. Burdick's influence increased further when he assumed the chair of the Environment and Public Works Committee. With an established institutional relationship with the Army Corps of Engineers, the Environmental Protection Agency, and the Fish and Wildlife Service, Burdick was in a unique position to ensure that they would cooperate in the development of this particular project. The strength of his position was evident in his remarks to the *Minot Daily News* on January 2, 1986. "His confidence is high," wrote Carl Flagstad, " . . . because of the fact his amendment not only has the backing of key Republican and Democratic senators, it also has the approval of the Corps of Engineers, the Office of Management and Budget and the Fish and Wildlife Service."[5]

In May 1987, an agreement in principle on the Operating Plan was reached by the five agencies most directly affected by the Rafferty-Alameda project: the Souris Basin Development Authority representing the government of Saskatchewan, the U.S. Army Corps of Engineers, the North Dakota State Water Commission, the Souris River Joint Water Resources Board (the local sponsor), and the U.S. Fish and Wildlife Service. Representatives of the five agencies signed a letter confirming the agreement in principle and sent it to Senator Burdick:

> We are pleased to inform you that an Agreement in Principle on the Souris River Operating Plan has been reached between the Saskatchewan - U.S.A. Negotiating Teams. The Agreement in Principle includes the issues of apportionment, and provisions for both non-flood and flood operations. Insofar as flood operations are concerned, all parties are satisfied that the Operating Plan will provide 100 year flood protection for the city of Minot and that the schedule of releases previously negotiated with water users downstream of Minot can be met. As well, this Operating Plan will be compatible with the operation of the two U.S. national wildlife refuges on the Souris River.[6]

The letter was sent to Burdick because we were concerned that the Fish and Wildlife Service might attempt to renege if it were left merely as a verbal understanding. While not legally binding, the letter constituted the most we could get under the circumstances. If nothing else, the Fish and Wildlife Service would be forced to pay a political price and answer to Quentin Burdick if it tried to back out.

Shortly after the letter was signed, Berntson wrote to Joe Clark, then secretary of state for external affairs, in an attempt to keep up the momentum:

> I am writing regarding the Rafferty-Alameda Project and the current state of negotiations between Saskatchewan and the United States negotiating teams. I am pleased to inform you that an Agreement-in-Principle on an Operating Plan for the Souris River has been reached between the two negotiating teams (attached is a copy of the letter sent to Senator Burdick in this regard).
>
> It is the intention of the Government of Saskatchewan to attempt to finalize all transboundary issues by the end of 1987. To this end, a draft agreement between Saskatchewan and the U.S. Department of the Army has been prepared and consultations between officials of the Souris Basin Development Authority and External Affairs have commenced. As well, Saskatchewan has attempted to facilitate the provision of information to the Province of Manitoba and to ensure that their concerns are addressed . . . [7]

Our approach had been to limit the involvement of governments and agencies that had, at best, a tangential interest in the project. The wisdom of this became obvious when the process was blown wide open and eighteen government agencies in both Canada and the United States became parties to the discussions, each with an increasing number of concerns that required resolution. One example illustrates the internalization of environmental issues and the willingness of those working in this policy field to politicize an issue in order to achieve their goals.

On December 14, 1988, I received a phone call from Jack Beard, head of the American delegation. He told me that a letter from Burdick regarding the Environmental Protection Agency (EPA) would be in the *New York Times*. Beard went on to tell me that people from the EPA were trying to stop the project, and they were using people from Winnipeg to "drive the wedge."[8]

A call to Burdick's office in Washington a day later confirmed that the EPA was trying to scuttle the deal by leaking information to *Winnipeg Free Press* reporter Barbara Robson. Robson had called Burdick's office, indicating that she had received a copy of the letter before it had appeared in the *New York Times*. The EPA's efforts to undermine the negotiations were sufficient to prompt Quentin Burdick, in his capacity as chairman of the Senate Environment and Public Works Committee, to write to then President-elect George Bush. The December 15, 1988, *New York Times* observed:

> The problem, it seems, is that the Reagan Administration has yet to negotiate an agreement with Canada authorizing United States payments to the Canadians to build a flood control project that would protect the North Dakota city of Minot. While the Army Corps of Engineers, the Fish and Wildlife Service and the State Department were giving the project the "fullest co-operation," the Environmental Protection Agency "was obstructing and delaying" an agreement with Canada, Senator Burdick complained.
>
> "Naturally I find this very disturbing," the Senator wrote. He added, "I would hope that this agreement could be initialed prior to the consideration by the Committee on Environment and Public Works of your nominee for the post of Administrator of the Environmental Protection Agency."
>
> Some environmentalists saw the letter as a thinly veiled threat to cause problems over the confirmation of Mr. Bush's nominee to head the agency.
>
> But Jean Brodshoug, a spokeswoman for Mr. Burdick, said that, "the Senator does not intend to sit on any of Mr. Bush's nominations." The letter, she said, was intended to show that the flood control project was a "top priority" of Mr. Burdick's and that if it is not dealt with quickly the issue would be brought up at the confirmation hearings for whoever is selected as the agency administrator.

The *New York Times* concluded that "the letter to President-elect Bush seemed to have the echo of heavy artillery booming between the lines."[9]

The City of Minot and the government of North Dakota were also critical in holding the Rafferty-Alameda project together. Minot, after all, was the reason the Americans were willing to participate in the first place. The city acted as a catalyst for public and political support throughout the negotiating process. As the fourth-largest community in North Dakota, Minot was able to lobby effectively at both the state and federal levels.

In addition to its role as both catalyst and advocate, Minot was the *de facto* local sponsor of the project. The *Flood Control Act* of 1970 had stipulated that "the construction of any water resources project by the Secretary of the Army shall not be commenced until each nonfederal interest has entered into a written agreement to furnish its required cooperation for the project,"[10] and the 1986 *Water Resources Development Act* required that, before any federal funds could be expended on a water project, a local sponsor was required to make a financial contribution. The residents of Minot, in a binding plebiscite and with the largest voter turnout on a single-issue election in city history, voted overwhelmingly in favor of the imposition of a 1 percent sales tax to pay for its share.[11]

As the negotiations progressed, the number of American government agencies involved increased. With their intervention came resistance to the project, particularly at the local level. Throughout the environmental assessment process in the United States, there was opposition from both government agencies and interest groups. And notwithstanding Quentin Burdick's efforts, there were problems in the Fish and Wildlife Service in North Dakota. It was at times difficult to know if we were dealing with an agency of government or an interest group that was opposed to the project. It depended on which hat an individual was wearing at any given time. The local staff of the Fish and Wildlife Service refuges on the Souris were ambivalent, at best. In January 1988, the *Minot Daily News* reported:

> A moratorium has been requested for the area below the Saskatchewan border in North Dakota, stopping any work on the Souris River international flood control project until a basin-wide environmental impact investigation has been undertaken. The statement would spell out potential harm to such things as fishing, wildlife habitat, wetlands and water quality...
>
> Duane Anderson of Minot, who served the past two years as [North Dakota Wildlife] federation president and is assistant manager of the Upper Souris Wildlife Refuge of the Fish and Wildlife Service at Lake Darling, said it was felt that the moratorium request was necessary in light of the facts. Part of the information, Anderson said, was furnished by the Saskatchewan Wildlife Federation.[12]

This was a common occurrence in both Canada and the U.S. Government agencies in support of the project often found their own employees working in opposition to it. This is one of the reasons the involvement of certain agencies in both countries was delayed as long as possible. Individuals and agencies frequently have their own agendas, which may or may not coincide with the policies of the government they happen to serve.

This was also an example of the frequent communications between the Canadian and Saskatchewan Wildlife federations and their counterparts in the

United States. When it comes to environmental issues, the border between the two nations is very permeable. This is why, when we were invited to Bismarck in January 1988 to address representatives from North Dakota wildlife groups, I suspected a setup. The meeting was held at the suggestion of the State Water Commission, which was having to deal with an increasingly vociferous environmental lobby voicing its concerns over the Souris River dams. In Saskatchewan we had made a number of attempts to reason with both the Canadian and Saskatchewan Wildlife federations, at considerable waste of time and money. They had their own agendas, and there was nothing we could do to change them. In light of that experience, I brought Keith Harde along from the Estevan Wildlife Branch to support our position.

Harde was a past president of the Saskatchewan Wildlife Federation and a past director of the Canadian Wildlife Federation. Like most members of the Estevan Branch, he was also a strong supporter of Rafferty-Alameda. When we walked into the meeting room at the State Water Commission Building in Bismarck, I was not surprised to see Ed Begin, the executive director of the Saskatchewan Wildlife Federation, sitting there. From the look on his face, though, he was certainly surprised to see Keith Harde.

Begin's presence suggested a continuing commitment to a strategy opponents of the project had used before. Unable to gain support among the people who actually lived in the Souris basin in Saskatchewan, they attempted to undermine the project by convincing their American counterparts to oppose it as well. They were never a serious threat to Rafferty-Alameda,[13] but they were an annoyance.

In Bismarck we made a presentation about Saskatchewan's legal right to 50 percent of the waters from the Souris River, the various components of the project, its anticipated effects on the environment, and our plans to mitigate its effects on wildlife to the point that there would be a 31 percent net gain in habitat after we were finished.

The Americans couldn't have cared less about what we were going to do for wildlife—or anything else, for that matter. The only thing they were concerned about was that we were proposing to take water from them. Will Rogers once said, "Whiskey's for drinking and water's for fighting." I can appreciate why. The Bismarck meeting provided an interesting perspective on both the politics of water and environmental interest groups. Opponents of Rafferty-Alameda in Canada have attempted to characterize the project as a sell-out to the United States, with a corresponding loss of Canadian sovereignty as a result of the agreement between the two countries. Listening to the wildlife interests at the Bismarck meeting, however, one got a fundamentally different perspective. They seemed to think it was the United States that was getting taken on the deal. They tried to make the case that their federal government was actually paying over $40 million for the privilege of giving up water they had been receiving for decades.

Virtually the entire discussion centered on the effects in North Dakota of Saskatchewan retaining its share of the Souris River waters. No doubt my describing as a "windfall benefit" the fact that they had been receiving Saskatchewan water for all these years angered many of the Americans in attendance,

who seemed to believe they had an inherent right to water that originated north
of the forty-ninth parallel.

Having Keith Harde with us tended to undermine the opposition from Canadian interest groups. No matter what they said about how bad the project was,
the fact remained that the branch of the Saskatchewan Wildlife Federation that
was most directly affected by the development was overwhelmingly in favor of
it. All in all, we thought the Bismarck meeting had gone as well as could be
expected. It got a little hot, but no hotter than many other meetings I had attended on the project. It certainly didn't get out of hand.

I was surprised, therefore, at the vehemence of the reaction from interest
groups on both sides of the border. Having had their strategy backfire, they
responded by not only attacking me, but Keith Harde as well. Grant Devine's
office received letters remarkably similar in syntax, structure, and tone, and all
written within two days of each other. Ed Begin of the Saskatchewan Wildlife
Federation wrote:

> Surely to God, Mr. Devine, there are competent people in this great
> province that could carry out their responsibilities without bringing
> shame on our province and government. I can assure you that I will be

*The opposition to the Rafferty-Alameda project never succeeded in attracting large
numbers of area residents. The caption accompanying this September 1989 photo noted,
"Many chairs remained empty when opponents of the Rafferty-Alameda dam project
gathered in Weyburn on Saturday."* Courtesy Regina-Leader Post

writing personal letters of apology to those people in North Dakota that
have been so abused by Mr. Hood's foul mouth and belligerent nature.

The North Dakota Wildlife Federation characterized events this way:

The chances that the purpose of the meeting could be achieved quickly
became nonexistent when Mr. Hood "took over the chair," interrupted
comments by several people, dismissed the comments of others as
wrong, uninformed or biased, and in general, behaved in a thoroughly
unprofessional manner.

The Wildlife Society complained:

Because of the manner in which Mr. George Hood of the SBDA conducted himself, the meeting frankly was a waste of time. Mr. Hood's
arrogant and abusive remarks detracted from the intent and purpose of
the meeting. His attempts to control the meeting and at the same time
belittle constructive comments prevented any useful exchange of information.[14]

My skin was sufficiently thick by that time that I felt no compulsion to
react. I was, however, getting fed up with all the controversy and the squabbles,
and I would likely have welcomed the prospect of being relieved of the job. If
there was a queue for it, it wasn't a long one.

Saskatchewan politics being what it is, I should have realized this was only
the beginning. Some months later, a man named Vince Hilbert wrote in a letter
to the *Saskatoon Star-Phoenix*:

. . . I suspect most Tory politicians, including Brian Mulroney and Grant
Devine and all their hacks, probably have not done an honest day's
work in their lives. For example, look at George Hood in Estevan, who
has no known qualifications to head up the Rafferty-Alameda Project
even though he and George Hill, President of SaskPower, "earn" sala-
ries more than any others have made in Saskatchewan history. No U.I.
problems for those two Tory hacks.[15]

I had never met Vince Hilbert, and he certainly knew nothing about my
salary, let alone my political leanings. More understandable, perhaps, were the
NDP's attempts to make political points at the expense of those working on the
project. What I noticed about these attacks was their utter lack of sophistication,
elegance, and civility.

As for Keith Harde, he found that he was *persona non grata* with the executive of the federation. Two days after the Bismarck meeting, Lorne Scott, then
president of the SWF and now an NDP MLA, wrote to Harde:

Effective immediately you are removed from the position of Sustain-
ing Membership Chairman for the Saskatchewan Wildlife Federation.
Furthermore, you will *not* be welcome at future Saskatchewan Wildlife
Federation President's Council meetings, unless invited to attend by a
future president.[16]

Ironically, it was Lorne Scott and Ed Begin who had signed Harde's honorary
life membership in the federation, citing his "long and outstanding contribution
to the aims and objectives of the Federation and to the Wildlife Resources of
Saskatchewan."[17]

The effects of Rafferty-Alameda on the Saskatchewan Wildlife Federation
did not escape public notice. In April 1989, Tom Loran editorialized in the
Saskatoon Star-Phoenix:

> There will be quite a few wildlife federation members cheering these
> days over the court decision gassing the Rafferty and Alameda dams.
>   They shouldn't cheer too loudly.
>   First of all, it's almost a sure thing the organization will lose mem-
> bers because it was the Canadian Wildlife Federation that took the case
> to court. There is a large contingent of provincial members—some of
> them extremely active—in the southeast corner of the province who
> are strongly in favor of the dams . . .
>   And the statement of executive director Ed Begin did not help
> matters at all. He made himself and the federation look a little ridicu-
> lous by talking about the government infiltrating the organization. It is
> quite obvious Keith Harde of Estevan was the leader of the pro-dam
> forces within the federation and anyone who knows anything of the
> SWF knows Harde has been a long and hard-working member. He's no
> "infiltrator" for the government. By trying to make Harde into something
> sinister, Begin simply widens the split already created in the federation.[18]

Once again, the strategy backfired. North Dakota Governor George Sinner
had been in attendance at the Bismarck meeting, as had State Representative
Orlin Hanson and Minot City Manager Bob Schempp, all of whom were quite
aware of what had actually transpired. Schempp, in fact, felt compelled to establish his version in writing:

> . . . You've been accused of being abusive, foul-mouthed and arrogant,
> and basically guilty of conduct unbecoming a representative of the Sas-
> katchewan government.
>   . . . from my perspective, that performance must have taken place
> at a different meeting. It certainly didn't happen at the Jan. 18th meet-
> ing that I attended.
>   Yes you did use one rather descriptive term following the word
> bull! As I remember, its use was appropriate.

During the course of the meeting, I asked that you become somewhat more forceful and blunt in order to get a message across to North
Dakota wildlife interests. I asked that you restate the fact that your
government is likely going to proceed with a project, with or without us.
And, in that event, the North Dakota part of the basin would be water short,
and would not have flood protection built into the Canadian dams . . .

It became obvious during the meeting that the above message was
not being heard (or admitted to) by some of those present and, that it
was necessary to explain (in no uncertain terms) that a project was
going to be built. You did, as requested, forcefully and bluntly state
that water management *was* necessary, Rafferty *would* more than likely
be built and that your government wanted to build it in conjunction
with us. In my opinion, you were not abusive, foul-mouthed or arrogant, but you did deliver the message.[19]

The attacks on Harde had the effect of solidifying support for the project
among members of the Estevan branch of the Saskatchewan Wildlife Federation. It almost certainly firmed up Grant Devine's resolve to see the thing through,
as Keith Harde was a friend and a well-known Conservative in the riding.

The City of Minot helped neutralize the local and state environmental lobby
by painting their position as inherently unreasonable, in that it would perpetuate
the flooding and favor ducks over people. This was no small feat considering
Minot was carrying the strategy out in the middle of the worst drought to hit the
Great Plains in 100 years. Minot was also the vehicle for mobilizing grassroots
support for the project from the United States. This was necessary not only
insofar as the assessment of the environmental impacts of the project in the U.S.
was concerned, but also for the various assessments that were carried out in
Canada. Minot was instrumental in rallying support for the project and making
appearances before the Canadian environmental tribunals reviewing the project.
A measure of the city's success is evident from the fact that, in 1992, it was
awarded the National Civic League's prestigious All America City Award, in
large part on the basis of the campaign it waged to acquire flood protection.

American states are not as powerful as Canadian provinces, nor do they
occupy the same role in water resource development. Despite this, the State of
North Dakota also played a key role in Rafferty-Alameda. In the early 1980s,
when the project was first under active consideration, the governor of North
Dakota was a Republican, Alan Olson. Olson, in 1981, had committed his administration to securing flood protection from Canada.

Orlin Hanson had been instrumental in gaining Olson's support for the
undertaking. When Olson was defeated by Democrat George Sinner, the state's
support for the project did not flag, largely because well-known local Democrats such as Dick Backes also supported it.[20] Both sides of the fence had
been covered, not only politically but geographically. Backes recalls testifying before the United States Congress with his brother Orlin. Orlin Backes
was the head of FOR DAM LTD, a Minot-based organization in favor of the

Burlington Dam, while Dick Backes, along with Orlin Hanson, headed the Citizens United to Save the Valley, which was against the dam. Orlin Backes, a Democrat in favor of the dam, opposed his brother Dick, also a Democrat, who was working with a Republican, Hanson, against the dam, and they were testifying before a Senate committee on opposite sides of the issue. Senator Bennett Johnson of Louisiana interrupted the proceedings to observe, in an animated southern drawl, "My God, sir, there sure are some strange politics in North Dakota."[21]

That both brothers were in support of the Rafferty and Alameda dams, as were many other well-known Democrats, obviously had an influence on Governor Sinner's position. When Sinner appointed Dick Backes to the State Water Commission, it significantly strengthened the coalition in support of the project. The participation of the State Water Commission was particularly valuable, in that they had experienced first-hand the loss of a transboundary issue, the Garrison Diversion. Many of the same officials were involved on Rafferty-Alameda. Their experience, along with the object lesson of how a controversial transboundary project can be stopped by internecine battles among government agencies, was enormously helpful. They offered indispensable strategic and tactical insights, and while it might be going too far to suggest that they had a score to settle, there is no question that they were determined not to allow the same thing to happen again.

The first indication that bureaucratic rules were being ignored on Rafferty-Alameda can be found in the minutes of an August 21, 1984, meeting in Minot between officials from Saskatchewan and representatives of various American government interests. Apparently, there was a strong political imperative behind the project on both sides of the border from the very beginning. In his opening remarks, Hill noted that "the Corps of Engineers had been invited by the Premier to proceed with a feasibility study." State Representative Dick Backes raised the possibility of a "crash program" the corps might undertake in order to meet Saskatchewan's schedule.[22] In response to a Saskatchewan proposal that the United States contribute to the cost of the studies then under way, State Representative Orlin Hanson proposed a means of getting around the problems the corps would have devoting resources to the project, given that Congress had passed an appropriation but that it had not, as yet, been authorized.[23] Hanson proposed that the City of Minot and the local citizens committee look at the possibility of funding the American share. Hill also noted during the meeting that Saskatchewan was facing stringent time restrictions, and that SaskPower had to have a new thermal generating facility in place by 1990–1991. The Corps of Engineers, not surprisingly, raised concerns about its ability to coordinate the necessary planning studies and still meet the deadlines Saskatchewan had imposed. The district engineer for the corps, Colonel Rapp, conceded that, "We have an unusual situation here."[24]

The immediate outcome of this first meeting was the transfer of technical information from SaskPower to the Corps of Engineers. More significant, the political people in attendance were clearly looking to make the thing work, and they were prepared to ride herd on the negotiations until they were concluded. The 1984 meeting established a pattern that was repeated throughout the negotiations. At virtually every bilateral meeting, the politicians in support of the project would know about it in advance, and no matter how technical the topic under discussion, there would be follow-up with the political people afterwards. Meetings strictly among officials, Canadian or American, were almost unheard of.

In any negotiations, it takes time to build trust among the participants. Sometimes it never happens, and for a while this appeared to be the case with these discussions. From the outset, we had reason to question the commitment of the Army Corps of Engineers to the Saskatchewan project. In the United States, the corps is the agency of the U.S. federal government responsible for flood control. It was the agency that had proposed the Burlington Dam. When that project was cancelled, the corps was directed to enter into discussions with Canada. If these negotiations proved unsuccessful, however, the corps would be authorized to undertake its own project and raise the elevation of the Lake Darling Dam above Minot. The corps has a reputation, deserved or not, for having dammed every dammable stream in the continental United States. By the 1980s, it had been some time since the St. Paul District of the corps had been involved in a major project. To some, it appeared there was a built-in incentive to see that the negotiations with Saskatchewan failed.

But the corps is a bureaucracy like any other organization, and as such it has a strong interest in self-preservation. Perhaps a glimpse of the political will behind Rafferty-Alameda was sufficient to convince the corps that it would be easier to back the project than to fight it because, in political terms, it was a fight it could not win. The first acknowledgement of this came in November 1985 when Robert K. Dawson, acting assistant secretary of the army, wrote to Quentin Burdick:

> I am responding to your letter of October 25, 1985, concerning substitution of flood control storage in two proposed reservoirs in Canada for the authorized flood control storage in Lake Darling, North Dakota. As noted during our October 1, 1985, meeting with you, Premier Grant Devine, and others, we believe such a substitution could be beneficial for interests in Canada and in this country.
>
> I am very pleased to report that the Corps of Engineers, using preliminary data available from their on-going study and from Canadian sources, has determined that up to 400,000 acre-feet of flood control storage could be used at the Rafferty and Alameda sites in conjunction with modified operation of the Canadian Boundary Dam and the existing Lake Darling to provide 100 year [flood] protection for Minot. Storage in the Canadian projects would eliminate the requirement for raising Lake Darling, but a new outlet at Lake Darling Dam and levees and other downstream measures would still be required to accommodate flood releases.

Subject to enactment of authorizing legislation, appropriation of funds and procedural approval by the Department of State, we are prepared to move forward with Saskatchewan in the construction of the Rafferty and Alameda reservoir projects. Based on our current estimates we would be willing to contribute $41.1 million during construction of the two projects . . . [25]

That the corps came on-side so quickly was no accident. "More than any other agency," one researcher has noted, the corps has become " . . . through its long and extensive ties with key congressional committees, associated with the concept of the pork barrel, linking local interests with federal programs."[26] Within the corps, a system circumventing at least two levels of the bureaucracy was established on matters relating to Rafferty-Alameda. The St. Paul office of the corps reported directly to Dawson's office in Washington, and to Burdick.

The United States Fish and Wildlife Service is a branch of the Department of the Interior, with a mandate to conserve and manage the nation's fish and wildlife resources. As the largest single holder of water rights in the Souris basin in North Dakota, the Fish and Wildlife Service had been the principle beneficiary of Saskatchewan's inability to store its legal share of the waters of the Souris. In light of the acute effects of the drought on waterfowl production on the prairies, the service had the most to lose from the construction of the Rafferty and Alameda dams. It came as no surprise, then, that there were elements within the service opposed to the project. But once again there is a paper trail outlining the handiwork of Quentin Burdick in establishing the importance he attached to Rafferty-Alameda. On November 15, 1985, the acting deputy director of the service wrote to Quentin Burdick:

The Service understands the necessity for prompt action on the proposal for reliance on two Canadian dams for the purpose of flood control in lieu of changes to the Lake Darling Dam . . .
. . . As the waters of the Souris River are developed and used in the Canadian dams, the priority for operation of Lake Darling will be dictated by its authorized water conservation purposes. From the point of view of the Service, it will probably be possible to have a combined operation of the Canadian dams and Lake Darling that will satisfy both conservation and flood control objectives . . . [27]

Recognizing that, by its nature, Rafferty-Alameda was a controversial project, and that the process would otherwise be too diffuse, a group was created consisting of representatives of the agencies and politicians who were committed to the project. This group comprised: the head of the North Dakota State Water Commission, State Engineer Dave Sprynczynztyk; City of Minot Manager Bob Schempp; Corps of Engineers St. Paul District Chief Planner Louis Kowalski; Bruce McKay, representing Senator Quentin Burdick; and me, representing Saskatchewan. Membership in what became known as "The Family" fluctuated depending on the issue of the day, but these people constituted its permanent members.

As with the environmental lobby, in the functioning of the Family, the international border did not exist. We had conferences over the telephone and we met face to face in Regina, Minot, Bismarck, Ottawa, Estevan, St. Paul, Denver, and Washington. Any member of the group could call a meeting. There was an explicit understanding that no issue would divide us; if one was identified as a "deal-breaker," a solution had to be found. Cognizant of the sensitivity of the issue, trust among the members was absolute.

An example of how well the group functioned can be seen in the decision to install a high-level intake in the Alameda Dam. A number of agencies in the United States had expressed concern about the quality of the water that would pass from the Alameda Reservoir into North Dakota. An analysis carried out in Saskatchewan, which was far more detailed than anything done by any American agency, indicated that post-impoundment water quality should not be a problem. But members of the Family were of the view that the issue was potentially serious enough to prevent American participation, so a decision was taken to construct a high-level intake in the Alameda Dam to ensure the capacity to "mix" releases from the reservoir. In light of the Saskatchewan position that, based on our technical analysis, there was no demonstrable need for this capability, the City of Minot agreed to pay the incremental costs. The principle elements of the deal were agreed to by Bob Schempp and myself over breakfast at the Holiday Inn in Minot. Confirmed by a handshake, the agreement was never in question, and was the easiest of all of the formal agreements on the project to reach and maintain.

As negotiations reached their most sensitive stage, communication among the members was a daily event. With eighteen agencies represented at the table, the exercise had become diffuse, and we were nervous about the efforts by some of the agencies to derail the thing. We decided to use the influence of the Family to help things along. On at least half a dozen occasions, when the international negotiations bogged down in the United States, at the prompting of the Family, Senator Burdick "invited" selected parties to a session in his private office in the U.S. Capitol.

Members of the Senate and House of Representatives have their main offices in buildings adjacent to the U.S. Capitol Building. A handful of senior senators and congressmen also have private offices within this building. These offices offer a venue for private meetings. Senator Burdick's private office was Room S 334. In this windowless room in the bowels of the Capitol, with threadbare furnishings and a photograph of Harry Truman on the wall, Burdick would call agencies of the U.S. federal government to account. I watched in fascination as he gently but firmly prodded generals from the Department of the Army, or officials from the Department of the Interior and the Environmental Protection Agency as to the reasons for the delays. It imposed discipline on a fragmented set of negotiations, and it all worked beautifully—until representatives of the State Department attended one of these meetings.

The Canadian government is decidedly nervous about representatives of Canadian provinces directly representing themselves in Washington. Provinces may represent themselves in other American centers—Saskatchewan had representatives in New York and Minneapolis, for example—but a province directly representing its own interests in Washington, unencumbered by a representative from the Canadian Embassy, is forbidden. Prior to November 1987, my visits to the accountability sessions in Senator Burdick's private office were made, as far as I know, without the knowledge of the Canadian government.

In early November 1987, the State Department was invited to send a representative to one of Burdick's accountability sessions. At the end of the meeting, I was approached by the State Department representative, who was concerned that there had been no representative of the Canadian Embassy in attendance. Diplomatic protocol obliged him to communicate the outcome of the meeting to the Canadian Embassy, and he was letting me know out of courtesy. I convinced him to hold off calling the embassy until we had a chance to talk to them.[28] After the meeting I hurriedly made my way to the Canadian Embassy, where I tried to make the whole thing look like much ado about nothing; officials at the embassy were not impressed. Relations between Saskatchewan and the Canadian Embassy in Washington were never the same on the Rafferty-Alameda file again.

About a year later, when negotiations on the international agreement were not going well on either side of the border, we decided that a face-to-face meeting of the members of the Family was essential. Given the sensitivity of the Canadian Embassy to our meeting in Washington, we chose Baltimore as the venue. By this time the controversy surrounding the project had grown substantially, and we wanted to avoid making it any worse. Accordingly, I took the precaution of ensuring that the only people from our end who knew my destination were my wife and George Hill.

It takes the better part of a day to fly from Regina via Minneapolis to Baltimore. When I checked into the hotel near the Baltimore airport in mid-afternoon, I was greeted by a flashing message light on the telephone. Jack Beard, with whom I was scheduled to meet, had called, and it was urgent. When I called him at his office in the Pentagon, Beard told me there had been a leak, and officials from the Canadian Embassy had called him to inquire if he was meeting with me today in Washington. Beard, a lawyer, answered the question literally and said no; he didn't volunteer that we were planning to meet in Baltimore instead. Beard said he was under incredible pressure, the embassy was really upset and were likely to call his boss, the assistant secretary of the army, as well as the State Department. The embassy had indicated to Beard that they were going to check a number of hotels in Washington in an attempt to reach me.

"If I were you, Hood," he advised, "I'd get the hell out of here as fast as you can." Which I did. I checked out, taking the first plane out of Baltimore. I spent the night in New York and eventually made it home around noon the next day. In a twenty-four-hour period I had flown Regina-Minneapolis-Baltimore-Pittsburgh-

New York-Toronto-Regina, all for nothing. I never did find out where the leak came from and even wondered if my international travel arrangements were being monitored.

The rewriting of bureaucratic rules was not limited to activities in the United States. The creation of the Souris Basin Development Authority as a single-purpose crown corporation together with the loose decision-making structure within the Saskatchewan government allowed us to remove the negotiations from the constraints imposed by a frequently hostile bureaucracy in Regina. This took the issue out of the hands of the officials who would normally have managed these kinds of water-related issues.

In any given policy area, there exists a cadre of government officials across Canada who manage specific issues. The same holds true on a regional basis between contiguous jurisdictions in Canada and the United States. These officials all know each other and, in the case of water resources, often work together as they make decisions on such things as apportionment agreements. Taking them "out of the loop" on Rafferty-Alameda had the effect of removing the issue from the conventional federal-provincial, inter-provincial, and provincial-state relationships among water managers. Bureaucratic access to the negotiations was thus limited to as few agencies and individuals as possible. While there were leaks during the negotiations, typically they came from Environment Canada, Manitoba, or the EPA, never from External Affairs or any member of the Family.

Notwithstanding the impending litigation of CWF II, by October 1989, everything seemed to be in order for the signing of the Canada-U.S. Agreement. The corps had completed a Supplementary Information Document (SID) to its Environmental Impact Statement. The U.S. Fish and Wildlife Service was finally satisfied with the project, and was prepared to sign the Certificate of Compatibility. The assistant secretary of the army, Robert Page, flew to Bismarck to execute the Local Cooperation Agreement. Once the corps had completed the SID, a formal Record of Decision pursuant to the *National Environmental Policy Act* was signed as the formal decision to proceed with the project. The State Department authorized the Department of the Army to sign the international agreement on behalf of the Government of the United States.

Timing on all these things was crucial. Even at this late date, we were concerned that the National Wildlife Federation would file a suit in the District of Columbia Circuit Court. According to Beard, it was not unheard of for representatives of environmental interest groups to have all the documents necessary to file an injunction prepared in advance of the Record of Decision (ROD) being issued. A runner would be waiting for the ROD to be issued by the proponent— in this case the corps—and then, with the decision in hand, would literally run to the DC Circuit Court and file the documents that would bring at least a temporary halt to a project approved only minutes earlier.[29]

The National Wildlife Federation had indicated to the EPA that in view of its limited resources it was questionable whether it would litigate. If the Rafferty-Alameda project had anything going for it in terms of staving off litigation south of the border, it was that the bill authorizing the project was the subject of a unique legislative strategy. Page's predecessor as assistant secretary of the army, Robert Dawson, was instrumental in getting the 1986 *Water Resources Development Act* through Congress. He did this by devising a local cost-sharing mechanism, and by the inclusion of water user fees in the bill:

> In pursuit of the legislation, which became law in November 1986, Dawson convened an unlikely legislative strategy session in his Pentagon headquarters the previous July: it pulled in most of the top Washington environmental leaders. Amazingly, Dawson and representatives of the Sierra Club, National Wildlife Federation, Environmental Policy Institute, Wildlife Management Institute, National Audubon Society, Izaak Walton League and Friends of the Earth came together.
>
> The subject was: how to get the House conferees to bend enough toward the Senate version of the omnibus water bill to avoid a presidential veto? Both the environmentalists and Dawson opposed the House bill because its cost-sharing provisions were too weak, and it was loaded down with 125 more projects than the Senate bill. The environmental groups endorsed the Senate bill because of the relatively limited number of new projects and because it would cast requirements for significant cost-sharing in legislation.[30]

Why would groups such as the National Wildlife Federation and the Sierra Club back the bill?

> Lynn Greenwalt, the NWF's vice-president for resource conservation, said: "The National Wildlife Federation cannot support the authorization of hundreds of new water projects with an estimated cost of more than $18 billion without significant cost-sharing and user fee requirements. Those reforms are absolutely necessary for the nation to set priorities and weed out the political boondoggles from the genuinely necessary projects that represent sound investment and wise natural resource management.[31]

Contained within the *Water Resources Development Act* was Rafferty-Alameda. While it was not out of the question that the National Wildlife Federation might initiate litigation against the project in 1989, given the strategic position of Burdick and the fact that the NWF had backed the bill in 1986 that contained authorization for the project, we thought we were on fairly solid ground.

The head of the Canadian delegation, Brian Buckley, and I spoke on October 2. Buckley's sense from people in the federal government who were working closely on CWF II was that the action would likely not succeed (where had we heard that before?). More important, there was nothing to prevent us from proceeding with the signing of the agreement posthaste. With October 25 and 26 set for the signing, bureaucratic concerns became critical: ensuring that External Affairs had the legal authority to sign on behalf of Canada, ensuring that equally valid French and English versions were ready. Both sides had to review both versions and ensure they were each correct. Given the technical nature of the agreement and the operating plan, this was no small feat.

The Canada-U.S. agreement was signed in Washington on October 26. Jack Beard, head of the American delegation, had overlooked nothing. A carefully coordinated chain reaction of U.S. document signings in the previous ten days as well as the issuance of the ROD had all been accomplished with clockwork precision. His attention to detail even extended to the location of the ceremony: a room in the Capitol with large windows overlooking the new Canadian Embassy.

The agreement was signed by officials of the Department of the Army and the Department of External Affairs on behalf of the United States and Canada. It struck me as incongruous that many of the people who had spent years negotiating the agreement were sitting in the audience, while two bureaucrats who knew virtually nothing about it were putting their signatures to the document. But neither that nor the litigation still hanging over the project could detract from the satisfaction derived from this event. It was directly proportional to the effort we had expended, which was as it should be. It was also a melancholy occasion, the kind that comes with any significant event when you recognize that a part of your life is over, and the people you had worked with so closely would never again meet as a group. And even if they did, it wouldn't be the same.

The signing of the agreement was greeted with considerable satisfaction by residents of the Souris River basin. Opponents of the project cried foul, but that was to be expected. Lorne Scott likened it to "going out and counting up the war dead after the project is built."[32]

We viewed the signing as a victory, along with the news that a representative of the U.S. National Wildlife Federation was quoted as saying the federation was "extremely disappointed and I guess we hope that the Canadian Wildlife Federation court case succeeds."[33] It confirmed that there would be no litigation in the United States.

The signing of the agreement was not, by itself, sufficient to start the flow of American funds to Saskatchewan. Considering that the agreement was signed by the government of Canada and it was the government of Saskatchewan that was building the project, a separate agreement between the federal government and Saskatchewan was necessary. As federal-provincial agreements go, it was not complex, nor did it take long to negotiate or sign; it is a one-page document with only two clauses. But while it is structurally simple, that doesn't make it insignificant. One very significant aspect is the clause in which Saskatchewan indemnified and saved harmless the Canadian federal government from any and all liabilities that might result from the signing of the Canada-U.S. agreement. What it meant was that, no matter how many times the federal government made errors related to the project—and more would be forthcoming—it could not be held responsible.[34]

CHAPTER SEVEN

POLITICAL GAMES

AND VERBAL DEALS

No issue raises more questions about the Rafferty-Alameda project than the meeting that took place between Grant Devine and Robert de Cotret on September 5, 1990. It is still impossible to reconcile the two versions of the meeting. Rarely do two politicians on opposite sides of an issue, let alone of the same political party, confront each other in such an open and adversarial fashion, and for such high stakes. But lost in everyone's desire to know "the real story" about this event, which is central to the resolution of the Rafferty-Alameda story, is how and why we got to the September 5 meeting at all.

When Saskatchewan signed the January 26, 1990, Agreement limiting construction on the project, Lucien Bouchard was quick to announce that a panel had been appointed. Within a matter of days, Robert Connelly, one of the most experienced people within FEARO, had been appointed to chair the five-member panel; the other four were either from private consulting firms or academia. Bouchard's actions were encouraging, as it seemed to confirm the federal commitment to a quick review.

We responded early in February, providing full documentation (the EIS and related documents now totalled between 5,000 and 6,000 pages each) and an offer of a technical briefing for the panel. From the outset of the panel review, we were encouraged by the signals we were receiving from FEARO. Bob Walker, vice-president of environmental programs at SaskPower, told me he had spoken with Robert Connelly on February 8. According to Walker, Connelly had indicated that Rafferty-Alameda was being acknowledged within the federal government as a "major federal screw-up" and that "this is the most embarrassing situation that and the environment minister have ever been in."[1] Connelly also indicated to Walker that he had sympathies for the people of southeastern Saskatchewan, and that he was under time pressure from Bouchard. We had heard media reports that Connelly's review would take at least a year, but we were convinced this was public posturing.

When the terms of reference for the panel review were made public early in February, I noticed that in one key respect, they were not consistent with the terms of the agreement reached on January 26 between Saskatchewan and the federal government. The panel had been led to believe that all work not explicitly referred to as permissible in the agreement was prohibited. The SBDA, on the other hand, took the view that all work not explicitly prohibited was allowed to proceed. The January 26 Agreement stated that Saskatchewan would cease construction on three components of the project: the Rafferty Dam, the Rafferty-Boundary Diversion Channel, and the Alameda Dam. Because all our licenses were still in place, and we had agreed to delay construction of only these three structures until the federal review process was complete, we felt we were within our rights to carry out work on any other aspect of the project. Indeed, since all the regulatory obligations still applied, it was arguable that we were legally obligated to continue with these mitigative responsibilities.

They were not insignificant. They involved building a causeway across the Souris River valley approximately two-thirds of the way up the Rafferty Reservoir, initial construction on a park and golf course, planting trees to replace wildlife habitat, archeological investigations, fencing the reservoir area, replacing government-owned community pastures, and, what proved to be the most controversial component, excavating a river channel below the Rafferty Dam.

Presumably as a result of the controversy surrounding the project, the federal and provincial environmental approvals contained interlocking clauses making them mutually dependent. Approvals from the Saskatchewan Water Corporation contained similar terms. With these interlocking provisions in the most critical licenses for the project, we were aware that if we did not live up to our mitigative obligations, we would risk losing not only one of the approvals, but all of them.[2]

In negotiating the terms of the agreement with Environment Canada, Hill had told Deputy Minister Len Good that Saskatchewan would be carrying out mitigative activity related to the project. While Hill outlined in general what we would be doing, Good apparently fell victim to his own lack of knowledge about the project. No senior official from Environment Canada had to that point bothered to visit the site. When the terms of reference were published, I informed the panel secretariat and, through our legal counsel, Environment Canada, that a discrepancy existed between the terms of the January 26 Agreement and the terms of reference for the panel. The response Tom Gauley got from Environment Canada was that the deputy minister had said to "let the agreement stand as is."[3]

By the middle of February, the panel had appointed a group of consultants to function as its technical committee. Only one of them was from the west, and she was not from Saskatchewan. Hill was beside himself. "Can you imagine," he asked, "how the government of Ontario would react if the Sky Dome was 'EARPED'—which of course it won't be—and all the technical experts reviewing it came from Saskatchewan?" The lack of western Canadian representation among the consultants was difficult to accept. There were numerous consultants in the west with the expertise to evaluate dams on prairie rivers.

By early March, FEARO began to receive correspondence from SCRAP, alleging that "destructive work continues in the upper valley area of the dam." In response, Raymond Robinson wrote to Len Good as deputy minister of the initiating federal department: "This allegation, I am sure you would agree, requires urgent investigation. I would be grateful if your officials would look into this matter immediately and establish whether there has been any contravention of the agreement."[4]

Within a day of the Robinson letter, an official from the Environment Canada Regina office contacted us to find out what work was taking place. It was now a full month since the panel had been appointed, and there had been no visible activity in terms of initiating the review. We had been informed, in fact, that one of the reasons for the delay was that one of the panel members had just begun a month-long vacation. This did not help the deteriorating relationship between ourselves and Environment Canada. It appeared that while the latter somehow found the time to investigate the "destructive work" that was allegedly going on, it couldn't arrange for the panel to get started.

Progress on the panel review was so slow that it prompted Hill, who in addition to his duties on the SBDA was also president of SaskPower and had other demands on his time, to write and personally deliver a letter to Len Good in Ottawa dealing with activities in the Rafferty Reservoir area. Hill also went to inquire into the lack of progress in the panel review, as well as the fact that the payments of $1 million per month were chronically late.

Excerpts from the letter Hill delivered further reflect the deteriorating relations between Saskatchewan and Environment Canada:

> . . . In his letter and its attachment, Mr. Robinson demonstrates a woeful lack of sensitivity towards the current situation the government finds itself in and Mr. Robinson's letter demands a response . . .
>
> It would seem to me that if Mr. Robinson, as he alleges, is concerned about establishing that no activity has occurred which may undermine the work of the panel, he would be well advised to start with the federal Minister of the Environment who has breached the Agreement with the Saskatchewan Water Corporation by failing to pay the funds to Saskatchewan that he was obligated to. The work which is currently occurring in the Rafferty-Alameda Project is work that Saskatchewan is fully entitled to carry out and in certain respects, is legally obligated to under existing federal and provincial licenses.
>
> The misplaced concern evidenced by Mr. Robinson on this matter demonstrates little if any remorse for the factors leading up to the situation that the Saskatchewan government has been placed in through no fault of its own. His concern over the issue of current construction activities on the project is, in my view, misplaced and constitutes an undue infringement upon the rights of the Government of Saskatchewan with respect to Rafferty-Alameda.
>
> . . . If Mr. Robinson is sincere in his concern about the environment, and I have no reason to believe that he isn't, it would seem to me that he would be well advised to focus his efforts on replacing the EARP guidelines with a clear and unambiguous federal environmental as-

sessment law. Cavalier interventions in matters of provincial jurisdiction do nothing to help matters and succeed only in exacerbating
resentment about the incompetence of the Federal Environmental
Assessment Review Office and the way it has handled the Rafferty-
Alameda Project.[5]

Hill later noted in a sworn affidavit:

> The only purpose of my visit to Ottawa was to see Dr. Good and one of
> the reasons was to point out to him the lack of progress on the environ-
> mental review and to point out that six weeks had expired since the
> Panel was appointed and that the Panel had not even visited the Project,
> and to remind him of his undertaking to see that the Panel would expe-
> ditiously carry out their duties. Dr. Good advised me that he was em-
> barrassed that nothing had yet happened concerning the Panel. As well,
> I informed Dr. Good that the Saskatchewan Water Corporation had yet
> to receive any funds provided for under the January 26 1990 Agree-
> ment. Before that day expired, two million dollars had been sent to the
> Saskatchewan Water Corporation in Moose Jaw.[6]

The environmental lobby, the NDP in Saskatchewan, and the federal government were all accusing Saskatchewan of making a mockery of the environment. It was our view that Environment Canada had made a mockery of things
by defending the EARP Guidelines when they were clearly indefensible as a
regulatory instrument. One of our lawyers, Bob Kennedy, began to refer to the
entire affair as "a mockery of a sham of a travesty."

At some point in the spring of 1990, we decided we weren't going to take it
any more. No specific event triggered this decision. It resulted from increasing
frustration over the mishandling of the issue by what we concluded was an incompetent federal government. If Environment Canada wanted to defend the
EARP Guidelines at the expense of the Rafferty-Alameda project, we would
turn the whole thing into a circus. Perhaps it wasn't the most constructive thing
to do, but under the circumstances it seemed our only recourse.

The task for us, and it was a relatively easy one, was to demonstrate how
badly the federal government had handled its review of Rafferty-Alameda and
how flawed the EARP Guidelines were. Clearly, there were differences between
our approach to the issue and Environment Canada's: both cultural and organizational. We valued the dams. The Ottawa bureaucracy valued process, consensus, and anonymity. The people working on Rafferty-Alameda were not civil
servants. We didn't approach the issue as civil servants would. In a bureaucracy,
process matters more than substance. To career civil servants, on-going relations are more important than any single project. But we had removed the project
from the grasp of the Regina bureaucracy. We had virtually complete freedom,
because we had nothing to lose. For us, it was the project or nothing. This was a
critical distinction that Environment Canada never did grasp.

As individuals, we had long since forsaken our anonymity. The high pro-files of Devine and Berntson meant that they could not respond to every issue related to the project and, in certain instances, they wanted to distance them-selves from it. This meant that Hill and I had to assume a much higher profile than would normally have been the case. It was, therefore, no great problem for us to turn the issue into a political battle. We decided to spell out who was to blame. In a bureaucracy like Ottawa's, which values anonymity more than any-thing, this must have cut like a knife. In their world, it was something that simply was not done.

George Hill fired the opening shot. On March 13, he addressed the Kiwanis Club of Minot and wasted no time in tearing into the federal government, charg-ing, among other things, that "the problem in Canada rests wholly and solely on the shoulders of the federal bureaucrats, but they spend more of their time cov-ering their butts than rectifying the problem they created."[7]

There was little support remaining for the project in the provincial Cabinet. It was still unclear who actually had ministerial responsibility. On paper, it was Harold Martens. When questions were asked in the House, as often as not George McLeod answered. We tolerated this situation for a while, but things came to a head when McLeod, during the week of March 26, told the House that the only work we were doing was that specified in the January agreement and by the engineering review board. He had forgotten, ignored, or misunderstood the cru-cial distinction between the Rafferty Dam and the Rafferty project, and that we were fully entitled to complete certain works related to the project. The situa-tion was particularly unfortunate considering that, the day the House opened, we had sent a briefing note to McLeod's office specifically dealing with this issue.

We drafted a statement for him to clarify his remarks, but he refused to read it in the House. He knew he had made an error but, as he told Berntson, it was better to let sleeping dogs lie. Hill made the point that, if the thing was liti-gated—and SCRAP was looking for any avenue to litigate—they would prob-ably go to McLeod's statement in the House rather than to what was contained in the agreement.[8]

Eventually, McLeod did issue the statement, but the whole episode diverted a great deal of our time and resources. The situation reflected the deteriorating state of the government. It wouldn't have been allowed to occur had Berntson still been in the Cabinet. As the issue grew more factional, Hill and I felt in-creasingly isolated. Without the necessary political backing, it became exceed-ingly difficult for us to manage the project. We, and Hill especially, found our-selves out front on the issue, constantly facing the media. We did not seek this high degree of notoriety, rather it was a function of the growing political turmoil within the provincial Conservative Party, made worse because no individual government member was willing to speak on behalf of Rafferty-Alameda.

In early April we began what amounted to a slow game of chicken with Environment Canada. It lasted the better part of six months, and it was surpris-ingly easy. We began to speak openly about all the work we would be doing on the project: downstream channelization, causeways, parks, fencing, golf courses, pasture, and wildlife mitigation. We also talked about virtually completing the Rafferty Dam. With all the media interest, we managed to create the impression that we had hardly even slowed down, despite the January 26 Agreement.

On April 2, Bob Connelly wrote to Bouchard on behalf of the panel, requesting clarification:

> ... some of this work may indeed be permitted under existing federal and provincial licenses or agreements. However, there can be no doubt that the integrity of the review would be seriously compromised should work continue which seems contrary to the spirit of the federal-provincial agreement and to the understanding of Panel members when they agreed to serve on the Panel.[9]

What was Bouchard to do? He and his officials had created this situation and they couldn't get out of it without our help. We were aware that SCRAP and the Canadian Wildlife Federation were putting pressure on the minister. But every time they complained, it helped demonstrate how ridiculous the whole thing was. "This is not acceptable," environmentalist Elizabeth May announced on *CBC Newsworld*:

> This is a scandal ... Why are Canadian taxpayers giving Saskatchewan $10 million? I mean, I would really like to know what we are compensating them for ... So much is very offensive about this process. Three different [court cases] have said that the Rafferty-Alameda Dam required full environmental assessment. The federal minister responded to the most recent of those decisions by arranging with the Saskatchewan government to halt construction to create the last shred remaining of credibility around this process, so that the federal environmental assessment process and review could be conducted during a time that construction had stopped. It is a thin reed of credibility, but it is all they had, and they agreed to do a federal environmental assessment of the dams. Construction was supposed to stop, and in exchange for the stopping of construction, Saskatchewan managed to get $10 million in compensation to be given out $1 million a month up to a maximum of 10 months. That was the arrangement.
>
> It was pronounced and announced by both Saskatchewan and the feds as an arrangement that would stop construction so that a full environmental assessment process, with as much credibility as you can have once the project is half-built, could be conducted. And what has happened now is that Saskatchewan has essentially found a loop-hole in their agreement. They have gone back on their word. They haven't stopped construction. They plan to bring it to nearly completion during the time that they continue to pocket the $1 million per month in compensation.[10]

We increased the pressure on Ottawa by announcing all the things we were planning to do throughout the 1990 construction season until we got our license back. Bouchard was in an awkward position. He either had to convince us to stop construction, which was hardly likely, or continue to run the risk that the panel might resign. His options were further limited by the fact that he could not arbitrarily cancel the license; his own officials had insisted that it be drafted in the form of a contract signed by both parties, and no one had breached the contract.

When the panel accepted our offer of a technical briefing, it had become obvious to them and their support staff that emotions among local residents were running high. In an attempt to keep things from getting out of hand, the panel decided that the briefing would be a by-invitation-only affair, and that only representatives of interest groups would be invited. The general public, therefore, would be unable to attend. According to the secretary of the panel, the officials were hoping to accommodate public interest in a "manageable" way.[11]

Political strategy aside, the notion of the panel attempting to hold this kind of meeting caused us great concern. It was obvious that the EARP Guidelines did not make provision for such a meeting, and because of this, any attempt to limit public input would create another opportunity for litigation. To us, this was simply one more example of the dysfunctional nature of the guidelines, and one more indication of the lack of expertise among environment officials in the federal government.

One interest group in support of the project was incensed as well, and sponsored radio announcements informing the public of the time of the briefing. Hill wrote to Len Good, denouncing the attempt to restrict public access to the review and, more important, questioning the slowness of the panel in conducting it.[12] The panel's response was to cancel the technical briefing and reconsider how best to proceed.

It did not take Environment Canada long to determine that it had no way out on the issue of continued construction on the project. On May 3, Bouchard wrote to Harold Martens:

> I am writing to you to make known my concern about the April 27 announcement by Saskatchewan of its intention to proceed with further construction on the Rafferty dam and associated works in the reservoir area. The announced construction would appear to extend beyond what is necessary to meet the requirements of the independent dam safety review board and will definitely be viewed as contravening the spirit of the Canada-Saskatchewan Agreement.
>
> . . . I have referred this matter for further investigation by federal officials. If activities are occurring that are contrary to the terms of the Agreement or the federal license for the project, I will take whatever steps are appropriate.[13]

When lawyers start citing the spirit of the agreement, it generally means they don't have a leg to stand on. Environment Canada was getting desperate, and would try almost anything to get us to stop construction. I had received calls from both Environment Canada and FEARO telling me that the panel might resign, and that would be bad for the project because it would mean additional delays. This was a familiar refrain; it had become apparent that the promise of a speedy review had been an empty one. The panel had been appointed at the end of January, and by the first week of May it still hadn't bothered even to visit the site. Besides, if the panel resigned it would only provide further proof that the EARP Guidelines were a mess and that Environment Canada was incapable of managing the issue.

Another example of the brinkmanship between Saskatchewan and Environment Canada involved the excavation of a channel below the Rafferty Dam. The original river channel from the dam six kilometers downstream to Estevan was so flat and poorly defined that the river actually "flowed" upstream during spring runoff due to the effect the dam had on water that flowed out of Long Creek into the Souris. To build the dam and not excavate the channel made no sense, as virtually any releases from the reservoir would have resulted in flows exceeding the channel capacity in this reach of the river. Besides, downstream channelization had been excluded from the terms of the January 26 Agreement, and by this stage, anything that wasn't explicitly cited in the agreement was being built with as much fanfare as we could muster.

When we awarded the contract for the downstream channelization we instructed the contractor to stay out of the old river channel. Given that, in some sections, the excavated channel would travel down the center line of the old meander loops, this was an inefficient way to do the work, requiring the machinery to "leapfrog" their way down the valley to avoid the riverbed. It made no sense from a construction point of view, but as long as the contractor didn't go into the existing channel, which was bone dry, no federal jurisdiction was affected and Ottawa couldn't do anything about it. The environmental groups reacted as we knew they would, raising a stink and putting more pressure on the minister. But that was the object of the exercise.

When we first awarded the contract for the downstream channelization and the panel didn't resign, we decided to increase the pressure. We ordered the bulldozers into the channel. I knew our construction activities were being closely monitored, and I immediately got a call from Bob Halliday, regional director for Environment Canada's Inland Waters Directorate in Regina—an individual I liked and respected. He asked me if we had ordered the machines into the river channel. "This morning," I said. Clearly feeling awkward about the message he was delivering, he told me that this action was being treated very seriously by the federal government and that charges under the *Fisheries Act* were a possibility for damaging fish habitat.

There was no water in this reach of the river. Because of the drought, there hadn't been for a number of years. After consulting our lawyers, I called Halliday back and asked, if there was no water, and obviously no fish, how could it be fish habitat? He said that if there ever was water there, then it would be fish habitat.

"Couldn't the same argument be made about the Sahara Desert?" I asked.

"Probably," he responded.

I thought for a moment, and then I said, "Bob, this project has been in court I can't even remember how many times. If the federal government wants to charge us under the *Fisheries Act* for working on a project that will result in a net gain of habitat, then go right ahead."

I didn't mention that it was somewhat paradoxical that an agency of the federal government, the PFRA, under contract to the SBDA, had done the initial routing and design for the downstream channelization.

During the week of May 7, we sponsored public meetings throughout the Saskatchewan and Manitoba portions of the Souris basin. Ostensibly, they were to inform the public of the current status of the project and what work was being proposed for the 1990 construction season. In reality, we wanted finally to spell out just how much of a mess the federal government had made of it and, more specifically, to buttress support for the project among basin residents. We used overheads and slides and quoted from various letters, reports, and decisions from the courts. We were quite deliberately tapping into the undercurrent of resentment toward the east, which always exists just below the surface in the west. The response was visceral and overwhelming. At the end of the meetings, people would shout out, asking what they could do to help. Strategically, we were securing the political base for the project. If we were going to fight the issue out on a political level, we had to be sure we had a solid base of public support.

The meetings confirmed what most residents of the Souris basin had managed to figure out on their own: Saskatchewan was being mistreated by the federal government. By this point, anything we did was guaranteed to get media coverage, and that was certainly the case with these meetings. Don Curren wrote in the *Regina Leader-Post*:

> The federal government's involvement in the Rafferty-Alameda project has been a "long litany of screw-ups," project official George Hood told a receptive audience here [Estevan] Tuesday night.
>
> Hood used handouts and overhead displays to chronicle Ottawa's involvement in the $140-million project for about 125 gathered in Estevan . . .
>
> "To say these EARP Guidelines were indefensible would not be an overstatement," he said.
>
> Hood said that the ambiguities of the EARP Guidelines could possibly result in additional legal challenges of Rafferty-Alameda.
>
> "I am convinced that we are not finished with the courtroom in terms of this project," Hood said.
>
> New federal environmental assessment review legislation expected this year should exempt existing projects such as Rafferty-Alameda through a "grandfather clause," he said.
>
> Hood depicted the five-member panel reviewing the project as slow-moving, saying that they had been in position for four months and still had not toured the Rafferty Dam site.[14]

By this point in Devine's mandate, Hill and I were fairly certain that the Tories were not going to be reelected. If anything, the realization strengthened our resolve to get the project built. Fear is a great motivator. The last thing any of us wanted was a half-built monument on how not to do something.

Noteworthy in all this is that Hill and I had not consulted with anyone inside the government, other than Berntson, before I headed out on our road show. The day after the meetings started, we sent copies of the material to be distributed at the meetings to Harold Martens and George McLeod—who were both speaking on behalf of the project at the Cabinet level. We figured it would be easier to apologize after the fact than to ask for permission in advance.

In May Lucien Bouchard resigned from the federal Cabinet over the Meech Lake Accord. Robert de Cotret became acting minister of the environment, but remained as president of the Treasury Board. De Cotret had not been in the position long before he was dragged into the middle of the mess Bouchard had left him. The Canadian Wildlife Federation was quick off the mark with the new minister:

> The Canadian Wildlife Federation is extremely concerned about ongoing construction of certain project features at the Rafferty-Alameda Project site. The current situation is totally unacceptable and must be rectified immediately. We refer specifically to the construction of downstream channelization, Mainprize Park and mitigation works.[15]

It was a classic example of how silly the exercise had become. Here was the Canadian Wildlife Federation complaining about our planting trees and grasses to create wildlife habitat and building a park. It was one more act in a soon-to-be-completed farce.

In early June, de Cotret received our written response to Bouchard's "appropriate measures" letter of May 3. To this point, the tension between Saskatchewan and Ottawa had been restricted to bureaucrats and officials. There wasn't much on paper at the ministerial level until our response reached Ottawa. Interestingly, the letter was signed by Hill rather than Martens, further indicating the growing distance between the provincial Cabinet and the project. That it came from Hill should have signalled to Ottawa just how far off the rails the project was, both procedurally—in terms of the environmental assessment— and in terms of the absence of ministerial accountability in Regina. The letter spelled out in blunt language some of the more egregious problems Saskatchewan had encountered with the federal government:

> . . . The accusation made in Mr. Bouchard's letter that activities that we have announced for the Rafferty-Alameda *Project,* "will be viewed as contravening the spirit of the Canada-Saskatchewan Agreement" is highly questionable given the fact that prior to the signing of the Agreement on January 26, 1990, I explained in considerable detail to the Environment Canada Deputy Minister, Dr. Len Good, the nature and

extent of the work that Saskatchewan would be carrying out.

. . . And while one raises the issue of breaching the Agreement one need look no further than the performance of the federal government and the fact that only one payment to date out of four has been made on time.

. . . However, as noted in Mr. Bouchard's letter regarding concerns about the continuation of work on the new Dr. Mainprize Park, the incongruity of the federal Minister of the Crown responsible for parks arguing against the creation of a park could not escape me . . .

It is questionable, notwithstanding the comments of Environment Canada officials regarding possible charges under the *Fisheries Act,* that there is any *bona fide* federal jurisdiction on this matter. Without this jurisdiction Environment Canada does not have unfettered discretion to amend the IRIA license so it is difficult to appreciate the nature of his concern, particularly given that there will be at least a thousand-fold increase in fisheries habitat *after* the Rafferty-Alameda Reservoirs are developed.

The letter concluded:

In all probability, Rafferty-Alameda will be litigated again. It is immaterial to us if it is the federal government or intervener groups. From the Saskatchewan perspective, we are far better off standing up for something we believe in than being brow-beaten by Ottawa as we attempt to conserve water in the worst drought of the last century. To this end, our construction schedule for 1990 stands as outlined . . .[16]

With de Cotret's appointment, there was a marked difference in the federal government's approach to the project. Lucien Bouchard, we had been told by contacts in Ottawa, was not really interested in issues that did not involve Quebec. Robert de Cotret proved to be much broader in his view, and with a sense of the inequities and injustices that had been committed on the project. After our response to the Bouchard letter, Len Gustafson, MP for Souris-Moose Mountain, advised us to give de Cotret a chance; we should not prejudge him because of what Bouchard had done to us.

Len Gustafson's role in Rafferty-Alameda has not received a great deal of attention. Gustafson, now a senator, is a lifelong resident of the Souris River basin, with a large farming operation based in Macoun just northwest of Estevan and less than twenty kilometers from the Rafferty Reservoir. He was one of the first members of the Conservative caucus to back Brian Mulroney's leadership bid in 1983. For his efforts, he was rewarded with the position of parliamentary secretary to the prime minister. Not completely irrelevant to the discussion is the fact that Mulroney himself was not unfamiliar with this area of Saskatchewan or the Rafferty-Alameda project. As a young man, he was an executive assistant to Gustafson's predecessor, Alvin Hamilton—also a supporter of water management in the Souris River basin.[17]

Gustafson had always been a steadfast supporter of Rafferty-Alameda, and was clearly upset by what had transpired on the project, but he carried little weight in Ottawa. Until the public meetings held in May he had escaped the wrath of his constituents. Then he became the focus of considerable criticism for what the federal government had allowed to occur. With the appointment of de Cotret, Gustafson, after much "encouragement" from Hill, became involved in virtually all our dealings with the federal government.

In the middle of June, Harold Martens extended an invitation to de Cotret to visit the project. Shortly after that, Gustafson told me that he had spoken with de Cotret, and the minister had a genuine desire, as far the project was concerned, to "move it." De Cotret had also acknowledged that Environment Canada officials did not share his view.[18]

By the third week in June, the panel that Lucien Bouchard had appointed five months earlier finally came west for its tour. While there was still talk about the members resigning, we were convinced those threats were vacuous. We were also convinced that the panel was not about to hurry for anyone. When it met with area residents, though, members were left in no doubt as to the level of frustration in the Souris basin. Jack Fingler, president of the Estevan Chamber of Commerce, addressed the panel:

I am trying to get some hold on the time element involved here. It would seem more realistic to me if you are going to do this study, for God's sake get your ass in gear and get at it. I am damn mad and other people out here are damn mad, and very frustrated and angry. And when you come to us now and you say you are working part-time, maybe a few days here and maybe an evening there, and I appreciate the time and effort you're putting into it but damn it, you're getting paid 450 bucks a shot [per day] to do that. For God's sake get at it.[19]

The political strategy we had decided to follow became more sophisticated during the latter part of June. We had reached a point where it had become necessary to educate the public not only inside the province, but across the country. Accordingly, we contracted with a Regina-based company, Film Crew Productions, to produce a documentary or "infomercial" about the project. It was not yet apparent when and where it would be used, but it was obvious that a more sophisticated means of disseminating information about the Rafferty and Alameda dams was necessary. We realized that we had a tremendous resource to tap into for the film—the area residents who so strongly supported the project.

By the last week in June, Len Gustafson had become directly involved in the attempt to get the federal minister to deal with the problems surrounding the review. When I spoke with him on June 26, Gustafson agreed that de Cotret needed to visit the site. In the first week of July, we unveiled our strategy for dealing with the federal government to Grant Devine. A briefing note laid out the suggested approach:

Rafferty-Alameda can no longer be finessed. It has gone too far in its development and construction and the mistakes that have been made by the federal government are far too serious.

While we have in the past, consistently sought ways to find win-win solutions to the problems created for us by the federal government, the current situation is, in my view, sufficiently serious so as to effectively remove such an alternative.

It is clear that any alternative that the federal government has put forward contravenes past verbal commitments that officials of Environment Canada and specifically the Deputy Minister of the Environment has made.

• (ie) the review is *not* going expeditiously, he is now saying that the FEARO and EARP panels operate at arms length and that he is not the appropriate individual for us to deal with;

• the federal Deputy Minister is now accusing me [Hill] of lying regarding whether or not we informed him about whether work would be ongoing on the project after the Agreement was signed.

"There are a number of alternatives which Saskatchewan would consider," the note went on:

... Our preferred alternative would be the recognition by the federal government that because of the Canada-U.S. Agreement and the fact that the U.S. is continuing to pay for both Rafferty-Alameda, that work must begin immediately on Alameda. Accordingly, either the Canada-Saskatchewan Agreement should be amended or cancelled and/or the Terms of Reference of the panel should be changed so that they could only make recommendations about the operation of the project while construction continues.

• Another alternative that we would consider is a deadline for the panel of August 1990.

• If either of these conditions are unacceptable to the Panel and it resigns then we should demand that a federal Order-in-Council be passed exempting the Rafferty-Alameda Project from the EARP guidelines.

• It is indeed ironic that Alberta is permitted by the federal government to continue all aspects of the Oldman River Dam despite that fact that no environmental impact statement has ever been done and we have done so much work and have been reviewed twice and are shut down ...

• The federal track record on Rafferty-Alameda is indefensible and it [Saskatchewan] has been the province that has borne the brunt of federal incompetence.

• No senior federal official including the Deputy Minister nor any federal Environment Minister has even bothered to visit the Souris Basin to see the project.

• Saskatchewan is bearing *all* of the real responsibilities because we have indemnified and saved harmless the federal government.[20]

Devine's instincts when dealing with the federal government were not to fight, but by July 1990, even his patience had run out. With Devine and Gustafson lobbying de Cotret, the minister agreed to visit the project during the last week of July. The visit was coordinated to ensure that he met opponents and supporters alike. We were ecstatic. Not only would we be able to give the minister a tour of the project and let him see what the source of all the controversy was, but he would also get a chance to meet the opposition. As far as the latter were concerned, we were convinced they would do as much to harm themselves and their cause as anything we could say or do.

De Cotret arrived in Saskatchewan on Wednesday, July 25, with his parliamentary secretary, Lee Clark, MP for Brandon-Souris in Manitoba. He and Gustafson met with Hill and then with the project opponents. The next day, Devine and North Dakota Governor George Sinner toured the project by air with de Cotret, Gustafson, Clark, Hill, and a number of other officials. According to Devine, when they flew over the Alameda Dam site, de Cotret's comment was, "This is it? This is what all the fuss is about? I could dam this with my briefcase." There was almost no water in Moose Mountain Creek.

In Estevan, there was a ground tour of the Rafferty Dam and then a luncheon. De Cotret didn't know it, but he was being set up. In consultation with Devine and Gustafson, we had decided to demonstrate how much support there was for the project, to show de Cotret that the people of the area were not unreasonable, but they were extremely frustrated by their treatment at the hands of the federal government. The task fell to Hill, as no Saskatchewan politician was willing to deliver the message. It was a speech

Grant Devine and Robert de Cotret tour the project in July 1990, along with Len Gustafson and Lee Clark, far right. Courtesy Regina Leader-Post

that no one in attendance would easily forget. Despite having written much of it myself, I can recall actually cringing as Hill delivered it.

We were able to demonstrate the strong support for the project when Hill introduced the mayors of virtually all the municipalities through which the Souris flowed—and not only in Saskatchewan, but in North Dakota and Manitoba as well. When Hill introduced these people, as well as many others, he asked them to stand to demonstrate their support for the project and that of the interests they represented. By the time he had finished, forty-six people had stood to be individually introduced to Robert de Cotret. The introductions were interspersed with an overview of the troubled history of the project:

> Mr. de Cotret, there are many more people here today that I have not introduced, and we could have had thousands here, but I think it can be safely said and you will understand that this project enjoys overwhelming support throughout the Souris Basin in Saskatchewan, North Dakota, and Manitoba. These people believe and they know what's best for themselves and their children. Procedural miscues and the bungling incompetence of insensitive federal bureaucrats who are more concerned with the thickness of the padding over their backsides than they are with Rafferty-Alameda dams in a place they likely never visited called *Saskatchewan*.
>
> Think of the situation that the federal bureaucrats have put your government in. You are attempting to apply a law
> • that was never drafted to be a law and was never passed by Parliament;
> • that defies application because it isn't clear;
> • that was drafted by federal bureaucrats who don't know what it means;
> • that was approved not by your government but by that of Pierre Elliot Trudeau;
> • that threatens up to forty thousand projects across Canada irrespective of their size, complexity, or environmental impact;
> • that denies water storage to people in the middle of a literal desert during the worst drought of the last century;
> • Saskatchewan receives 50 cents on the dollar from the United States to store water that it historically has had a right to store but has never had the ability to do so.
>
> Mr. Minister, I ask that you, as a new minister, reach a decision as soon as possible and I conclude with the words of Mr. Justice J. Fontana: "There is no legal canon prohibiting the application of common sense."
>
> Please sir, apply common sense, bring this matter to an early conclusion and let us fulfil the dreams of the people in the Souris Basin.[21]

De Cotret had the good grace to use humor in his response. He also acknowledged the need for new legislation to replace the EARP Guidelines, and that there were thirteen projects that had been "caught." I left the luncheon with a SaskPower vice-president who remarked, "That was brutal."

While all of this was going on, of course, work on the project continued, the panel continued its work, and we were putting the finishing touches on the Rafferty-Alameda documentary. Within a week of de Cotret's visit, the panel issued a request for additional information. We were informed that there had never been an EARP Panel that did not issue a request for additional information. They had published a draft list of questions in May, so there were few surprises when the final list was issued. There were forty-five questions for which the panel wanted answers. The questions themselves did not pose a problem, as the answers to many of them were contained in information we already had available. As part of its request, the panel acknowledged that it would "engage the services of experts in at least two areas, water quality and social impacts, to provide advice on matters raised during the public review process. The experts will review existing studies and, if appropriate, gather additional information to assist the panel in completing its review."[22]

I couldn't recall any section of the EARP Guidelines that made provision for a panel to conduct its own studies. Suspecting that there was no such provision, I called Gauley and Kennedy and asked them for a legal opinion. I was right. The guidelines, in fact, were quite explicit for once: if the panel wanted more information, it was obliged to ask Environment Canada, as the initiating department, to ask the SBDA, as the proponent, to get it.

Our concern was not with the proposed investigations. By this point in the process, the social impacts of the project were well known. There were over 100 landowners affected by the project, and we had yet to resort to expropriation. We didn't need polls to tell us that public opinion in the area was overwhelmingly in favor of Rafferty-Alameda. As for the water quality issue, we had already concluded a number of supplementary studies. We also had far more expertise at our disposal and had completed many more analyses than the panel or Environment Canada were likely to amass. Our concern stemmed, rather, from the realization that Rafferty-Alameda was being used as a test case, and any procedural error could result in additional litigation.

Immediately after de Cotret's visit, I left for my annual summer vacation. It didn't last long. In a matter of days Hill was on the phone and we were working via fax on the text of a letter Devine would send to de Cotret. We wanted to keep the pressure on before de Cotret became a captive of his department. By August 10, the text of the letter was agreed to, and copies were sent to the prime minister and Len Gustafson as well as de Cotret. It stated, in part:

I believe there are alternatives favourable to both governments which would resolve this unique situation. Please consider the following options:

    1. A fall deadline could be imposed on the panel for the conclusion of its review;

    2. The terms of reference of the panel could be amended to review

the operation of the Rafferty-Alameda Project and construction could resume immediately;

3. Because of its transitional nature, all previous hearings and stage of completion, the Rafferty-Alameda Project could today, very legitimately, be exempted from the EARP Guidelines altogether by means of a federal Order-in-Council.

In particular, I would request that the agreement of January 26, 1990, be opened and renegotiated so that this project could be treated the same as the Oldman River Dam Project.

... there is the matter of the uneven application of federal decisions. I am now speaking of the decision to allow the Oldman River Dam Project to proceed with construction while a review is undertaken. This matter is particularly upsetting here in Saskatchewan given that no environmental assessment of the project has been undertaken in Alberta while we have gone through this unworkable process several times.[23]

The news of the Oldman River Dam had not yet broken, but we were aware of the decision, and from our perspective the timing could not have been better. For in the middle of all the controversy over trying to shut down Rafferty-Alameda in the name of maintaining the integrity of the EARP Guidelines, the federal government had decided not to halt construction on the Oldman River Dam while a panel review was under way. We could not have imagined a more contradictory situation. Rafferty-Alameda had successfully undergone two environmental reviews, and the federal government was working to shut down construction during a third, while the Oldman River Dam project in southwestern Alberta had never been subjected to a formal environmental assessment.

Groups opposed to the Oldman River Dam had initiated litigation before the Federal Court, arguing that the EARP Guidelines applied to that project, given its impact on matters within federal jurisdiction such as fisheries, navigable waters, and Native people. While the Friends of the Oldman were unsuccessful in the Federal Court—Trial Division, the decision was overturned by the Federal Court of Appeal, and a review pursuant to the EARP Guidelines was ordered.[24] The only substantive difference between the two projects was in the federal licenses required for each. Rafferty-Alameda required an *International River Improvements Act* license before the project could proceed. The Oldman River Dam did not require federal licenses as a condition to proceed, although such licenses would be required eventually. The projects were at roughly the same stage of completion, so Ottawa's decision to allow construction to proceed during the review of the Oldman seemed to us particularly hypocritical. It confirmed our opinion that Environment Canada was not concerned primarily about the environment; if it were, it would not have decided to delay the Oldman review until after construction was complete. It also confirmed our opinion that Rafferty-Alameda was pure politics—not that we needed any further confirmation. Finally, it confirmed our assessment of the capabilities of those at the senior level of Environment Canada. They had created a situation in which Saskatchewan had no option but to fight back.

Saskatchewan has traditionally occupied a position among the provinces as an honest broker. Its small population has prevented it from carrying any real weight on the federal-provincial stage, but its progressive stands on many issues have often led to its politicians occupying positions of prominence on the national stage far out of proportion to the actual size and importance of the province itself. This was particularly true during the 1970s, when Allan Blakeney and his deputy premier and minister of intergovernmental affairs, Roy Romanow, carefully forged positions and sought consensus on the national issues of the day, notably the constitution.

With the election of Grant Devine, a fundamentally different approach was taken in regard to federal-provincial relations. In large part, this was attributable to the fact that Regina and Ottawa were both now represented by Conservative governments. This putative partnership would have made it much more difficult for Saskatchewan to occupy its traditional role as a broker even if it had wanted to, which it manifestly did not. Grant Devine placed a very personal imprint on relations between Regina and Ottawa. One of his first acts on assuming office in 1982 was to eliminate the Department of Intergovernmental Affairs. The most important elements of the department were rolled into Devine's own department, the Executive Council, and for the majority of his years in office Devine functioned as his own minister of intergovernmental affairs.

The most significant single factor in Saskatchewan's relationship with the federal government was Grant Devine's personal relationship with Brian Mulroney. While there can be no question that this relationship had its benefits, it also had its drawbacks. Devine unapologetically supported federal initiatives such as the Meech Lake Accord and the GST that were unpopular in the west. His unstinting support for Ottawa contradicted a long-standing historical reality in Saskatchewan: the tendency to vote for one party provincially and another federally. For years, many Saskatchewan voters supported the CCF of Tommy Douglas provincially and the Conservatives of John Diefenbaker federally, and saw nothing inconsistent in doing so.

Running against Ottawa frequently makes for a good political strategy in the west. It was something Allan Blakeney was not above doing, for example, on the issue of federal taxation of the potash industry. This approach was suggested to Devine on a number of issues, but to no avail until Rafferty-Alameda. Because of Devine's approach to federal-provincial relations, it appeared to Hill and me that Saskatchewan had little capital with other provinces or the federal bureaucracy when it came to garnering support for its initiatives. Environment Canada's inconsistency in handling the Rafferty-Alameda project and the Oldman River Dam confirmed in our minds how little respect there was for the current Saskatchewan government within the federal bureaucracy.

Later in August, Devine and de Cotret discussed by telephone the letter we had sent. De Cotret indicated he was willing to impose a deadline on the panel of December 31, 1990.[25] This was of little value, in that it would not allow us to

begin the Alameda Dam that fall. Devine said the deadline was not acceptable.
We couldn't afford to ease the pressure, so a meeting between Devine and de
Cotret was scheduled for September 5 in de Cotret's West Block office. A briefing note on the intent of the trip was prepared for the provincial Cabinet. In part,
it echoed our briefing note to Devine in preparation for de Cotret's visit in July:

• meetings have been scheduled for Ottawa on September 5, 1990, with:
• Federal Minister of Environment—Robert de Cotret
• Chief of Staff—Norman Spector
• the purpose of the meetings is to insist upon changes to the Terms of
Reference of the Rafferty-Alameda Federal Environmental Panel so
that construction on all aspects of the project can begin immediately.
• Saskatchewan is seeking this course of action because Rafferty-
Alameda can no longer be finessed. It has gone too far in its development and construction and the mistakes that have been made by the
Federal Government have been far too serious.
• while we have in the past, consistently sought ways to find win-win
solutions to the problems created for us by the Federal Government,
the current situation is sufficiently serious so as to effectively remove
such an alternative.
• prior to signing the January 26, 1990 agreement with Ottawa, Saskatchewan was promised an expeditious Panel review by Federal bureaucrats. This is not happening.
• the Panel will not likely report until the end of 1990 which may bring
into question whether the Alameda Dam will be built as well as the
Rafferty-Boundary Diversion Channel.
• while this review is going on, Saskatchewan continues to receive funding under the Canada-U.S. Agreement for both the Rafferty Dam and
the Alameda Dam.
• we are told by External Affairs that the Canada-U.S. Agreement is still
binding yet the Panel could make recommendations which would call into
question the Agreement (i.e.) whether the Alameda Dam should be built.
• given that the Saskatchewan Government has indemnified the Federal
Government with respect to the Canada-U.S. Agreement, the Federal
Government's intransigence places the province in an impossible situation vis à vis the United States.
• on a more political level, all Saskatchewan is seeking from Ottawa on
Rafferty-Alameda is equal treatment to the major projects such as
Oldman River Dam in Alberta and the Point Aconi Thermal Electric
Power Plant in Nova Scotia where sources indicate that construction
will continue while panel reviews take place.
• to the best of our knowledge, Rafferty-Alameda is the only project
halted in mid-construction by the Federal Government.
• the Federal Government has overwhelmingly applied the EARP guidelines against the interests of Western Canada. Of the 44 federal envi-

ronmental panel reviews that have been held, 6 have occurred in Ontario and Quebec and 28 have taken place in the West . . .
• Ottawa must deal with Rafferty-Alameda by:
    a) amending the Panel's Terms of Reference.
    b) amending the January 26, 1990 Canada-Saskatchewan Agreement.
• the timing is ideal because:
    i) the Federal House is not sitting.
    ii) the Provincial Legislature is not sitting.
    iii) other projects such as Oldman River are going ahead, projects which have far greater impact than Rafferty-Alameda.
    iv) the Federal Government can blame Lucien Bouchard for screwing up the process.
    v) the Canada-U.S. Agreement is binding and the U.S. is becoming increasingly concerned because it is continuing to pay funds to Saskatchewan for both Rafferty and Alameda.
    vi) the Federal Panel review of Rafferty-Alameda is taking so long and has been so flawed, thus further confirming the need for new legislation.[26]

By this point, Hill and I had become thoroughly cynical about the entire affair. It had been six weeks since de Cotret had visited the site; nothing had happened and we were convinced that nothing would. The panel would muddle along, perhaps getting its work done some time in 1991. The Saskatchewan government would not take a stand and, in all likelihood, would go down to defeat in the general election that had to be held in 1991. The Alameda Dam would, as a result, probably never be built. Without Alameda, the Rafferty Dam as designed made little sense. There was precious little reason for optimism as we headed to Ottawa.

The meeting had been scheduled by the Premier's Office, and both Hill and I thought it was a waste of time. We took the last plane out of Regina, arriving in Ottawa around 12:30 AM. Since the meeting with de Cotret was not scheduled until noon, we had brought a rough copy of the project documentary for Devine to view in the morning. We had decided on the title "Dreams in the Dust." After the viewing, the balance of our time with the premier was spent reviewing the material in the briefing book I had prepared. There was an extra copy for the federal minister. In addition to the standard briefing material, the packages for Devine and de Cotret contained: a newspaper report about the Point Aconi thermal electric power station in Nova Scotia that had been allowed to proceed without a federal panel review; a copy of the January 26, 1990, Agreement; a draft of a new agreement that would allow the panel to review the operation of the project; new terms of reference for the panel; and a draft Order-in-Council exempting the project from the EARP Guidelines should the need arise. The new draft agreement also allowed for the cessation of the payment to Saskatchewan of $1 million per month. The reason for all this documentation was simple: in the unlikely event that the minister was actually going to do something, we knew that his department could not be depended on to correctly prepare any of the necessary papers.

Devine, his assistant Doug Mallo, George Hill, and I arrived at de Cotret's Parliament Hill office at noon. Devine was ushered into the minister's office. The three of us were left in an ante-room to wait along with an Environment Canada official, Ralph Pentland. In the half-hour we spent waiting, I gently chided Pentland about what a mess Environment Canada had managed to create. Then one of de Cotret's secretaries invited us into an adjoining room where a table had been set up for lunch with eight place settings.

Devine and de Cotret, all smiles, entered the room from the opposite side. Devine looked at me, winked, and said *sotto voce*, "It looks good." No sooner were we seated around the table, with the addition of two of de Cotret's assistants, than the minister advised us that he and the premier had reached an agreement that would settle everything once and for all. De Cotret said that he and Devine had agreed to amend the January 26 Agreement, removing all restrictions on continuing construction and allowing all components of the project to proceed immediately.

The minister went on to say that the terms of reference for the panel were to be amended to limit the scope of the review to the operations of the project once it was complete. He said that he and the premier had reached a further agreement to establish a mitigation trust fund of $10 million, consisting of the $8 million Saskatchewan had already received and the $2 million still pending from the federal government. Proceeds from the fund were to pay for any mitigation the panel recommended that the minister was prepared to accept. De Cotret then asked Devine if he had correctly stated the terms of the agreement, and Devine indicated that he had. I looked across the table at Hill. Both of us were incredulous. We couldn't believe what we had heard. I remember thinking that the nightmare was finally over.

Throughout the lunch it became apparent that, while de Cotret may have been pleased with the agreement, his two assistants and Ralph Pentland were not. There was discussion about the panel, which, ironically, was finally touring the project that day, and whether its members would resign over the issue of downstream channelization. De Cotret remarked that if the panel did resign, his options would actually increase.[27]

In light of this new agreement, it was necessary to amend the text of the draft agreement we had prepared to make provision for the mitigation trust fund. It was agreed that I would stay and work with federal officials to reduce the agreement to writing, and that no announcement would be made until after the following Tuesday, September 11, the day of the Manitoba general election. The lunch concluded on a congenial note, with a handshake between Devine and de Cotret on the agreement that had been reached. Hill wrote a memo to file:

> We left—I was absolutely ecstatic. I congratulated the Premier in the hallway and told him that I didn't know how he did it but it was fantastic. We proceeded to Len Gustafson's office for a debriefing. Helen

[Gustafson's secretary] ushered us in to Len's private office [Gustafson was at home in the constituency], where Devine indicated he had simply explained to de Cotret what was in the briefing notebook, went through it and how important the Project was to Saskatchewan. With that, de Cotret read the proposed agreement and said it was fine, but how about including a $10 million mitigation trust fund. He explained what he had in mind and Devine said it was a great idea. It was fine with him. De Cotret said, we have a deal. They then, according to Devine, left the room.

Devine said in Gustafson's office that the mitigation trust fund was a great idea and he wished he had thought of it.[28]

We called Gustafson at his home in Macoun. His wife, Alice, told us that he was out combining. He later recounted on CBC Radio that Devine had called him at about 2 o'clock on September 5. He had been out harvesting and his wife called him to the phone. Devine, he said, was "very elated that an agreement had been reached" and that "the work would be going ahead." Gustafson concluded: "That's what I understood."[29]

From Gustafson's office in Ottawa we called Bob Kennedy in Saskatoon, who had drawn up the original draft agreement Devine had discussed with de Cotret. We told him about the agreement and asked that he amend the document to provide for the mitigation trust fund. With an intervening stop at the Prime Minister's Office, where Devine had a meeting scheduled with Norman Spector, chief of staff to the prime minister, who was told about the agreement, Devine, Mallo, and I eventually ended up at the Government of Saskatchewan office in Ottawa where Kennedy faxed a draft of the revised agreement.

There were still some changes I wanted to make to the document to make it consistent with the agreement that had been reached between Devine and de Cotret. I told Kennedy that I would be spending the evening at my cottage, two hours south of Ottawa, and that if he would make the necessary changes, I would call him in the morning and make arrangements for him to fax me a copy.

It became apparent that something was amiss within twenty-four hours of the meeting in de Cotret's office. Kennedy faxed me a copy of the written text the morning of September 6. Satisfied with its contents, I started trying to contact officials in Environment Canada and the minister's office in order to get an agreement on the wording. No one would take my calls. It was obvious they were stalling for time, trying to figure out what to do. By that afternoon, it was equally obvious that officials of Environment Canada had no intention of meeting with me to work on the text of the written agreement. There was nothing I could do but head home to Regina.

CHAPTER EIGHT

DAM BREAK

I wasn't sure what was going to happen, but I knew it was going to be significant. De Cotret was caught on the horns of a dilemma. On one side, he had the government of Saskatchewan and the parliamentary secretary to the prime minister arguing that the issue must be brought to a conclusion. On the other side he had his own officials, who were obviously opposed to the agreement. The symbolic importance of the project to the environmental movement coupled with a broad base of public opinion demanding that the federal government take a more active role in protecting the environment put further pressure on the minister.

Throughout September there was a flurry of activity on the agreement. On the 10th, Hill and I spoke on the telephone with a noncommittal and anxious Martin Green, executive assistant to de Cotret. The only thing he would agree to was our sending him a copy of the amended agreement via fax. By the 19th, there was still no word from Ottawa. We must have placed eighteen phone calls to de Cotret's office, all with no response. If the stakes hadn't been so high, it would have been laughable: senior government officials afraid to answer their phones in case it was Saskatchewan calling.

At 7:20 on the morning of Saturday, September 24, I got a call from Hill. He said he'd been up all night thinking, and he had something he wanted to run by me. He spoke for ten minutes in carefully measured tones. He laid out a strategy whereby we would announce that we had a deal with Ottawa, albeit verbal, and that we were going ahead. This would place pressure on the minister, who would then be forced either to agree or to say it was not the case. If the latter, it would make his course of action difficult because of the number of people who already knew about it.

By the time I travelled the two blocks to Hill's home, he had spoken to Gustafson, who was "65 percent on-side" to appearing at a press conference with Devine when the announcement was made.[1] The whole strategy was predicated on the fact that no one, so far, had told us the deal was off. As the days passed and there was still no word from Ottawa, announcing the agreement became our only realistic option.

Throughout the week of September 24 the pace of preparations increased even though we hadn't yet cleared it politically with anyone in the provincial Cabinet. On Tuesday the 25th, I was in Vancouver editing "Dreams in the Dust." I called Regina to find out the latest dealings with Ottawa. When I called, Hill was on the phone with Devine. Apparently, Gustafson had convinced Environment Canada to start answering the phones. Devine had spoken with de Cotret, who had told him there was nothing he could do.[2] Devine's response was that he was going ahead anyway. De Cotret asked Devine if there was anything that could make the panel resign, because if it did, he would have more options. Devine later told Hill that he had never been that angry before.[3] His anger couldn't have come at a better time. The strategy of announcing the deal was entirely premised on nerve.

On the 26th I again spoke with Gustafson, who indicated that the federal government was about to take the interest off the advance payment to western grain farmers, and that there might be an attempt to get Saskatchewan to make a trade-off for provincial capitulation on Rafferty-Alameda. Cash advances are made to grain farmers in the spring. Until 1990, farmers had been able to borrow money interest-free against the grain stored in their bins for the costs they would incur in planting their upcoming crop. When this provision was changed, the advances became, in effect, commercial loans. Now Gustafson was warning Saskatchewan not to be coerced into a trade-off for Rafferty-Alameda on the removal of the interest provision, as it was coming off anyway.

A day later, Gustafson was still trying to get the deal signed. He told Hill that he had spoken with the deputy prime minister, Don Mazankowski, who had then spoken with de Cotret and advised him to sign the agreement. By Friday, the 28th, the lobbying seemed to have paid off. Devine spoke again with de Cotret, who indicated that he was willing to make provision for putting the Oldman River project, the Point Aconi generating station in Nova Scotia, Rafferty-Alameda, and an Alcan Smelter in Quebec [sic] (the smelter was likely BC's Kemano hydroelectric project) "all on the same footing."[4] According to the premier, construction would go ahead and the review would go on. De Cotret indicated to Devine that if the panel resigned a new one would be appointed, and that he would be making the announcement the following Monday, Tuesday, or Wednesday.

By Tuesday, October 2, Bill McKnight, the federal cabinet minister from Saskatchewan, had become involved. Gustafson had spoken with McKnight, who said that the issue had been discussed by Cabinet and the agreement was going to be signed. There was only one problem: the panel didn't want to quit. Ottawa's political logic was that the occasion of the panel's resigning would provide the political cover necessary to allow the project to proceed. We had heard this refrain before. We had our doubts.

Within the federal bureaucracy, meanwhile, the possibility of the panel resigning was apparently being used as a means of trying to *prevent* the politicians from signing the deal. Gustafson called at 8:05 Wednesday morning, October 3, to tell me that he had attended a special meeting of caucus at which Raymond Robinson, executive chairman of FEARO, had said that the EARP Guidelines had the force of law and should not be tampered with.[5] This was obviously a preemptive move by the bureaucracy to keep the politicians from signing the agreement. Gustafson later confirmed that this was indeed the case. The bureaucrats had dug in their heels for one last stand.

Hill spoke with Bill McKnight on the same Wednesday, October 3. McKnight read Hill the text of a draft press release that had obviously been prepared by Environment Canada. Dated October 1, it read, in part:

> Environment Minister Robert R. de Cotret today announced the resignation of the Rafferty-Alameda Environmental Review Panel.
> In a letter to the Minister, the Panel said Saskatchewan's continued construction of the project compromised the review and made it impossible for members to continue their work. Mr. de Cotret said he fully accepts the Panel's reasons for resigning.
> "Members had been appointed with the clear understanding that no work, other than that necessary to render the Rafferty Dam safe, would proceed during the review," Mr. de Cotret said. When it became apparent that Saskatchewan was proceeding with construction beyond that necessary for safety, the Panel was compelled to resign.
> Despite federal efforts to bring about an understanding with Saskatchewan, the Province has chosen not to honor the terms of the ministerial agreement restricting construction, the Minister said.
> "Had it completed its task, the Panel would have provided valuable recommendations to the benefit of the environment and the people of Saskatchewan, Manitoba and North Dakota. The resignation is a loss for all concerned."[6]

That evening, we went over to Devine's house to discuss the strategy that Hill had first suggested only the week before. It was obvious that Environment Canada wasn't going to give in, and that the federal Cabinet wouldn't buck the bureaucracy on this, no matter how many assurances de Cotret gave Devine. We were also aware that time was not on our side. It was early October. If we were going to start the Alameda Dam it would have to be before freeze-up, which could occur any day. We had to decide if we were going to announce the agreement or back down. If we backed down, the odds were—given the deteriorating political fortunes of the Devine government—that the Alameda Dam would never be built.

Events were gathering a momentum of their own. We were preparing for a unilateral announcement of the agreement. Concurrently, we had to ensure that contracts were ready for the Alameda Dam and the Rafferty-Boundary Diversion Channel, and that we had a process in place for their tender, evaluation, and award. We also had to set in motion a system for rapid land acquisition at Alameda, for if the deal was announced, we would have to buy land quickly. Where voluntary acquisition was not possible, we had to be prepared to expropriate.

To this point, we had not expropriated any land. Every parcel of land we acquired—tens of thousands of acres from dozens of landowners—had been through negotiated settlement. A generous purchase policy coupled with the depressed state of agriculture in the west meant that we were able to offer many people a way out of a life at which they could no longer make a living. In the end, though, we would have to expropriate five quarter-sections of land owned by Ed and Harold Tetzlaff.

In the midst of all this, we were also readying an advertising campaign. We purchased air time in Alberta, Saskatchewan, and Manitoba (for western solidarity), in Ottawa (the federal government), and in Montreal (de Cotret's riding) for "Dreams in the Dust." We prepared print and electronic advertising to get the province's side of the story out. We wanted to tell the history of the project first, and then utilize the independent consultants who had worked on the project to attest to its environmental soundness. These testimonies were juxtaposed with past statements from representatives of the federal government—Lucien Bouchard in particular—extolling the environmental virtues of Rafferty-Alameda. When the story of the September 5 agreement broke, we would be ready.

In light of the draft press release and on the advice of Berntson and Gustafson, Devine agreed to speak with de Cotret again. If he couldn't get a firm commitment, we would go ahead and announce the agreement. On the morning of October 5, de Cotret assured Devine that there was still a deal, but there were one or two problems with the agreement we had drafted. Dr. Good, his deputy minister, would be calling "within minutes" to clear these up.[7]

De Cotret told Devine that he would be ready to sign the agreement on the following Tuesday, October 9. Devine said that any further delay was unacceptable, but perhaps the federal government should consider the strategy of having Saskatchewan announce the agreement in order to take some of the heat off Ottawa. When the premier called Hill on Friday morning to tell him of his discussion with de Cotret, we agreed that we would give Len Good until 1 PM Regina time. If he hadn't called by then, Devine would call de Cotret back.

To no one's surprise, 1 PM came and went without a call from the federal government. At 2 PM we received a call from Raymond Robinson of FEARO. By this time, after taking legal advice and in anticipation of further hypocrisy from Ottawa, we had begun to record our phone discussions with Environment Canada officials. The verbatim transcript of the discussion between Hill and Robinson, compared to Devine's account of his conversation with de Cotret, demonstrates how different the minister's agenda was from that of his officials:

Robinson: The purpose of my call is very, very simple. We've . . . essentially come to the end of the road with the existing panel.
Hill: Yes.
Robinson: And I thought out of courtesy, if no other reason, that I should talk to you about that, although we don't anticipate that becoming public for a few days yet.
Hill: I see.
Robinson: I'd be grateful if you would respect that, for obvious reasons. But the situation very simply is that, at the minister's request and following the discussions that he has had with your premier, we have attempted to resolve basically two problems with the panel. The first one was the problem they had with channelization, and we were successful in

persuading the panel that if we remove that from the terms of reference that it would no longer create a conflict in terms of their position. That is to say, if they were not required by virtue of the definition of project—that is, the terms of reference—to review the downstream channelization, then they would not be in a position to object to the fact that it has begun. Which might seem a little bit contrived but I think that you would recognize as at least correct. And that we were prepared to do that, however, they naturally were concerned over what would be the situation with regard to the Alameda [Dam] and, as you know, there have been some discussions with Premier Devine, and he has indicated that you are likely to be moving with the Alameda in the near future. Is that, first—perhaps I should make it clear—is that correct? 'Cause if it's not then the point of what I am about to say is lost. Is that, in fact, correct?

Hill: Well, from my standpoint, what is correct is that firstly, dealing with the downstream channelization, there never was an undertaking on the part of Saskatchewan not to do the downstream channelization. Furthermore, it was always understood—and at the time of the January 26 Agreement—that we were required to do the channelization and we were going to do it, that we were required to do mitigation insofar as building a golf course is concerned and we were going to do it, and that we had to build causeways and we were going to do it. So whatever the panel was told by the department [has] absolutely no resemblance to what was understood between Dr. Len Good and myself and what was contained in the Agreement of January 26. Now, insofar as the other part is concerned, the people of Saskatchewan are sick and tired of the delays that have taken place insofar as the panel is concerned, and as a result of negotiations that took place between the premier of Saskatchewan and Mr. de Cotret, there was an understanding that the Agreement of January 26 would be amended to remove the restrictions that Saskatchewan had entered into . . .

Later in the discussion:

Hill: . . . what we should be talking about is the agreement that the federal minister and the premier came to, and we should be talking about doing the amending agreement and, as both the premier and the federal minister said, they would prefer that the panel didn't resign, but if they did resign because of a changed terms of reference, so be it. There are other panels. There are other people who are prepared to serve on panels, and they would. The federal minister would deal with that and, if necessary, would appoint a new panel with new terms of reference. There wasn't anybody at that meeting who really had any concern one way or another if the panel resigned or didn't resign. That's entirely up to the panel. And we do not view that the world revolves around what the panel wishes. We, as far as we're concerned, and insofar as everything that we've been told, the federal minister has confirmed and reconfirmed the fact that, yes, he made a deal with the premier of Saskatchewan. And we don't understand why this agreement has not been entered into.

Robinson: I hear what you are saying, and I will relay that to the minister.

Hill: And that was confirmed between the premier and the minister this morning. It was confirmed between the premier and the minister yesterday morning. It was confirmed between many people and cabinet ministers at every level, but they don't seem to be able to get this matter dealt with. We could care absolutely less out here what happens to the panel. There was an agreement between the federal minister and the premier, and let's get it reduced to writing. Now the federal minister told the premier this morning that you had one or two points about the amending agreement that you wanted to discuss with us, and that you would be in touch with us within minutes. What are the one or two points about amending the agreement, Ray?

Robinson: I'm very sorry, I have no idea.

Hill: Well then, we'll just have to get a'hold of the premier and he'll have to phone de Cotret again.

Robinson: Yes, I think, quite obviously, they're going to have to discuss at that level. Clearly the debriefing that we are receiving from the minister doesn't accord with what you are telling me, and we're clearly at a loss. Clearly, we cannot function effectively under those circumstances. What I was merely instructed to do was alert you to this development and to indicate that we do believe both our Department of Justice and ourselves, here, that there is a high risk we will be back in court. We also believe that it may be very difficult to put together another panel simply because of the image problem this might create for panel members, given the fact that they'd be seen as a kind of second line or—

Hill: I think the image creation is—there are far too many people in Ottawa who are more concerned about covering their ass than about images of panels . . .

And then later in the discussion:

Hood: And Ray, just so you don't think that this is something we've concocted, this was discussed afterwards with the chief of staff to the prime minister, a guy by the name of Spector; you might have heard of him. It's subsequently been discussed with the member of Parliament [from] the area and confirmed as well [by] the minister of national defence as well as the deputy prime minister, and their understanding is identical with what ours is, and, in fact, has been confirmed with your minister.

Robinson: Well, I will convey all of that back to the minister, and obviously there has to be a further discussion between him and the premier.[8]

At 2:30 PM, Robinson called back. The transcript is picked up in mid-discussion:

Hill: Okay, we'll try and find out where the premier's going to be between—you say between 5:30 and 6:00 your time?

Robinson: That's probably when our minister would be available to make the call, given that he will probably, undoubtedly want to touch base with me for a moment so that I can bring him up to speed. See, the minister himself does not yet know that the panel is resigning.

Hill: Well, I don't know, the last I heard was on Monday they were, on Tuesday they weren't, and on Wednesday they were.

Robinson: We were able to persuade them to change their minds, but what he doesn't know is that the latest approach to them has led to their decision to resign. He doesn't know that yet. So I have to tell him that before he talks to the premier.

Hood: Can I just ask you a philosophical question, Ray?

Robinson: Sure, I might even give you a philosophical answer.

Hood: Doesn't it strike you as a tad bit odd that given all of the background to this, given that these things were never intended to be mandatory and so on, that you are going to such extraordinary efforts to make this thing work? Particularly on a project where we've gone through two separate environmental reviews and there are other projects, like Oldman River, that have never [been] environmentally assessed at all? And that they get to go ahead? Doesn't that strike you as being somewhat incongruent?

Robinson: The answer to that in a word is, sure it does. And, in fact, quite obviously if we had the hindsight, we might well have approached it differently.[9]

Robinson's second call did not make any difference to our position; we knew after talking with him the first time that the die was cast. He presumably did not know that we had seen the draft news release and that we had a pretty good idea of their strategy, such as it was, to deify the panel and hang us out to dry.

Tuesday, October 9—the date that Robert de Cotret had said he would be ready to sign the agreement—passed without event. On Wednesday, October 10, we were in Devine's office in the Legislative Building listening to his end of a conversation with de Cotret. It became clear early on that de Cotret had no intention of signing the agreement. Devine went at him hard, saying that de Cotret's bureaucrats didn't give a damn about anybody but themselves—not Saskatchewan, not the Tories in Ottawa. It was a bitter pill for Grant Devine to swallow.[10]

While Devine met with the provincial Cabinet, we drafted a letter for his signature. The letter confirmed the agreement made on September 5 and the fact that de Cotret had reconfirmed it in subsequent discussions with Devine on September 28 and October 5:

> Please confirm by 4:00 PM central standard time today that you will execute the attached Agreement and will participate in a joint press conference in Regina on October 11, 1990. In the event that we do not receive your confirmation, we will proceed with our own announcement of the Agreement.
>
> We continue to thank you for your cooperation in arriving at this Agreement, which will as you stated, be the blueprint for all projects which were under construction when there was a court ordered review.
>
> It is our desire that the present Panel continue with the new Terms of Reference; however, should they resign, I am sure there exists qualified people in Western Canada who would accept an appointment to a new review Panel.
>
> We trust that we will hear from you in the time limit indicated.[11]

We were past the point of no return. The letter put things in writing for the first time. It had been composed with a view to the draft press release that the federal officials still, presumably, did not know we had seen. It was also written with the knowledge that all this would become public very soon, and the more we had on paper about what had occurred over the past six weeks, the better our position would be after the announcement.

The letter was hand-delivered by Len Gustafson to make sure that de Cotret received it. Copies were sent to Don Mazankowski and Bill McKnight.

On Thursday, October 11, the federal government announced that the panel reviewing the Rafferty-Alameda project had *suspended* operations. In their letter to the minister, the panel wrote:

> The Panel understands that the Canada-Saskatchewan ministerial agreement, signed in January 1990, restricting construction on the Project, has been interpreted differently by the federal government and the government of Saskatchewan. The Panel also recognizes and appreciates your attempts to reach an understanding with Saskatchewan on the agreement. It is this difference in interpretation, and the incompatibility it causes with the Terms of Reference, however, which has given rise to the difficult situation in which the Panel has been placed.
>
> ... the Panel is seeking your guidance on how best to proceed with the review. In the interest of preserving the integrity and credibility of the process and the review, the Panel feels compelled to suspend its operations until the matter is clarified.
>
> The Panel deeply regrets the further delay and uncertainty this decision will cause the people of the Souris basin.[12]

There are two interesting things about this letter. The first is that it was dated October 4. The secretary to the panel told me that she had hand-delivered it to de Cotret's office the day it was written. De Cotret spoke to Devine on the 5th and promised that the agreement would be signed. As far as I can determine, de Cotret did not mention to Devine that the panel had already suspended its operations. In his phone conversation with us on October 5, Raymond Robinson had used the phrase "come to the end of the road," which seemed to imply that the panel members had resigned. It is not clear whether de Cotret knew that the panel had suspended its operations when he spoke to Devine on the 5th. It sure didn't sound to us as if they had resigned.[13]

The second interesting thing about the letter is that the members of the panel must have been aware of the difference between the terms of the January 26 Agreement and their own terms of reference. For one thing, we had drawn it to the attention of the panel secretariat and legal counsel for Environment Canada in early February. Environment Canada was aware that construction on the downstream channelization had begun on August 21. The panel toured the project on September 5, the day of the Devine-de Cotret meeting in Ottawa. Yet the issue of downstream channelization, as far as I know, was never a major issue between the federal minister and Devine. And while there is no question that the downstream channelization was a concern for the panel, one would have thought they would have come to their decision somewhat earlier, given that earth-movers were excavating the channel and that we had gone to considerable lengths to publicize it.

In any event, all hell was about to break loose. Our deadline was ignored by de Cotret. On Thursday, October 11, Devine's office issued a news release without comment:

> Premier Grant Devine today instructed the Souris Basin Development Authority (SBDA) to begin or resume construction on all aspects of the Rafferty-Alameda project in south-east Saskatchewan.
>
> Devine said he issued the instruction in response to the announcement by the federal Rafferty-Alameda Environmental Review Panel that it had suspended its operations pending clarification of its terms of reference.
>
> "The Panel's announcement is final proof the entire review process is an abject failure and has played havoc with an issue of vital importance to the people of the Souris valley," Devine said. "It also negates the agreement we considered to be in force since January between the federal and provincial governments.
>
> "At the outset, federal bureaucrats promised the Saskatchewan government the Panel would complete its work expeditiously. But it took a full five months before the Panel even visited the site. Let's not forget the taxpayers of Canada are paying the Panel members $450 per day each. With today's announcement by the Panel, there is still no end in sight to its deliberations, mainly because of the complete ambiguity of the terms of reference originally set by the federal bureaucrats."

Then, two-thirds of the way through the release, there was an almost oblique reference to the September 5 agreement:

"Mr. de Cotret displayed great regional sensitivity by actually visiting the project site," Devine said. "He can now reinforce that sensitivity by giving the review Panel the new terms of reference which he and I agreed to at a meeting on September 5."

Devine said those new terms allow for the completion of the Rafferty Dam and for the acquisition of land for and construction of the dam and reservoir at Alameda. The new terms also change the Panel's scope to the operation of the Rafferty-Alameda dams after they have been completed.[14]

By the following day we were ready to recount in detail what had happened between Devine and de Cotret on September 5. A news conference was held in the SaskPower board room, and who wasn't in attendance was more interesting than who was. George Hill and I were present, along with Bob Lawrence, senior vice-president of SaskPower. No elected politician from the government was in attendance. Even Devine was putting distance between himself and what was about to happen.

Devine, in fact, was 200 kilometers northeast of Regina, goose-hunting with actors Patrick Duffy and Steve Kanaly from the prime-time soap opera, *Dallas*.[15] Prior to the announcement, Devine had made one final attempt to get the agreement signed. He spoke to de Cotret from Wadena and, after finishing his

This editorial cartoon by Cam Cardow reflected the changing public perception of the Rafferty-Alameda issue in Saskatchewan. Courtesy Cam Cardow

call, concluded bitterly that "it was apparent from de Cotret's comments that his bureaucrats had got to him."[16]

The night before the news conference we had worked late, preparing Hill's statement as well as the background documentation, and photocopying the unsigned agreement that would be issued to the media the following day. Our strategy was to document the issue in detail, placing the blame on the federal bureaucracy rather than the politicians so as not to back the federal Tories into a corner. Driving home around 2 AM, Hill said to me, "You know, Hood, if this doesn't work, there won't be enough room on this planet for you and I to get far enough away from this." "It's like the old saying, Victory has a hundred fathers, but defeat is an orphan," I answered.[17]

We had a laugh about it, but we were concerned about what was to unfold in less than twelve hours. Considering there were no political fathers planning to attend, and that a chasm existed between us and virtually all of the Cabinet, we couldn't help wondering if we were about to become orphans.

Walking into the news conference, I was tired and scared. Lawrence and I let Hill do most of the talking, and he was at his best. At first I'd thought it was a mistake that no members of the Cabinet were there. But as I listened to Hill, I realized there was no one left in the provincial Cabinet with the ability or the guts to deliver this message. In a room packed with reporters who could have had only the barest idea of what was about to occur, Hill wasted no time ripping into Environment Canada. Excerpts from the media release reflect the tone:

> The Souris Basin Development Authority (SBDA) today responded to the announcement yesterday that the Rafferty-Alameda Federal Environmental Assessment Panel had suspended its operations due to continued construction on the Project. The Authority placed the blame for the predicament that the Panel had been placed in completely in the hands of the federal bureaucracy in Ottawa. The federal government was told by SBDA at the time that the Terms of Reference were issued for the Panel, that they did not conform to the Terms of the Agreement that Saskatchewan and the Federal Government reached on January 26 of this year.
>
> Saskatchewan has not in any way contravened the terms of the January 26 Agreement. The Agreement in question limits construction on three aspects of the Rafferty-Alameda Project and three aspects only. Saskatchewan agreed not to acquire land nor initiate construction of the Alameda Dam, not to initiate construction of the Rafferty-Boundary Diversion Channel, and only do such work on the Rafferty Dam as was necessary to stabilize the structure and to ensure public safety as specified by the Rafferty-Alameda Independent Engineering Review Board. A road crossing the valley is not the Rafferty Dam nor is the Mainprize Park and Golf Course, and the Government of Saskatchewan does not need the approval of the Federal Government or the

Environmental Assessment Panel to carry out this work . . . The extent of the work that Saskatchewan intended to carry out was explained to the federal Deputy Minister of the Environment *prior* to the signing of the January 26, 1990 Canada-Saskatchewan Agreement and *prior* to the Terms of Reference for the Panel being issued. The fact that the Panel is now having problems with these Terms of Reference is completely the fault of the federal bureaucracy who once again have demonstrated that it is incapable of administering the federal government's ill-conceived environmental assessment policy.

On September 5 of this year, a meeting took place in Ottawa between Premier Grant Devine and Environment Minister Robert de Cotret along with a number of Saskatchewan and federal officials. At this meeting, an agreement was reached between Premier Devine and Mr. de Cotret whereby the Federal Government agreed to allow construction on all aspects of the Rafferty-Alameda Project to proceed immediately and the Terms of Reference for the Panel reviewing the Project would be amended to limit its scope to the operation of the Rafferty-Alameda Reservoirs once the Project was completed. It was further agreed that the $10 million that the Federal Government agreed to pay Saskatchewan for the delays that have resulted in the federal review of the Project would be allocated to a trust fund administered by the federal Environment Minister to finance further mitigation identified by the Panel and agreed to by the Minister.

In light of yesterday's developments with the Environmental Assessment Panel, it has become abundantly clear to anyone who objectively reviews the history of the Rafferty-Alameda Project that the entire blame for the delays lies with the federal bureaucracy. The Federal Court of Canada has already concluded that the civil servants reviewing the Project were "silly and inattentive." Once again this has proven to be so painfully true. In light of this and in accordance with the September 5, 1990 Agreement between Premier Devine and Mr. de Cotret, Saskatchewan will be proceeding with all aspects of the Project as soon as practicable.[18]

And in his statement, Hill was even more blunt:

We will be making a number of statements that are critical of federal public servants. We will lay before you incontrovertible evidence of bureaucratic incompetence in the administration of the Federal Environmental Assessment process. We will clearly demonstrate insensitivity on the part of the environmental [*sic*] public servants in Ottawa to the needs of Western Canada.

As well, we will document for you our dealings with the senior public servants in the federal Department of the Environment over the past year and how we have been deceived and lied to.

If at times, it sounds like we are presenting excessive detail, we are doing so to document our case and to prove beyond doubt that the blame for all of these problems lies with the federal bureaucracy itself.[19]

The news that Devine and de Cotret had struck a handshake deal on September 5 exploded onto the national stage. For once, we controlled the timing and the agenda, and, most important, we were ready. When the announcement was made, we opened a land acquisition office in the town of Alameda. The response was overwhelming. Area landowners were so concerned that work on the project would be stopped again that there was a virtual around-the-clock queue of people waiting to sell their land. In two weeks we were able to acquire 13,500 acres, or 70 percent of the land required for the Alameda Dam and Reservoir.[20]

Environment Canada, as we had assumed, was not ready for the announcement. But while officials in Environment Canada may not have believed that Saskatchewan was prepared to announce the deal, senior members of the federal Cabinet certainly were. McKnight, Mazankowski, and Gustafson all knew what was about to happen. Gustafson told us the federal Cabinet had discussed the issue, but de Cotret, for reasons known only to him, had chosen to side with his officials.

Despite our efforts to direct the criticism at the bureaucracy rather than the politicians, the minister faced a torrent of questions from the media and in the House. The complexity of the issue and the confused history of the project meant that there was no great understanding of it on either side of the House. Demands were made for de Cotret to obey the existing court order, to revoke the IRIA license, to take the Saskatchewan government to court and seek an injunction to stop construction. A sampling of headlines from across the country reflects how widespread the coverage was:

De Cotret searches for way to halt Saskatchewan dam *(The Financial Post,* October 18, 1990)

A dam mess *(Toronto Star,* October 18, 1990)

Grits gunning for de Cotret *(Winnipeg Free Press,* October 17, 1990)

De Cotret waffles on Rafferty threat *(Saskatoon Star-Phoenix,* October 17, 1990)

De Cotret backs down on Rafferty *(The Globe and Mail,* October 17, 1990)

De Cotret still hopes to halt dam *(The Globe and Mail,* October 18, 1990)

Ottawa must stop Rafferty dam: Paradis *(Montreal Gazette,* October 18, 1990)

Maybe Devine is right about the Rafferty Dam *(Toronto Star,* October 25, 1990)

As far as the court order was concerned, technically and legally it had been complied with. De Cotret threatened to pull our federal license, but that wasn't an option either, given that we had not violated any of its terms. He denied there had been an agreement on September 5. In the TV coverage of de Cotret in scrums outside the House of Commons he looked disoriented and nervous.

On Thursday, October 18, de Cotret announced that Environment Canada would be seeking an injunction to stop construction on Rafferty-Alameda. The minister and his officials swore affidavits denying that an agreement was reached on September 5. One day later, before the federal government was able to file its application for the injunction, Devine held a news conference in Saskatoon to announce that the Saskatchewan Water Corporation and the Souris Basin Development Authority were suing Environment Canada, and that the applications had been filed in both the Federal Court of Canada and the Saskatchewan Court of Queen's Bench. The Saskatchewan suits were claiming tens of millions of dollars in damages and arguing that the federal minister did not have the legal right to stop the province from building the project. Such a move, the suits claimed, would violate the international agreement between Canada and the United States.

A quick glance at those in attendance at the news conference was enough to tell me that the politics of the issue had fundamentally changed. It had the potential now to be used as part of a reelection strategy. For in addition to the media, members of Devine's political "brain trust" were also in attendance.

Suing Ottawa. Saskatoon lawyer Robert Kennedy, far right, *along with Hill and Hood, brief Premier Grant Devine on the impending legal battle in which Saskatchewan sought compensation from Ottawa.* Courtesy Chris Dekker

Two weeks earlier, before the announcement of the September 5 agreement, they were nowhere to be seen. If the project were the political orphan that Hill and I had feared it would become, these opportunistic political handlers would not have been anywhere near the news conference.

Hill and I flew to Alameda immediately after Devine's announcement. A $1.5 million contract had been awarded to begin construction on the dam. In the early morning hours of October 19, Panteluk Construction moved its giant Caterpillar 631 E yellow scrapers from Estevan to the Alameda Dam site. On our arrival we were greeted by clouds of dust from the machines racing over the valley, and by over 200 cheering supporters who were there to watch the construction begin. While the majority of area residents were obviously pleased, there was an ominous sign for anyone who cared to look. Parked on the edge of the valley was a blue half-ton with two men standing beside it: Ed and Harold Tetzlaff.

On Tuesday, October 16, de Cotret faced a feeding frenzy about Rafferty-Alameda—inside the House by the Opposition and outside by the media. He was not in command of the file and it showed. It would get worse for him. In the midst of the controversy, the story leaked that the federal government had exempted from the EARP Guidelines the Kemano hydroelectric project being built by Alcan on the Nechako River in British Columbia. While Environment Canada was in a confrontation with Saskatchewan over the applicability and integrity of the EARP Guidelines, an Order-in-Council had been passed by the federal Cabinet exempting the BC project."[21]

Within a matter of days, de Cotret's office announced that federal public hearings on the Oldman River Dam in Alberta would not begin until after the Supreme Court had heard the appeal that had been filed concerning the Alberta project. This announcement meant that the review would not take place until construction of the dam was complete. De Cotret's media assistant was quoted in the *Regina Leader-Post*:

> There will be no review or public hearings into the Oldman River Dam in southern Alberta until the project is completed and the reservoir filled, says an aide to federal Environment Minister, Robert de Cotret.
>
> "The whole thing is on ice until the Supreme Court of Canada rules on the lower court ruling that called for the review," said Terry Collins, de Cotret's executive assistant . . .
>
> Officials with the Federal Environmental Assessment Review Office said they had verbal assurances from the Minister's office that hearings would begin immediately because the Federal Court of Appeal had ordered them.
>
> But Raymond Robinson, executive chairman of the review office, had no comment . . . [22]

Ottawa's hypocrisy became even more apparent when it came out that, unlike Rafferty-Alameda, which had already undergone two environmental reviews, the Oldman project had not been subjected to any formal review at all. For the first time, Rafferty-Alameda began to get some sympathetic treatment from the national media:

The Financial Post

The odds are that you think Premier Grant Devine is trying to pull a fast one with the Rafferty-Alameda Dam project in southeastern Saskatchewan. After all, he's on one side while Ottawa and the environmentalists are on the other. Devine can hardly be the one in the white hat, right?

Wrong. The federal Environment ministry has visited an appalling amount of delay and red tape on Saskatchewan. Devine is entirely justified in moving ahead with the project and taking Ottawa to court for damages this delay has cost.[23]

The Globe and Mail

No one should doubt Saskatchewan Premier Grant Devine's integrity in trying to ram through the completion of the Rafferty-Alameda dam project, even though it happens to be in his own riding.

The provincial argument is that Rafferty-Alameda has to go ahead because of contractual obligations with the United States, which is paying nearly $50 million of the cost for water management downstream. And that federal environmental officials botched the process by not getting their act together on precise guidelines.

There is more than just a grain of truth to this charge, as Ottawa's environmental policy has been in a state of suspended animation for some time. But regardless, Rafferty-Alameda has become a tremendous symbol for environmentalists across the country and is being watched with great interest by every provincial government with a dam or a power project up its sleeve.

People tend to forget that the project has already passed two environmental assessments—a public provincial inquiry in September 1987, and a three-month federal review in the summer of 1989. They recall only that it has been halted twice now by the Federal Court of Canada on the novel grounds that Ottawa has not adhered to its own regulations under the Environmental Assessment and Review Process.[24]

Western Report

There is something distasteful about the manner in which Premier Grant Devine and the people and government of Saskatchewan are being pushed around with respect to the Rafferty dam. I have said in this space that my personal view is that we should be hesitant to dam or reroute rivers. I hold that view very strongly. But I feel even more strongly that governments must be bound by their commitments and must not use their political muscle to change terms of reference in the

mid-point of an agreement. And that is precisely what the government
of Canada, frightened by environment groups, is attempting with respect to the Rafferty-Alameda dam project in south-eastern Saskatchewan.
    . . . Perhaps Mr. Bouchard concluded that Saskatchewan should
not be forced to accept something that every observer knows in a similar situation would not even be proposed to Quebec or, for that matter,
Ontario. If the Rafferty-Alameda works were in either of those provinces—and the same presumably is true of the Oldman in Alberta—the
political equation is such that interference in either case would have
been so politically disadvantageous it would not have occurred.[25]

Maclean's
    . . . for de Cotret, the controversy could not have been more ill-timed.
He has recently been completing the Tories' long-awaited master plan
for the environment—known as The Green Plan—which is likely to be
released next month. But de Cotret's credibility suffered badly during
last week's exchanges with Devine. His biggest problem centered on
whether, as Devine claimed, de Cotret had agreed early in September
to allow all construction to go ahead while the federal review took place.[26]

We ran advertisements in the electronic and print media. The advertising
campaign, coupled with the airing of "Dreams in the Dust," was designed to
solidify public opinion behind the project. It was not the easiest thing to do,
given the complexity of the issue and the tortuous path the project had taken.
Our first objective was to point out the inconsistencies in what the federal government had said and done on the project. These ads were based on the slogan,
"They've said it before, we'll say it again." Comments from the federal government—from Lucien Bouchard in particular—extolling the virtues of the project
were juxtaposed with comments from professional biologists working on the
project attesting to its environmental soundness.
    Our second objective was to make the public aware that Saskatchewan
had been treated differently than other jurisdictions. This not only crystallized support for the project, but it gave Devine at least a potential issue on
which to base his sagging electoral prospects. "There's no question that this
fed-bashing is good for Grant Devine," reported Dan Oldfield of CBC Radio.
"In fact, many of his handlers have been urging him to get on this bandwagon a long, long time ago. Whether he can tie his can to this one particular issue, whether it has broader appeal outside of [the] southeast corner of
the province is another question."[27]
    Our third objective was to solidify support for the project in the other west-
ern provinces and plant some seeds of doubt in central Canada about the track
record of the federal government on the Rafferty-Alameda project. This was the
rationale for the purchase of air time for "Dreams in the Dust" in Alberta, Saskatchewan, and Manitoba. Airing the documentary in the Ottawa and Montreal
markets was aimed at delivering a message to Environment Canada and to de

Cotret, who represented the Montreal riding of Berthier-Montcalm. The federal government paid Saskatchewan $1 million per month because it was incompetent, we were merely using some of that money to prove it.

"Dreams in the Dust" did little to endear us to Ottawa. The ending involved the story of Oxbow resident Bob Pegg. A long-time supporter of Rafferty-Alameda, Pegg had decided to enter the debate by writing a letter to the community newspaper, *The Oxbow Herald*. Upon completion, he took the letter to his friend, Glen Gibson, in the neighboring community of Alameda. In Gibson's oil-field servicing firm office, Pegg read him the letter expressing his dismay over all the delays, and then he dropped dead from a massive heart attack.

The ending of "Dreams in the Dust" shows Pegg's widow, Betty, a proud and distinguished lady, telling of her husband's life on the river, how he had experienced both drought and floods, his support for the project, and the anguish he had felt in drafting the letter. Gibson relates how Bob Pegg had read him the letter and then suffered the coronary, and he describes the steps he took in trying to revive his friend. The film ends with Betty reading Pegg's letter over visuals of a photograph of her husband superimposed on aerial footage of the Moose Mountain Creek valley.

It was powerful stuff—so powerful, in fact, that we wondered if we should use it at all, given how far it intruded into what was obviously a private grief. In the end, we decided to use it because of Betty Pegg's dignity in telling the story and because she agreed to leave it in. But there was no question that it was playing hard-ball.

The political benefits to Devine began to manifest themselves immediately. He was in the midst of his post-harvest tour of the province, and while he was entering the fifth and final year of his mandate and the Conservatives were far from popular, the feedback he received on the Rafferty-Alameda issue was almost universally positive. "Judging by the reaction the premier gets from ordinary rural folk who have experienced drought," *Regina Leader-Post* columnist Murray Mandryk wrote, "you immediately get the impression that they are no more sympathetic to the concerns of bureaucrats and environmentalists over process than Devine is."[28]

For the first time on the project we began to poll. The response was overwhelmingly positive.[29] While I was gratified to know that there was widespread support for the project across the province, I was skeptical of the strategy being proposed by the Tory brain trust to use Rafferty-Alameda as a launching pad for an Ottawa-bashing provincial election campaign. Devine had been too tight with the federal Tories for too long to be able to mount such a campaign with any degree of credibility. We were suspicious that his advisors might try to manipulate the issue for political gains at the expense of the project.

Hill was disdainful of many of the advisors Devine had surrounded himself with, as well as their practice of using out-of-province firms to conduct polls and devise political strategy. He felt, and I agreed, that we needed an independent basis to evaluate how the project was tracking politically. To that end, we asked the following question: "Considering the upcoming provincial elections next year, which one of the three provincial party leaders do you think would best stand up to the federal government for western Canada and Saskatchewan interests?"

The question produced the following results:

Just over one-half of those respondents expressing an opinion (53.8%) feel that Roy Romanow would best stand up to the federal government for western Canada and Saskatchewan, just under one-third (31.9%) feel that Grant Devine would best serve this interest and 14% think that Lynda Haverstock (Liberal) would best serve this interest. Note that almost 40% of respondents were undecided, indicating both or either an unwillingness to express an opinion and a large amount of indecision several months before an election.[30]

We were interested in the answer to this question not only from the perspective of defending the project from political manipulation, but also because we felt it gave a proxy indication of how much time we had left to get the various components of the project started. We were now certain that the Devine government was going down to defeat. If the Alameda Dam was going to be built, therefore, it had to be taken past the point of no return prior to the provincial election.

The announcement of the September 5 agreement not only unleashed a storm of controversy, it prompted numerous lawsuits as well—so many, in fact, that the *Regina Leader-Post* began publishing a chart to enumerate who was suing who, on what basis, and for how much. Some of the suits were filed by supporters of the project, and I was struck by how events on the project were coming full circle. When we first started out, it seemed that every time we turned around we were getting sued. It was the environmental lobby's favorite strategy. The environment as an issue to be litigated was so recent and so vague in terms of jurisdiction that it was unclear as to where it fell in terms of the courts. Given the interdependence of the various approvals for the project—international, national, and provincial—the tactics were quite clever. Writs on different legal issues but all obviously pertaining to the same project were filed in either the Saskatchewan Court of Queen's Bench or the Federal Court, and because of their interdependence, this multiple-suit strategy had the effect of tying the project in knots.

The suits became so numerous that we lost count. Some were frivolous, some not. There were two we had to treat seriously: the federal government's attempt to get an injunction (halting construction pending completion of the panel review) in the Saskatchewan Court of Queen's Bench, and Ed and Harold Tetzlaff's appeal in the Federal Court of Appeal of Mr. Justice Muldoon's decision of December 29, 1989. We had been concerned that Muldoon's decision to grant the federal minister until January 29 to appoint the panel was incorrect and that, on appeal, it would be overturned and the

IRIA license quashed. This consideration had been a significant part of the rationale behind the January 26 Agreement in which we had agreed to halt or delay construction on the three components of the project.[31]

When the September 5 agreement was first announced, there was considerable speculation that it had been staged by the federal and provincial Conservatives to give Devine an election issue. Speculation quickly died when the federal government filed its request for an injunction to halt construction.

The federal request for an injunction pending completion of the panel review was to be heard in the Saskatchewan Court of Queen's Bench. Ignoring for the moment that Ottawa was asking the court to exercise an extraordinary measure in the form of an injunction, we anticipated a fairer hearing in the Court of Queen's Bench than in the Federal Court. The view was that the Federal Court had, in a manner of speaking, "gone green" on a number of cases, including Rafferty-Alameda.[32] If we were ever to get such a thing as the benefit of the doubt, we hoped we would get it from a Saskatchewan court.

Our preparation for the case was meticulous. For three days, three lawyers, two secretaries, and the "Two Georges" locked themselves in the Royal Suite of the Hotel Saskatchewan preparing the necessary documents. The cornerstone of our case was the affidavit Hill would swear before the very court on which he once sat as a judge. In a ninety-four-paragraph, thirty-five-page document, we painstakingly recounted what had happened on the project with the federal government since 1985. Copies of the letters from the federal government indicating that the EARP Guidelines did not apply to the project were affixed as exhibits. Devine and I swore affidavits as well.

Most of what is contained in the Hill affidavit has been recounted here and does not bear repeating. What is worth noting is the situation itself, for here was a former justice of the very court in which the injunction application was being heard filing an affidavit of such minute detail that only someone skilled in the law and intimately involved in the issue could have prepared it. My journals helped immensely in the process as we were able to document in detail what had occurred over the previous three years. The affidavit was so detailed, in fact, that the federal government could not ignore the issues it raised. Our affidavits sparked a second round of questioning in the House of Commons, and this time the headlines were more pointed:

De Cotret shook hands on deal, Devine says *(The Globe and Mail,*
    October 31, 1990)
Devine's affidavit indicates Rafferty deal with de Cotret
    (Saskatoon Star-Phoenix, November 2, 1990)
De Cotret accusing Devine of lying: Opposition *(Saskatoon Star-*
    Phoenix, November 3, 1990)

After two delays to allow the lawyers to prepare, the request for the injunction was heard in Regina before the Chief Justice of the Saskatchewan Court of Queen's Bench, D.K. MacPherson. The federal government's arguments were fairly technical. There were two types of issues in question. The first centered on whether injunctions could, as a matter of legal principle, even be issued against an agent of the Crown in right of Saskatchewan. The second involved whether the federal government had a *prima facie* case for the injunctive relief. When the decision came down on November 15, Chief Justice MacPherson determined that the injunctions could not be issued against the Crown in right of Saskatchewan; the request for interlocutory relief failed, and the injunction was denied.

But MacPherson didn't leave it there. He gave reasons why the federal government had failed to prove a *prima facie* case. The minister of the environment had failed to fulfil his obligations under the January 26 Agreement by not reappointing a new panel after the first one resigned. Even if an injunction were granted, the minister was not in a position to fulfil his part of the agreement simply because he did not have a panel in place.

An agreement had been struck between Canada and the United States that obligated the government of Canada to "expeditiously" construct the Rafferty and Alameda dams. In the accompanying Canada-Saskatchewan agreement, Saskatchewan had agreed to indemnify and save harmless the Canadian government with respect to any liability of Canada to the United States. If the Canadian federal government was successful in its attempt at obtaining an injunction, "expeditious construction would not be possible and liability would result." This, too, MacPherson concluded, weakened the federal government's case.

Section 7 of the *Department of the Environment Act* stipulated that federal-provincial agreements respecting the carrying out of programs can only be entered into with the approval of the Governor in Council—that is, the federal Cabinet. David Wilson had one of his articling students check the list of Orders-in-Council passed by the federal government and discovered that the January 26 Agreement had never been ratified by the federal Cabinet. MacPherson concluded that the January 26 Agreement fell under the meaning of the word program:

> that where there is a statutory requirement of an order in council or other formal approval to authorize a contract, any contract that does not meet that requirement is unenforceable.
>
> ... the January Agreement is, therefore, unenforceable by virtue of the said s. 7 and the undisputed absence of the approval of the Governor in Council. Again a severe weakening, if not a fatal blow, to the plaintiff's *prima facie* case.[33]

In the injunction application, the federal government was seeking an order from the courts on the basis of the January agreement and, in so doing, requested that "the injunction continue until the panel had completed its report and made recommendations in accordance with the process of the Guidelines."[34]

MacPherson pointed out the inconsistency in the federal government's position on Rafferty-Alameda compared to the position it argued before the Federal Court in the *Naskapi-Montagnais Innu Association v. Canada (Minister of National Defence)* case. In the Naskapi case, the federal government intended to use portions of Labrador for NATO training exercises that involved low-level flying. The Naskapi-Montagnais Innu Association represented interests that could be injuriously affected by these flights. The minister of national defence followed the EARP Guidelines Order by appointing a panel. During the panel review, the Naskapi-Montagnais-Innu filed suit in the Federal Court to prevent any low-level flights pending the final report of the panel.[35]

When the issue was argued before Madam Justice Reed of the Federal Court, Ottawa took the position that there was nothing in the EARP Guidelines Order to preclude the activity that was being assessed from going ahead while the review was in progress. MacPherson noted:

> I agree with the conclusions of Madam Justice Reed as set out in her decision and would simply add that the concern she expresses . . . is remarkably similar to the situation in which the parties find themselves in our case. Because the defendants in our case did something (i.e., downstream channelization) which, as I have stated, is permitted, or at least, not prohibited, under the January agreement, but is contrary to the wording in the terms of reference, the Panel chose to suspend its operations and to continue the suspension until the matter is "clarified." The matter could not be clarified, and in theory at least, the suspension could have gone on forever. As it turned out, when the defendants proceeded with the Alameda Dam construction, the Panel resigned . . .
>
> In the notice of motion herein, the plaintiff seeks an interlocutory injunction on the basis of the January Agreement, and asks that the injunction continue until the Panel has completed its report and made its recommendations in accordance with the process of the guidelines. Oddly, the plaintiff now seeks basically the same kind of order which its Minister of National Defence opposed in Naskapi six months ago. Should an interlocutory injunction be granted, it would have the same effect as the kind of "stop order" which was applied for in Naskapi which holds that no such stop order is permissible under the guidelines in these circumstances.
>
> . . . It is unfortunate that the Panel did not contemplate these results when it first suspended its operations and then resigned—notwithstanding the construction which occurred and which the Panel's terms of reference said would not occur, better it should have carried on so that the parties and the public would have the benefit of its recommendations.[36]

Another interesting aspect to the MacPherson decision is what he had to say during oral arguments and in the decision about the EARP. It was fairly clear from the first day of oral arguments that the federal government was going to get a rough ride. As *The Globe and Mail* reported:

A senior Saskatchewan judge says Canada's environmental review process is faulty and the federal government is to blame.

"It's been a pretty flawed process up to this point and the flaws have been on the part of your client," Chief Justice Donald MacPherson of the Court of Queen's Bench told federal lawyers arguing for a stop work order on the Rafferty-Alameda dams yesterday.[37]

In the decision, MacPherson reiterated the point:

> As for irreparable harm to the plaintiff, on the material before me, it has not been proven that any such harm has or will occur; at best it is purely conjectural. Further, I see no merit in enjoining the defendants in order to preserve a badly flawed process, and in any event, I fail to see how such action would, in fact, under the circumstances of this case, have the effect of preserving the process.[38]

At the end of all this legalese, the most critical point was that the MacPherson decision allowed us to continue construction of the Alameda Dam. It was also the first significant case to go our way. It did so in a sweeping fashion, and in the process it confirmed what we had been saying about the federal government. MacPherson's comparison of the Rafferty-Alameda situation with the Naskapi case provided one more illustration of the double standard the federal government was applying to Rafferty-Alameda. In the context of all the other actions before the courts and the manner in which the media covered them, this was an important decision and certainly we received positive coverage. The decision also bolstered the momentum that had been building behind the project.

Our jubilation over the MacPherson decision was short-lived, however, because the federal government would launch an appeal in Saskatchewan, and within a week we were in the Federal Court of Appeal in Winnipeg for the Tetzlaffs' appeal of the Muldoon decision. We drew an experienced panel made up of Allan Linden, John Urie, and the chief justice, Frank Iacobucci, now of the Supreme Court of Canada. At issue was whether Mr. Justice Muldoon had erred in December 1989 in not revoking our license in CWF II.

Early in the proceedings, it became apparent we would not be run out of the place. On the first day of oral arguments, the chief justice interrupted the presentation of the Tetzlaffs' lawyer, Alan Scarth, to ask, "Wouldn't you agree, Mr. Scarth, that the EARP Guidelines are pretty difficult to interpret?"[39] The oral arguments were not without moments of levity, such as when Scarth was extolling the virtues of his clients as stewards of the earth and lamenting that there was no way to mitigate the fact that there was going to be 120 feet of water on top of their land. After allowing Scarth considerable latitude, Mr. Justice John Urie asked Scarth how tall his clients were.

The contradictions were bizarre, to say the least. A week earlier, we had been in the Court of Queen's Bench fighting the federal government's attempt to get an injunction to halt construction on the project. Now we were in the

Federal Court of Appeal trying to save the license, and the federal government was supposed to be on our side in doing so. Lawyers for the federal minister of the environment had prepared their argument in written form in a memorandum of fact and law. In the majority of instances, counsel arguing the case use the memorandum as the basis on which to make their oral arguments. When the court called upon counsel for the minister of the environment, Brian Saunders, to make his presentation, however, Saunders indicated that he was prepared to answer questions, but beyond that his argument was contained in his memorandum of fact and law and he was not proposing to say anything else.

The judges went into a huddle, leaving Saunders to cool his heels at the podium for about three minutes. Then Iacobucci, who used to be federal deputy minister of justice and therefore Saunders's boss, said, "Very well, Mr. Saunders, we understand that you have received your instructions. You can sit down."[40]

While we were disappointed in the actions of counsel for the federal government, they did not come as a complete surprise. Through the course of the litigation on Rafferty-Alameda in the Federal Court, we had come to like and respect Brian Saunders. We knew, as did the court, that in all likelihood he was under instructions not to make an oral presentation. By this time, there wasn't much new law left in Rafferty-Alameda. Most of the justiciable issues had been determined, and certainly the federal government's position on these matters had already been stated. It appeared that Environment Canada was again concerned about public perception; Ottawa was attempting in one court to shut down construction on the project and, in another, to defend the project's license. While these were substantively different legal issues, the distinction would be difficult for the general public to make.

In an interview, John Urie, now retired from the bench, avoided speaking about any aspect of the Rafferty-Alameda case. On the issue of federal counsel's avoidance of making an oral argument, he would only acknowledge that he deplored, "in a general sense, the tactic of federal counsel not taking positions of either opposing or supporting motions."[41] That federal counsel avoided making oral argument did not hurt us. In fact, it probably helped us, for it likely meant that we were given greater latitude than would otherwise have been the case.

Lawyers from the Justice Department, with few exceptions, act as legal counsel for the line departments of the federal government. Environment Canada was therefore not solely to blame in its misinterpretation of the applicability of the EARP Guidelines. Part of the responsibility must be shouldered by the federal Justice Department. As Ottawa's difficulties in dealing with Rafferty-Alameda mounted, it became increasingly apparent that the federal government, the Environment Department in particular, was receiving questionable legal advice.

The question is, given its involvement in what almost everyone has acknowledged to be poorly drafted EARP Guidelines and subsequently on the matter of their status as a mandatory federal instrument, how could such fundamental errors be made by the federal government's legal counsel? All that a circumspect John Urie would offer in this regard was that the EARP Guidelines were not unique, and there were "hundreds of others that were not masterpieces."[42]

The Federal Court of Appeal ruled on December 21, largely on the basis of Madam Justice Reed's decision in the Naskapi case, that Muldoon had not erred in allowing the license to remain in place. In his decision for the three-judge panel, Chief Justice Iacobucci wrote:

> The determination of these issues is of considerable importance not only to the parties and a wide group of affected people but also to the scope and effect of federal environment legislation and regulations. Despite the importance of the environmental issues before us, Counsel for the Minister informed the court he took no position on the appeal or the cross-appeal, apparently being satisfied with the judgement of Muldoon, J., and willing to put himself to the guidance of this Court.
>
> ... The EARPGO [Environmental Assessment Review Process Guidelines Order] does not contain express language that a license cannot issue until the Panel has reported following a public review nor can such an obligation be inferred from the provisions and scheme of the EARPGO.[43]

The implications of this decision were best described by Lorne Scott of the SWF. "What we did get," he told *CKTV News Service*, "was the Federal Court of

The design for the spillway of the Rafferty Dam was one of few sources of disagreement between Saskatchewan and the U.S. Corps of Engineers. Low construction prices made it possible for Saskatchewan to accommodate the corps' concerns. Courtesy Souris Basin Development Authority

Appeal upholding the previous court decision that a federal environmental review has to be done on the project. This is what we've said for the last several years and the courts have always come down on our side. So I guess we're right but we've lost, if you can make sense out of that."[44] The national environmental lobby's dissatisfaction with the results was summed up by Julia Langer of Friends of the Earth: "On the one hand, go ahead, do an impact study. You're required to. On the other hand, you don't have to wait until the study is done to issue a permit. The environment is lost in the dust, in the courts.[45]

Although this was obviously not the end to litigation on the project, the importance of the Iacobucci decision—to us and the environmental lobby—should not be underestimated. To the environmental lobby, the decision meant that the EARP Guidelines had been weakened by the courts; to us it meant that construction could continue on the Alameda Dam. By December 21, we had managed to get Alameda to the point where work was being carried out on the low-level outlet and spillway, where hoarding had been assembled so that work could continue throughout the winter.

While it would be logical to conclude that these court victories would have shored up support for the project within the Saskatchewan government, this was not the case. As a single-purpose crown corporation created by Order-in-Council, the SBDA did not have the legal authority to expropriate land. We had to rely on our parent crown, the Saskatchewan Water Corporation, to do this for us. Yet we encountered resistance from the SaskWater Board of Directors to a resolution authorizing the expropriation of land from Ed and Harold Tetzlaff. After considerable persuasion, the board eventually passed the resolution. The most disturbing aspect of this was that the minister responsible for the SBDA was also the minister responsible for SaskWater, Harold Martens. Martens, in attendance at the meeting, offered little help in getting the resolution passed.

Our confidence in the government was further undermined when the Iacobucci decision was announced. If the decision went against us—and our track record in this court was certainly not in our favor—it would have had disastrous results not only for the project but for the government as well. The court took the extraordinary step of announcing that the Rafferty-Alameda decision would be brought down on December 21, so we knew in advance when it was coming. But once again, Hill and I were left to deal with the media. The premier was skiing in Montana, and our minister was nowhere to be seen. That Devine had been out hunting with a pair of TV stars when the critical announcement was made regarding the September 5 agreement, and away in Montana when the Federal Court issued its decision, was not a healthy sign. It was apparent to us that the government had reconciled itself to losing the next provincial election, and had given up.

Throughout 1991, the game of musical chairs in the courts continued with the federal appeal of the MacPherson injunction decision and a new application by the Tetzlaffs in the Federal Court seeking an order for the minister to appoint the panel. The Saskatchewan Court of Appeal refused to hear the federal appeal on the injunction while the matter was still before the Federal Court. For us, as long as construction continued, it was a victory of sorts, although it was still very much a race against time. Environment Canada still sought to stop construction on the Alameda Dam but, apparently out of fear of having the federal minister cited for contempt, a new panel, with noted Saskatchewan historian Dr. John Archer as chair, was appointed in the first week of February, before the Federal Court could hear the case. Its mandate was to review the operations of the project, assuming that it would be completed. Having achieved this, we had finally succeeded in putting Rafferty-Alameda on the same footing as the Oldman River Dam.

On April 9, 1991, the Saskatchewan Court of Appeal overturned the MacPherson decision and agreed to issue an injunction halting all construction on the Alameda Dam if the federal government was willing to compensate Saskatchewan for the amount of $1 million per month while the injunction was in effect. This the federal government was unwilling to do, considering all of the technical difficulties and legal liabilities looming if it were to assume responsibility for stopping construction of a dam as far along as Alameda. The federal government was, once again, confronted with stinging criticism from a court. The Court of Appeal provided one of the most definitive statements as to what had transpired on the entire Rafferty-Alameda issue to this point:

George Hood with John Archer, chair of the second federal Rafferty-Alameda Environmental Assessment Panel. Archer's considerable skills were put to the test during the public meetings. Courtesy Estevan Mercury

... the delays and confusion surrounding this project were wholly the fault of federal officials. Initially the Federal Department of the Environment advised the Authority that the *Guidelines* did not apply to this project, when in fact they did. Thus the federal Minister granted a license without appointing an environmental review panel, and that contravened the *Guidelines*. Then, when ordered to appoint a panel by the Federal Court, the federal Minister refused to do so without the January 26 agreement. Then, when setting the terms of reference for the review panel, the Minister created an anomaly between those terms of reference and the terms of the 26 January agreement, which led to further confusion. Finally, when the Review Panel resigned, the Minister waited in excess of four months before appointing a new panel—all this in the context of a consensus between the federal Minister and the respondents (but not the Tetzlaffs) that the Rafferty-Alameda project itself would ultimately be completed and would be beneficial to the residents of Saskatchewan. In all of this, the only fault which can be laid at the feet of the respondents [Saskatchewan] is that they acted precipitously on their entirely understandable frustration when the Review Panel suspended its operations, and prematurely began to resume full construction of the project.[46]

The Tetzlaffs did exercise their right to an injunction ordering Saskatchewan to give up possession of the land that had been expropriated. But while this protected their land, it did not stop construction work on the Alameda Dam. From the SBDA's point of view, the Tetzlaff land would eventually be required for the Alameda Dam, but not before the structure was over 80 percent complete. On June 12, 1991, two months after the Saskatchewan Court of Appeal decision on the injunctions, the Moose Mountain Creek channel was closed off. We had succeeded in getting the Alameda Dam past the point of no return, save the possibility that someone decided to tear the thing down. So absurd were things by now, I wouldn't have bet against such an occurrence. It was a bittersweet victory. We had succeeded in the face of considerable adversity, and in this we took justifiable pride. It was, however, impossible to savor. We knew that, while Rafferty-Alameda was past the point of no return, neither Hill nor I would still be working on the project when it was completed. The impending provincial election would see to that.

CHAPTER NINE

NEWS AND TRUTH

It was inevitable that, with all the controversy Rafferty-Alameda generated on its own, it would attract additional controversy from a number of disparate sources. We were not prepared, however, for the barrage of attacks from groups and individuals attempting to graft their issues onto Rafferty-Alameda. An environmental activist, a naturalist opposed to the project but earning his living on a reservoir in the middle of Regina, the Canadian Broadcasting Corporation, the United Church of Canada, a citizens' group against free trade, even a former minister in the Devine government—all fit this description. People with causes often only tangentially related to the project attempted to raise the profile of their own issue by imputing some kind of causal linkage with the two Saskatchewan dams. The project was a lightning rod for controversy.

To successfully carry out their grafting strategy, these people had to ensure their claims were not so outlandish as to go beyond the pale of being at least remotely plausible. They also had to ensure that their message was conveyed to the public. Often the media provided this outlet and seemed singularly incapable of discerning what was and was not a fact when it related to the Rafferty-Alameda project.

Given the politics of Saskatchewan alone, there is no question that the Rafferty-Alameda project would have been controversial. As it progressed and the legitimate controversy surrounding it increased, so too did the nonlegitimate controversy generated by proponents of grafted issues. In many cases, the media reported on the latter without any attempt to distinguish them from the former.

Controversy makes all aspects associated with a major project more difficult. Acquiring land, relations with contractors, dealing with the public, and virtually everything else associated with the project becomes more expensive, as most of these difficulties somehow get translated into money. As we have seen with Rafferty-Alameda, the controversy frequently has to do with procedural questions relating to the nature and extent of the environmental assessment of the project. Environmental assessment processes are designed to be sensitive to public opinion. Therefore, the more controversy that can be created about a development, the greater the likelihood the environmental assessment process will be lengthy and detailed, and the greater the potential to stop the development.

On September 11, 1988, the Elizabeth May story broke in the *Winnipeg Free Press* under the by-line of environmental reporter Barbara Robson. May, a lawyer and former advisor to federal Environment Minister Tom McMillan, charged that the reason for her resignation from the minister's office was an alleged trade-off between the federal and Saskatchewan governments for the federal license for the Rafferty-Alameda project. In the process, she claimed, Manitoba's interests were given short shrift. "I left because they traded Rafferty-Alameda for Grasslands [National Park] . . . and that's the only reason," she said. She was also quoted as saying, "Manitoba's interests have really been shafted."[1]

The story was picked up by Canadian Press and carried across the country. It seemed to confirm what many people had suspected—that the project was rife with political machinations.

The May allegation raises a number of troublesome issues. If "Manitoba's interests have really been shafted," for instance, why did she wait three months from the date of issuance of the IRIA license to make her complaint public? She had already left the employ of the minister, so she had nothing to lose. And it wasn't as if we were trying to hide the fact that construction on the Rafferty Dam was under way.

The "how" of it is even more interesting, in that Robson offers no corroboration of Elizabeth May's allegations. The only thing that *might* have pointed to a possible substantiation of the story was a briefing memorandum from Environment Canada to the federal minister speculating that Saskatchewan might attempt to make a Grasslands-for-Rafferty deal. The author of the memorandum, a federal official, speculated that such a deal might be proposed on the basis of suggestions that had been made by environmental interest groups.

In a March 23, 1988, Letter to the Editor of the *Winnipeg Free Press*, the communications advisor to the federal minister of the environment, Terry Collins, wrote:

> . . . Ms Stuemer [the federal official] flagged what Saskatchewan environmental groups had been telling our officials for months: that the province may offer concessions on Grasslands in return for the federal dam license.
>
> Your readers should know:
> • The December 1987 memo was written for a scheduled meeting between Mr. McMillan and Saskatchewan Deputy Premier Eric Berntson that didn't take place.
> • That by the time that the rescheduled meeting took place three months later, the question of Frenchman River water rights— the last stumbling block in the forty year old Grasslands issue— had been resolved thanks to a federal concession. The concession allowed the province to retain the river bed rights within the park.
> • That when Mr. McMillan and Mr. Berntson met, Saskatchewan had nothing to bargain away on Grasslands—if that had been the province's intent. Let me repeat, however, once again: Saskatchewan did not seek to obtain the dam license in an exchange nor was it offered by Mr. McMillan as the proceeds of a dam for a park deal.[2]

There is no evidence to corroborate May's allegation. As Tom McMillan pointed out, "I think there are five billion people in the world and she is the only one who has said that."[3]

Three days after the story broke, May inexplicably added a new twist to it. While she had initially charged that the only reason for her leaving the federal minister's office was the trade-off of Grasslands National Park for the Rafferty-Alameda IRIA license, she then put an additional variable into the equation: a *quid pro quo* for French language translation in Saskatchewan. Randy Burton pondered the situation in the *Saskatoon Star-Phoenix*:

> May resigned her job in June, saying later she believed Ottawa traded Rafferty approval for provincial approval on the Grasslands national park and now she says the French translation deal was also part of a three-way swap . . .
> The federal government was sorely disappointed in Saskatchewan's Bill 2 passed this spring, which abrogated French language rights in the province, while promising partial French translation of laws in the future.[4]

There were problems with the change in May's story. If there were a trade-off for French language translation, then presumably the *quid pro quo* for the federal government in return for issuing a license for Rafferty-Alameda would be for the provincial government to rescind its French language law. It never happened. *Regina Leader-Post* columnist Dale Eisler commented:

> It is an interesting assertion but one that doesn't necessarily make sense.
> The reason is that the program to translate laws and to establish a minority language institute at the University of Regina is almost completely funded by Ottawa. At the same time, the Devine government did not back down from its English only language legislation.[5]

The federal government's response also cast doubt on the May story. "I think it is reprehensible for her to say that, because if she left for that reason she didn't tell anybody," McMillan stated. "It is a *post facto* explanation by her that serves her purposes [to return to the environmental movement]."[6]

In an interview with the *Estevan Mercury*, the minister backed up his position:

> McMillan added the federal director-general of inland waters recommended to him that the license for Rafferty-Alameda be approved. He said also putting their stamp of approval on the concept were the deputy minister of the environment, the assistant deputy minister for the conservation and protection service as well as all the senior people in the bureaucracy, including May.[7]

The seriousness with which the May allegations were treated by the federal government was apparent when Environment Canada officials held their own news conference to point out "that proper procedures were followed before the June 17 approval of the license."[8] A more damaging revelation occurred when it became public that May, "was in the room when Environment officials recommended Rafferty proceed and she made no objection."[9]

As for the provincial government, responses to the May allegations were swift and strong. "Who is she?" Grant Devine wanted to know. "I mean, who really is she? She drew a long bow and took a cheap shot while betraying the federal minister in an election year. What the heck would she know, or if she knew that, why didn't she raise it earlier ... why?"[10]

Deputy Premier Eric Berntson made equally strong denials, but perhaps the most persuasive comment, and the one most difficult to refute, came from Colin Maxwell, the minister responsible for parks, who was negotiating with the federal government on the Grasslands National Park. (Maxwell is now the executive vice-president of the Canadian Wildlife Federation.) A September 24, 1988, article in the *Saskatoon Star-Phoenix* reported:

> Allegations made by a former policy adviser to federal Environment Minister Tom McMillan "are really testing all credulity," he [Maxwell] said in an interview Tuesday ... The Rafferty-Alameda issue was entirely separate matters [sic], "and we never discussed Rafferty/Alameda in our discussions." May also linked the deal to French language translation which Maxwell called "just the most incredible thing I have ever heard in my life." He says he's "somewhat privy" to the real reasons May left McMillan's office "and I don't want to get into any mudslinging with some woman that I've never met in my life before, but that is really stretching the imagination beyond all credulity."[11]

In a November 16, 1990, Letter to the Editor written in response to an "Op-Ed" piece May had written in *The Globe and Mail* entitled "A Tangled Tale Set on a Tiny River," former federal Environment Minister Tom McMillan wrote:

> ... at no time while in my employ did Ms. May express to me, to my chief of staff or to anyone else on my political or government staff that she was resigning on principle over the Rafferty-Alameda dams or for any other policy related reason. The first I heard of this rationale was in an interview to the *Winnipeg Free Press* some six weeks after she left my employ. Indeed, in a letter of July 11, 1988, to Evan Armstrong, assistant deputy minister, Finance and Administration, Environment Canada, she stated: "the ... termination [of my employment] is not a resignation ... but the result of an agreement that [my] work is no longer required."[12]

If McMillan's communication adviser, Terry Collins, is correct, the only basis for the trade-off rumor actually came from environmental groups in the initial instance as a means of clinching the Grasslands deal. After securing that, so the argument goes, the rumor that was initiated by environmental groups as a means of getting Grasslands National Park, which they wanted, became a means of attempting to kill the Rafferty-Alameda project, which they clearly did not. If true, it is not only brilliant, it is duplicitous.

The significance of Elizabeth May's allegations can be easily seen. Within three weeks of the story first appearing in the *Winnipeg Free Press*, the Senate announced it would be holding hearings into the circumstances that led to the granting of a federal license for the Rafferty and Alameda dams in southeastern Saskatchewan. The chair of the Agriculture and Forestry Committee, Senator Dan Hays, conceded, "the chance of a federal election being called any day played a role in the committee decision to review the project urgently . . ."[13] The hearings were a waste of time. The federal election was held and the investigation was never heard from again.

It is not unreasonable to question why Elizabeth May didn't participate in any of the various environmental assessments of the Rafferty-Alameda project. Given that she was in the employ of the federal minister of the environment at the time, it is understandable why she would not have participated in the Saskatchewan environmental review. It is less clear why she did not take an active role in either the Initial Environmental Evaluation in 1989 or the federal panel review in 1991, given her high profile on the issue. If the project "trashes the environment," as she alleged, why didn't she take the opportunity to make her case against it?

Another example of the misinformation that surfaces on these kinds of projects happened after the CWF II decision. In the spring of 1990, a controversy arose over how much work Saskatchewan was permitted to do on the project. On April 30, 1990, Mark Wyatt of the *Regina Leader-Post* quoted Lorne Scott as saying that he didn't object to any additional work that might be required to secure the dam:

> "The fact is the environmental damage was done and if it requires more dirt or cement on top, so be it," he said in an interview.
>
> But the ongoing construction projects on causeways and downstream channelization are not necessary for public safety, he argued.
>
> About 2,000 acres of forest will be bulldozed in the causeway construction, Scott estimated.[14]

Information that had been published more than two years earlier in the Environmental Impact Statement indicated that there weren't 2,000 acres of forest in the entire Rafferty Reservoir area. I contacted the *Leader-Post* to make sure that Scott had been accurately quoted. We then decided to rebut the claim by means of a Letter to the Editor, including a photograph:

> An opponent to the Rafferty-Alameda project, Lorne Scott, is quoted as saying that causeway construction in the Rafferty Reservoir would result in the removal of 2,000 acres of forest. The above photograph is the site of the causeway to which Scott refers.

There are not 2,000 acres of forest within the Rafferty-Alameda Reservoirs combined, let alone at the Rafferty causeway site.

There are two trees of any size at the causeway site, as shown in this photograph and these will have to be removed. In the last three years, the Souris Basin Development Authority has planted well in excess of 250,000 trees in the vicinity of the Rafferty Reservoir. This far exceeds the number that will be lost through inundation.

Responsibility for accurate depiction of the facts lies not only with project proponents such as SBDA, but with representatives of interest groups opposed to Rafferty-Alameda such as Scott. Inaccurate statements such as Scott's regarding 2,000 acres of forest being destroyed do nothing to help the public better understand the impacts and mitigation programs associated with Rafferty-Alameda, nor do they contribute to informed debate about the environment.[15]

In 1990, rather late in the development of the project, a group calling itself Citizens Concerned About Free Trade (CCAFT) launched a concerted effort to oppose the Rafferty and Alameda dams. The group presented an interesting argument, and one that had particular appeal at the time. During the debate over free trade between Canada and the United States, CCAFT waged a high-profile media campaign from its base in Saskatoon. One of the issues raised was whether the Free Trade Agreement between Canada and the United States prohibited or

This photo, taken in 1993, shows the results of tree planting undertaken by the SBDA as part of its mitigation program. Over 35 percent of the project's initial budget was devoted to environmental protection. Author photo

permitted the exportation of Canadian water to the United States. This issue was the source of no small degree of controversy, as individuals who were involved in the actual negotiation of the agreement fell on opposite sides of the issue.

In the midst of the controversy over Rafferty-Alameda, CCAFT tried to make the case that Rafferty-Alameda was not really limited to the Souris River basin. These two dams, so the story went, were actually part of a multi-billion dollar plan called the North American Water and Power Alliance (NAWAPA) that had been formulated by an American engineering firm in the 1960s. According to CCAFT, NAWAPA involved diverting twenty Canadian rivers into the United States, and the Rafferty Dam was an integral part of the strategy. The group contended that the natural water supplies for the Rafferty Reservoir were inadequate:

> The most obvious place [for the water to come from] is the Qu'Appelle River a short 100 miles away which is linked to the South Saskatchewan River system, a secure mountain-fed stream. By looking at a map it becomes clear how simple such a diversion would be—a short pipeline or a channel less than 100 miles long, through easily moved dirt from the Qu'Appelle to the Souris . . .
>
> We believe the Rafferty Dam is part of something much bigger. The Rafferty, along with the Oldman River Dam under construction in Alberta, only make sense as part of a water diversion to the United States . . .
>
> Once the Rafferty and Oldman dams are in place all that is required is a drought in the U.S., a media blitz about the desperate U.S. need for our water, and the primary structures are all there to divert our waters south with the simple opening of the gates.[16]

It's an interesting theory, and in the abstract it was at least plausible. It was also based on an alleged conspiracy, which is always good for creating controversy. The problem was, it made no sense in the context of the Rafferty and Alameda dams. If someone wanted to export massive volumes of Canadian water to the United States, it would have been much easier to do it before the Rafferty Dam was built. Prior to the Rafferty-Alameda project, the United States was receiving the vast majority of Saskatchewan's share of the Souris waters. This was not the case after the dam was built, when Saskatchewan was finally able to retain a share closer to its legal allotment. The Canada-U.S. agreement for the Souris River project, which would need to be amended in order to implement the NAWAPA, is in effect for 100 years from the date of signing. The operating plan portion of the agreement can only be amended every five years, and then only with the mutual consent of the Canadian and American federal governments. The IRIA license for the project is in effect for fifty years from the date of issuance, and contains a specific clause restricting the importation of water into the Souris basin.[17] The IRIA license cannot be amended without the mutual consent of the Saskatchewan and the Canadian governments.

But perhaps the most compelling arguments against the conspiracy are those provided by the limitations of government. Building a project the scale of NAWAPA would almost certainly constitute one of the largest civil works ever undertaken. It was all the combined governments of Canada and the United States could do to get the Rafferty and Alameda dams built, let alone secretly plan a project that would fundamentally alter the existing hydrological patterns of North America.

As with all good grafted issues, the NAWAPA conspiracy is technically feasible, has a high degree of political symbolism, and does potentially involve the Rafferty Dam. Largely because of these factors, the media treated CCAFT's interest as a *bona fide* concern, the print media even going so far as to publish the group's lengthy Letter to the Editor in a number of Saskatchewan papers.

Not all the issues grafted onto Rafferty-Alameda were on such a grand scale. The elixir of politics, water, and the blending of fact and fiction was sufficiently volatile to prompt interest from the arts community. In the summer of 1989, the SBDA received a letter from an associate producer with the CBC in Toronto. The letter, in part, read:

> During August and September of this year we are planning to film a two-hour television drama in and around Weyburn. The majority of our locations are in Radville, Saskatchewan, and there is one scene we would like to shoot on land that belongs to the Souris Basin Development Authority.
>
> I have enclosed copies of the title searches so that you will know exactly where it is we wish to film. I understand that this land might be leased to someone at the moment, in which case we would have to obtain their permission as well.
>
> Our story concerns a young minister newly posted to a small Saskatchewan town and the scene in particular involves an Easter sunrise service that the minister has planned to "boost his ratings" as it were.[18]

The overture from the CBC did not come as a complete surprise. We had for some time been aware of the parallels between Rafferty-Alameda and the Garrison Diversion project, and the fact that people involved in opposing the latter were also involved in the coalition against the Saskatchewan dams. In anticipation, we had screened a CBC television drama on the Garrison Diversion. Part of the *For the Record* series, it featured the noted Canadian actor John Vernon portraying a Manitoba farmer who was to be injuriously affected by the North Dakota project. The character led an emotional fight against Garrison, including the use of civil disobedience in the United States as a means of opposing the project.

It was, then, with circumspection that we considered the request from CBC. By 1989 we were sensitive to things being said about and done to the project, so out of curiosity and an abundance of caution we requested, in writing, a copy of the script before acceding to the request. We received no response from the CBC.

Something about this didn't ring true, and we knew we were on to something on September 13 when one of the SBDA staff learned from area residents that the CBC out of Toronto were in the area and proposing to shoot some scenes the next day on land owned by the SBDA. It didn't take long to find out where they were staying. Our inquiries were met with assurances that the CBC was shooting a drama about a gay United Church minister who was experiencing difficulties being accepted in the community. As a means of boosting attendance, he decides to have a sunrise service in the valley. We were told by one of the CBC coordinators that "there was nothing in the movie about the Souris River, dams, or reservoirs."[19]

Unknown to the CBC, we had been contacted by the *Weyburn Review* for our response to the CBC being in the basin shooting a film that had a town hall scene in which members of the public had congregated to deal with a major dam on the Souris River, and a gay minister was instrumental in swaying public opinion against it.[20]

After some discussion, we came to the conclusion that if we refused access, the CBC would simply shoot somewhere else. We were also of the view that if the *Weyburn Review* was right and this was what the film was about, the premise was such that it would not hurt the project in Saskatchewan. It might also dispel the notion, prevalent in central Canada, that the Souris basin was comparable to an Amazon rain forest, or that Rafferty-Alameda was on a similar scale to the James Bay II hydroelectric project.

It did not come as a complete surprise that what became "The Greening of Ian Elliot" was not only about a gay United Church minister attempting to boost his ratings through a sunrise ceremony, but that it was also about a United Church minister who moves to a small town in southern Saskatchewan to lead a new flock, but winds up instead leading a fight against the construction of a controversial dam project that will destroy the beautiful nearby valley.[21] There was no mistake: this was about Rafferty. The producer of the drama later acknowledged:

> "What interested me was this small group of people . . . getting together against this big project," she said.
>
> "On environmental issues, it's very difficult for people to feel they can do something about such an overwhelming problem and to band together to fight against it."[22]

A year later a controversy arose within the CBC over the appropriate date to air the film. Those involved in its development accused the CBC of postponing the airing of "The Greening of Ian Elliot" for political reasons. According to the CBC, the date was pushed back because of fiscal considerations. SCRAP suggested, without proof, that the province was behind the attempt to derail the airing—which was laughable, given that we were of the view that the film might actually benefit us by dispelling misconceptions in central Canada about what the area, and hence the project, were like.

From a poorly veiled attempt at anticipatory revisionism, the film had been transformed into a debate on what the producer described as "a case history of the sad state of public broadcasting in this country."[23] Not only was Rafferty-Alameda an issue about the environment and the politics of water, now it was a symbol of political interference in the role of public broadcasting. That such political interference from the province never occurred was, of course, irrelevant. What the CBC sought to do with "The Greening of Ian Elliot" was take a real project with a completed dam and change the ending—revisionism on the fly. There was no mistaking what the drama was about; the producer herself acknowledged, "it's clearly the Rafferty dam we're talking about."[24]

As television drama, "The Greening of Ian Elliot" is typical of many CBC productions. The quality of the filming was superb, providing glorious footage of a part of the country that many of those watching had likely never seen. But it raises the issue of whether it is a good idea to fictionalize issues that are still before the public. I don't know the answer, but at a time when the line between fiction and reality on television is becoming increasingly difficult to discern, it is a question that should be raised.

There were complaints to the Canadian Radio-Television and Telecommunications Commission (CRTC) when the SBDA-sponsored documentary "Dreams in the Dust" was aired. Opponents of the project wanted equal time. Curiously, these groups did not register the same concern when the CBC eventually aired "The Greening of Ian Elliot." If nothing else, it demonstrates that one's position on these matters would seem to be entirely dependent upon "whose ox is being gored" rather than a matter of principle.

The United Church of Canada couldn't leave the project alone, either. In August 1991, the United Church *Observer* waded into the fray with an article entitled "Lament for a Valley."[25] With no pretensions toward objectivity, the article chronicled the fight against the project by three area families and compared their plight with that of a California farmer who was in need of water to irrigate his crops. It relied entirely on information that supported arguments against the project, and conveyed no real sense of the overwhelming support for Rafferty-Alameda within the affected area. It disregarded virtually all the independent evaluation of the data that had been produced as a result of the two environmental assessments, which had been completed by the time the article was written, and it also, knowingly or not, ignored the fact that two senior lay members of the Anglican Church in Saskatchewan were deeply involved in the project. Dr. John Archer, former president of the University of Regina, noted historian, and chair of the Policy Committee of the Diocese of Qu'Appelle, acted as chair of the Federal Assessment Panel. George Hill was chancellor of the Anglican Diocese of Qu'Appelle. Archer did not conclude that there were overwhelming reasons why the dams should not be built, and Hill certainly did not suffer from moral pangs over the issue of whether flood control for the Saskatchewan portion of the Souris went against his deeply held religious beliefs.

Not surprisingly, the article succeeded in alienating a number of United Church members from southeastern Saskatchewan:

I cannot understand the reasoning of the reporter who wrote on the Alameda Dam in such a negative way. I am sure he could have found many individuals to interview who were in favour of the project, rather than interview two [sic] families who were against the undertaking. Your reporter's evident bias does not add credibility to the article.[26]

Was the article in the United Church *Observer* "news"? Clearly not, because by making no serious attempt even to suggest there may be another side to the story, it does not subscribe to one of the fundamental tenets of objective journalism. In the conclusion to the article, for example, the author notes that "from the start, opponents of Rafferty-Alameda have gone to great lengths to show how the stated objectives of the project could be achieved through a series of small pond-sized reservoirs strategically placed along the river valleys."[27] That a few area residents did attempt to make this argument is true. What *The Observer* omitted from the article was that a series of small dams had been considered and dismissed as not being technically feasible by the Rafferty-Alameda Board of Inquiry in 1988.[28]

From examining these cases, it would be convenient to assume that "grafting" is just another way of describing collateral attacks by groups that were directly or indirectly opposed to the Rafferty and Alameda dams. For the most part, this conclusion would be correct. One of the best examples of this grafting phenomenon, however, is provided by a former Saskatchewan Cabinet minister, Colin Maxwell.

Maxwell had been the minister responsible for wildlife in the Devine government. Throughout his tenure, he proved to be very popular with wildlife interests in Saskatchewan. In the shuffle that bounced Berntson from his position as deputy premier, Maxwell became the multiculturalism minister. It was widely believed at the time that he resented the loss of the wildlife portfolio.

In 1990, Maxwell resigned to assume the position of executive vice-president of the Canadian Wildlife Federation, the most senior permanent position within the federation. His animosity against the Devine government spilled out even before he was able to resign his seat in the legislature:

The Saskatchewan government has been wrong in its decision to ignore proper environmental review of the Rafferty-Alameda dam project, says a former Progressive Conservative cabinet minister.

And Colin Maxwell—now wearing the hat of Canadian Wildlife Federation executive director [sic]—said he will meet with federal Environment Minister Robert de Cotret to discuss what action should or shouldn't be taken against the Saskatchewan government.

Although he does not officially start his new job until next week, Maxwell said in an interview Wednesday he basically supports the CWF's call to revoke the Rafferty dam license because of Saskatchewan's decision to allow work on the project to proceed.

"The federation believes the Souris Basin Development Authority has gone beyond the spirit of the agreement," Maxwell said. "Given the fact that the federation has been to court twice before [to challenge the license], I believe there is still cause for concern—not with the project, but with the way they are doing things."

The wildlife federation released a statement Monday condemning the province for making "an absolute mockery" of the federal government's environmental assessment process by allowing work to proceed on the $140 million Rafferty-Alameda project near Estevan . . .

Maxwell—who resigned his position as multiculturalism minister last month, but still remains an MLA—said he did not know the CWF was releasing the statement Monday.

But the former Tory minister said he believes the concerns his new employer raised this week were totally legitimate . . .

"I've always felt an EIA (Environmental Impact Assessment) should have been done for the project," he said. "I think we should follow our own rules."[29]

Maxwell's comments might have been understandable were it not for the fact that, as minister of parks, recreation, and culture, he had been involved in licensing decisions involving Rafferty-Alameda. When the story broke over his apparent concerns regarding the environmental assessment of the project, it came as a bit of a surprise, especially in light of correspondence he had sent to the Canadian Wildlife Federation in his capacity as minister:

. . . significant integrated mitigation proposals have been developed which will minimize and in some cases eliminate the negative impacts on the Project.

. . . Regarding your request for the combination of the Environmental Impact Statements, extensive consultations have taken place between U.S. agencies and the agencies of the Government of Saskatchewan on the Environmental Impact Statement. Recognizing the jurisdictional realities on this issue, I am confident that every effort is being made to ensure that environmental concerns are being addressed.[30]

What these examples, including the Elizabeth May incident, have in common is that they were played out not before the official processes aimed at assessing the environmental effects of the project, but rather on the public stage provided by the media. In an age when the political definition of environmental assessment subsumes the scientific, the role of the media has arguably become more important than the assessments themselves. After Elizabeth May had made her allegation and it had been reported by Barbara Robson, despite the contradictions in the story and the absence of any corroborating evidence, the story was repeated *ad infinitum* in the media as a statement of fact. Participating in the assessment process and participating in the gathering of scientific data were important, but they weren't what counted on Rafferty-Alameda and they weren't what counted on a number of other projects.

The best example of this phenomenon involves the James Bay II project and the Cree of northern Quebec. Hydro Quebec learned this lesson in a much more painful manner than we did on Rafferty-Alameda. While officials of the Quebec electrical utility were meeting with officials of the environment ministries of the province and the federal government, hammering out the terms of reference for the assessment, the Cree of northern Quebec hired one of the largest public relations firms in the world. Soon afterward, the Cree were paddling canoes down the Hudson River in front of the cameras of the major American TV networks and holding news conferences in New York City, spelling out for the world the impacts of the James Bay II project not as determined by an environmental assessment but as they saw them.

The watchword on environmental issues has become: get your version of the truth out first. There is only one opportunity to make a first impression, and once you've made it it's virtually impossible to change. In the case of the Great Whale project, the Cree had their own "spin doctors" at work before Hydro Quebec even knew the rules of the game had changed. The Cree's version of the project's impacts was what got reported, and it was what the public of North America saw. Hydro Quebec never stood a chance.

In the midst of Rafferty-Alameda, when these collateral attacks were an all-too-frequent occurrence, the role of the media in interpreting and defining perceptions of the project became apparent. It was with this critical factor in mind that we set out to determine just how the media was covering Rafferty-Alameda.

In October 1991 we completed an analysis of every print and electronic media report available that dealt with the Rafferty-Alameda project from the period January 1, 1989, to December 31, 1990. In all, 1,234 separate reports were evaluated, and three specific questions were examined:

Which issues, events, and major players received the most media attention?

Did the media consult a wide range of credible, reliable sources to support both pro and anti-project views?

Did the media adhere to journalistic objectivity, or was coverage slanted towards a particular side of the debate?

Eleven media sources, representative of the project area and the provinces of Saskatchewan, Manitoba, and Ontario were analyzed as part of the study. Seven sources in the print media were analyzed: the *Estevan Mercury,* the *Regina Leader-Post,* the *Saskatoon Star-Phoenix,* the *Winnipeg Free Press, The Globe and Mail, The Ottawa Citizen,* and Canadian Press. The coverage of three radio stations was also analyzed: CBC Radio (Saskatchewan), CKCK Radio (Regina), and CFSL Radio (Weyburn). The coverage of two television stations completed the analysis: CBC (Saskatchewan English language service) and CKTV (Regina).[31]

It is important to keep in mind the events of the period in question, 1989 and 1990:

- the license on the project was quashed in CWF I; the second IRIA license was issued on August 31, 1989.
- construction on the project was restarted.
- the CWF II decision came on December 29, 1989.
- the Canada-Saskatchewan Agreement of January 26, 1990, halted construction on certain aspects of the project.
- there was a lack of progress in the federal panel review of the project.
- the Saskatchewan government realized that Rafferty-Alameda had developed into a federal-provincial political issue and was no longer, from its perspective, an environmental issue.
- the slow game of chicken between Regina and Ottawa was played throughout the summer of 1990 on what work was actually allowed on the project.
- Robert de Cotret toured the project in July 1990.
- on September 5, 1990, the Devine-de Cotret was-there-or-wasn't-there-a-deal meeting took place.
- in October 1990 Saskatchewan announced that an agreement had been reached between Regina and Ottawa to allow construction to proceed.
- the Saskatchewan Court of Queen's Bench refused to grant an injunction to halt construction.
- the Federal Court of Appeal on December 21, 1990, refused to overturn CWF II and allowed the IRIA license for the project to stand.

The study broke down the media reports into categories of principle issues discussed. All the data that follows is drawn from this study. In percentages, the reports throughout this period are as follows:

Legal Issues—42.9 percent
Politics and allegations of malfeasance—23.7 percent
Opinion—12.9 percent
Process of environmental review—8.3 percent
Project background—7.6 percent
Environmental issues—2.8 percent
Comparisons with related projects—1.7 percent
(Note: Does not total 100 percent due to rounding)

The analysis of the coverage throughout this period reveals that for each media type (print, television, and radio) the subjects covered are similar, with legal and political issues receiving a high proportion of the total. This is not surprising, given the events of the period. What we found surprising was the low amount of attention paid to substantive environmental issues.

The events-driven nature of the coverage is further reflected in a different break-down; if the coverage is broken down by the actual players involved in the issue at the time, one finds that the Saskatchewan and federal governments dominate, garnering approximately 26 percent each of all of the media reports during this period. Opposition interest groups were the subject of 12.2 percent, while interest groups in support of the project received 10.2 percent of the coverage. Coverage of all other players was much less significant.

The use of sources was also analyzed. For sources in favor of the project, fully 50% were from the government of Saskatchewan. This, too, is somewhat surprising, given the widespread support for the project throughout the southern portion of the province, particularly among the wildlife groups. For anti-project sources, the media relied most heavily on issue-specific interest groups (25.9 percent), members of the Opposition (23.3 percent), representatives of the Canadian Wildlife Federation (15.6 percent), and the federal government (14.3 percent).

The source analysis reveals only one deviation from this trend. The Manitoba and Ontario newspapers used Saskatchewan Opposition members less than did their Saskatchewan counterparts. The *Winnipeg Free Press* relied on Manitoba representatives, while the Ontario papers, *The Globe and Mail* and *The Ottawa Citizen*, relied more on federal and professional sources. This latter finding is not insignificant, as during this period we were frequently frustrated by the tendency of the media to report as fact unsubstantiated (and untrue) allegations about the project. This tendency is, in my view, a function of the politicization of the environmental assessment process. The plain fact is, things get said about the project all the time that are simply not true. The potential loss of 40,000 acres of wetlands through reservoir-induced drainage, 2,000 acres of forest to be cut down for the construction of a causeway, the loss of 2,500 whitetailed deer and 15,000 ducks—these are all claims that have been made about the project at one time or another. To this day, none of them have been proven, but they were still reported.

Plausible deniability is not a luxury that most developers have. Consequently, independent third-party sources take on added importance. On Rafferty-Alameda, we continually lamented that the media rarely went to an expert third-party source for an opinion as to what constituted a reasonable interpretation of the facts, particularly on the critically important issue of the actual environmental effects of the project.

What the results of this portion of the study reveal is that reporters do little information seeking. Sources on Rafferty-Alameda were used and re-used, with little consideration for the potential use of anything other than the same sources if for no other reason than variety. This propensity for lack of substantial information seeking was confirmed in an interview with Don Curren of the *Regina Leader-Post*, arguably the most informed reporter covering Rafferty-Alameda on a regular basis. Curren conceded that even he had not read all of the SBDA Environmental Impact Statement.[32]

The Globe and Mail acknowledged its tendencies and shortcomings in covering environmental issues. A December 18, 1991, editorial stated:

> . . . the media deplore uncertainty. Mired in lazy habits, we prefer the cut-and-dried to the complex, the cry of outrage to the cautious rumination.
>
> Realizing this, many environmentalists have learned to serve up clear, unambiguous opinions preferably couched in terms of angry accusation. Rather than try to determine the veracity of what they hear— as deadlines approach and editors scowl—reporters seek reaction from the accused party (usually a government or company) and print it along with the accusation. This is known as objectivity.[33]

Media bias is a sensitive issue for any project developer and, like most, we held the view that the prevailing bias in the media was against the project. Given the way events unfolded, there was perhaps some justification for a siege mentality. As a result, we were not prepared for some of the results of the study. Most media sources relied on conventional methodologies in covering the Rafferty-Alameda issue over the 1989–1990 period. Few articles or news items referred to an issue related to the project that did not give the other side a voice. This is not to say, however, that the other side was always given equal time or space.

In the print medium, the newspaper with the greatest degree of favoritism

The clash between Regina and Ottawa prompted the usual spate of editorial cartoons, such as this one by Brian Gable (October 26, 1990). Courtesy The Globe and Mail.

was, not surprisingly, the *Estevan Mercury*, which printed almost two-and-a-half times more supportive than opposing views. So supportive of the project was the *Estevan Mercury* that one of its staff actually appeared before one of the assessment reviews and expressed support for the dams on behalf of the paper. On the opposite end was the *Winnipeg Free Press,* which gave anti-project views three times more space than pro-project views. Given its locale, this too is not surprising. The two Saskatchewan dailies were relatively neutral in terms of the length of their coverage, but the same cannot be said for either of the two central Canadian dailies or of Canadian Press, all of whom gave more coverage to interests opposing the project.

As a whole, the electronic media were neutral. It is difficult to find any discernable trends within the data other than on an individual station basis, and any biases that radio and television have tend to be less extreme relative to newspapers. CFSL Radio coverage from Weyburn was, understandably, slanted in favor of the project. Slanted against was CKCK Radio (Regina). Its television counterpart, CKTV, was essentially neutral. What was really surprising for us were the results of the analysis of the coverage given to the project by the CBC. The project team was convinced that the CBC was biased against Conservative governments. Consequently, we were surprised at the results, which showed that, if anything, CBC television coverage was slanted towards pro-project coverage while CBC Radio was essentially neutral.

What does one infer from these results? The first thing is that the media have considerable difficulty in covering complex environmental issues such as Rafferty-Alameda. The difficulty manifests itself in two forms. Given the technical nature of the project, it was somewhat surprising that a greater effort was not made to explain these. The other indication of the media's difficulty in dealing with complex issues such as Rafferty-Alameda is its reluctance to rely on independent expert sources. While this relates to the substantive environmental effects of the project, it applies to the legal dimensions as well. The legal issues raised in many of the cases involving the project were anything but simple. There was evolving strategy in many of the cases. Why were certain things done or not done? To use but one example, why didn't the Canadian Wildlife Federation appeal the December 28, 1989, decision of Mr. Justice Muldoon, and why did the Tetzlaffs? There are good reasons for this but, as far as I know, they were never raised in the media. What was the importance of venue when certain cases were heard? Independent legal expertise could have provided the media with the capacity to deal with these kinds of issues and to educate the public at the same time.

From the perspectives of the newspaper coverage, there is another disturbing trend. Apart from the obvious biases of the *Estevan Mercury* and the *Winnipeg Free Press*, the degree of neutrality appears to decrease with distance. For this project, the apparent distortion in coverage by the central Canadian press is particularly disconcerting, given two factors. The first is that the vast majority of readers would know little of the area or the issue other than what they picked up in the media. The second is that, given that the greatest concentration of the population in this country is in central Canada, the existence of a significant bias against the project will likely have a disproportionately damaging effect. As University of Calgary political scientist Barry Cooper has noted:

Environmentalists are not an ordinary interest group which can be satisfied with a pragmatic compromise. Lots of environmentalists in Toronto and Montreal will fight to the last beaver in Saskatchewan.[34]

It is a reasonable question to ask how the opinion developed against the project in central Canada. If it did not come from the media, where did it come from? Recall that federal Environment Minister Robert de Cotret told us at the September 5, 1990, meeting in Ottawa that his problem with Rafferty-Alameda was not what the people of Saskatchewan thought about it but what the people of Toronto did. Roger Needham of the University of Ottawa reached these conclusions:

A group from the University of Ottawa is touring the Rafferty Dam site today. They are trying to get a better understanding of the project. Geography professor, Roger Needham, says after looking at the project, he believes that the eastern media is mainly responsible for the bad publicity over Rafferty and he also says that people in the east do not understand the project. "There are about 15 or 16 different interpretations of issues in the [eastern] media—but I'm getting one or two fundamental interpretations of this project here and everybody here seems to be talking with a singular voice."[35]

This is not to suggest that those outside the affected area do not have a stake in a project such as Rafferty-Alameda, which is of some national importance. Having conceded this, I would make the point that those most directly affected by a development certainly have the most to gain or lose if it goes ahead; accordingly, their opinions should count more. But that is not what appeared to happen on Rafferty-Alameda. In a distortion of this relationship, those least affected by the actual development appeared to have the stronger voice in determining what the federal government did on the project, and they did not necessarily have the most accurate information when reaching conclusions. And one thing is certain: virtually all knowledge about the project outside the affected area came via the media. It is for this reason that the inability of the media to accurately cover environmental issues is critical, not only for the public but for the developer as well.

When Grant Devine was interviewed by CBC Radio Calgary producer Susan Cardinal for the *Ideas* program "Rivers of Change" and he said that what the people in downtown Toronto thought about Rafferty-Alameda was not his problem, he was wrong.[36] On these kinds of projects, there is no such thing as someone else's problem. What they think in Toronto does matter, whether you like it or not. And if what they think in Toronto is almost exclusively obtained via the media and the media is unable or unwilling to tell the story accurately, then as a project developer your problem is much larger.[37]

I have attempted to deal sensitively with the issue of the news coverage of the Rafferty-Alameda project because it is perilously easy to fall into the trap of media-bashing. This is not a good idea at the best of times. The task of dealing with how the media cover environmental issues is made easier for me by virtue of the fact that two respected journalists have dealt much more persuasively with the matter than I ever could.

In 1991, Saskatchewan expatriate and noted Canadian journalist Eric Malling delivered the James M. Minnifie Lecture at the University of Regina. In his remarks, Malling dealt for the most part with the television news media and how it covers environmental issues:

> . . . it's hard to make wise ones [choices] when a few zealots spoon feed lazy reporters who get the public hysterical and push quavering politicians into bad decisions. We're being used.
>
> . . . We must make smart choices, but people don't know who or what to believe any more. In our zeal for criticism, we've convinced them to revile all politicians; ignore bureaucrats; and of course, distrust anyone in business or even science.
>
> It leaves special interest groups . . . be they amateurs parading around with their placards or the paid lobbyists and publicists . . . whose main skill is manipulating the media with emotional, dramatic stories or pictures too good to resist . . .
>
> Enter the single interest groups with simple emotional causes and a flair for the dramatic. We just couldn't resist. We helped create these monsters and now they are eating us alive. They've taken over much of the agenda. And what they offer is simplistic responses to complex problems. Unbending dogma when trade-off and compromise are needed more than ever . . .
>
> I interviewed a very wise professor at the University of Toronto earlier this year who . . . had been a founder of the environmental movement and hero of it. Philip Jones was one of the originals in Pollution Probe. He started the Institute of Environmental Studies at U of T and, most important, he had a key role in getting phosphates out of soap.
>
> But Jones has split with the environmental leaders now, split bitterly and gone to Australia because he says his old allies have begun to view their use of the media to create public hysteria as an end in itself.
>
> Eco-terrorists he calls them, dependent on scaring the dickens out of people by telling them everything is dangerous so they'll keep sending money. They have their own vested interests and some have turned into the ecological equivalent of TV preachers. Most important, they've often prevented practical solutions to environmental problems by demanding perfection, by bringing out the placards and with them the cameras any time anyone proposes doing anything, even something to help clean up.

... This isn't investigative reporting, this isn't being a public watchdog. It's being a stooge for people who often know more about writing press releases than they do about science.

The process goes something like this. Interest groups use the media to dramatize an issue; pollsters measure emotional response as opposed to considered views; politicians react; and it suddenly becomes conventional wisdom so the people back on the protest line can say, "See, I told you so."

It's a closed circle often bereft of common sense. But we play our part in it because we're just such suckers for the scare story, the dramatic headline ... and sometimes too lazy to get the perspective that would distinguish between significant and trivial.[38]

After I had read Malling's remarks, I called him on the telephone. I told him I had just read his remarks about the environmental movement, and that this was exactly what was happening to Rafferty-Alameda. I invited him to do a story about the project, promising full disclosure. He didn't take me up on my offer—he probably thought I was nuts—but there was much he said that I agreed with.

Malling is not alone in his criticism of the media and its reporting of environmental issues. Dale Eisler, political editor for the *Regina Leader-Post* and the *Saskatoon Star-Phoenix*, seems to support much of what Malling says. In November 1991, Eisler spoke to an environment and mining conference in Saskatoon:

So when it comes to a complex subject like the environment, which inevitably is a mixture of scientific, technological, social, economic and political issues—all tempered with a heavy dose of subjectivity— you can see where the media might have their problems.

... I think the media's coverage of environmental issues has at best been inconsistent, and at times even irresponsible. In fact, I hazard to say that too often we have done a poor job in objectively reporting and analyzing environmental issues. Regularly we seem to be little more than mouth pieces for interest groups on both sides of the debate— whether industry, government, or environmentalists, and have not done enough to adequately assess and counterbalance the information we pass on to the public.

... Far too often, I think you can describe the media's approach to the environment as "Chicken Little Journalism." That is, the sky always seems to be falling. Each incident involving the environment, whether it's an oil spill or the level of dioxins released by a pulp mill, is presented as a grave and immediate crisis to the environment and people.

... Into this media environment—where immediacy and drama sell and rapid production of stories is important—I add the final factor ... namely, our lack of expertise on environmental issues.

The simple reality is that most Saskatchewan news organizations don't have the human resources to put into environmental coverage. Reporters and editors find themselves stretched to their limits simply trying to cover the basics. With reporters scientifically and environmentally illiterate, I believe there is the potential for a great deal of misinformation on both sides of the environment issue being spread. We in the media become dependent on others to explain environmental issues to the public. The dependency is such that those who know how to use the media to get their message out can have a great impact. But as I said, protecting the environment is motherhood, which means that there is a natural bias towards the environmentalist's position amongst reporters. As such, there is the potential for overstatement and oversimplification to get public attention.

As you can see, we in the media become caught in a situation that is partly of our own making. Driven by the need for immediacy and drama and without the time or expertise to report on often complex environmental issues, we become the captives of interest groups.

I would argue that nowhere is the manipulation of the media greater than when it comes to the environment. Invariably there are assorted agendas behind the environmental debate that go far deeper than merely doing what is environmentally the right thing to do.

And we don't have to look far to see examples of this right here in Saskatchewan.

While I don't for the moment want to dismiss the environmental relevance of the story, I do believe that the Rafferty-Alameda debate ultimately had far more to do with political agendas than environmental ones. Had this not been in Grant Devine's own constituency, I am sure the outcry would not have nearly been as great. That isn't to say there does not need to be a rationalization of conflicting federal and provincial jurisdictions over the environment. That much should be obvious. But for many people the primary motivation behind opposition to the Rafferty-Alameda project was intensely and almost purely political. The environmental angle merely added legitimacy.

It's not surprising that partisan agendas often wrap themselves in the guise of the environment. It makes perfect tactical sense because instinctively people—as the polls tell us—see themselves as environmentally friendly. Thus, when one group declares itself as motivated by a desire to protect the environment against a proponent for a development, it makes it easy for the public to pick what side they are on.

. . . support for Rafferty-Alameda was clearly greatest in the Souris valley region where the project was being built. The opposition tended to be from environmentalists elsewhere and it often seemed politically inspired. In fact, at one point, SCRAP, the group opposing the project, hired the Saskatchewan NDP's pollster to do a poll in the Estevan constituency. It found that Grant Devine was trailing the NDP. What relevance this had to the environmental impact of Rafferty-Alameda was never clear. But what was clear were the negative political implications the poll done by the environmental group had for Devine and his government.[39]

While public concern over environmental matters may have waned recently in light of the economic circumstances confronting the country, environmental issues are not going to go away, nor should they. With any new issue, it is reasonable to assume that the media will require some time to adapt to covering it. Rafferty-Alameda was at the forefront as an environmental issue. It is in this context that the media coverage of Rafferty-Alameda should be seen. As the level of abstraction and the complexity of environmental issues increase, the ability of the media to explain them decreases. At the first level of abstraction—describing who said what—reporters are able to identify the issues. At the second level of abstraction—the description of what the issues are—the media do less well. Finally, at the third level of abstraction—the evaluation of the issues—the media are almost completely incapable of operating with any degree of expertise.[40]

The significance of the media in interpreting and dealing with environmental issues is likely to continue for the foreseeable future, particularly on matters relating to the assessment of the environmental effects of major projects. The symbolic importance of these kinds of economic activities—cathedrals in the wilderness—the ease with which they are attacked because of their inherent complexity, and the ambiguous structure of the assessment processes are, in combination, sufficient to ensure that there will always be opposition to these types of projects. And the opposition will not be expressed through scientifically valid arguments but rather through induced emotional responses, many taking the form of what I have referred to as "grafted" issues. If this is the case, how the media responds will be critical.

As Walter Lippman wrote, "News and truth are not the same thing and must be clearly distinguished . . . The function of news is to signalize an event, the function of truth is to bring to light the hidden facts."[41]

CONCLUSION

In the spring of 1993 an agreement between the Saskatchewan government and the Tetzlaffs was reached and the last of the major lawsuits against the Rafferty-Alameda project were withdrawn. For the first time in over five years, there is no litigation and the dams will likely be finished, some 25 percent over the estimated control budget. This milestone presents an opportunity to address a few questions raised by the project.

What does all of this mean? Why the different perceptions of the project? What significance does it hold for other developments? What does it say about the environmental movement in Canada? What does it say about politics in Canada and Saskatchewan, and about the way we are governed?

In trying to answer these questions, it makes sense to start with the different ways people viewed the project. It seems to me that the primary reason for the differing perceptions of the Rafferty-Alameda project is to be found in politics and symbolism. One cannot help but notice that virtually every major stakeholder had a different agenda, so a consensus in terms of language never developed. Groups and individuals all used the term Rafferty-Alameda, yet the words meant fundamentally different things to each of them. Flood protection, a sell-out to the Americans, a sell-out to the Canadians, an international conspiracy, jobs, a solution to the drought of the century, a landmark legal case, an economic panacea, a political boondoggle, a political asset, a wildlife destroyer, a wildlife boon, an environmental holocaust, and that most frequently used modifier—controversial. All of these terms have been used, many of them here, to describe two dams in the middle of a virtual desert. The question is, Why?

There is no simple answer, but I will lay the foundation for my explanation in the partisan nature of Saskatchewan politics. Gaining momentum as it did during the 1970s, partly because of the frequent flooding that occurred throughout the basin during this period, the dams immediately became caught in the partisan vice of Saskatchewan politics. The decline of the Liberal Party, the ascendancy of the Tories from the heart of the Souris basin, and the latter's positioning on the issue ensured that the Rafferty and Alameda dams would be difficult, if not impossible, for an NDP government to support. As the records from the Blakeney government attest, the issue was politicized in a partisan sense almost a full decade before construction began. There are no clean hands; responsibility falls on both the NDP and the Tories.

Just how much Rafferty-Alameda was politicized is obvious when one considers that a similar project was developed in the 1970s in Saskatchewan at Poplar River with not nearly the degree of political spin, even though an international controversy resulted that arguably had more serious ramifications than did Rafferty-Alameda. The reason for the difference between the two projects lies in the decision of Grant Devine to run in Estevan, the increasing political fortunes of the Conservatives prior to 1982, and Devine's close personal attachment to the issue.

Rafferty-Alameda was born into a zero-sum environment when it was announced on February 12, 1986. The project's future was not helped by its announcement as part of the Conservative strategy leading up to the 1986 provincial election. Fundamental questions remained unanswered, and the environmental community took offence at the politically opportunistic manner in which the project was announced. The political spin was compounded by how the project was managed in its early stages. Many of the mistakes major project developers traditionally make were repeated on Rafferty-Alameda. We made them and, to the extent that I am to blame, I accept my full share of responsibility.

The complexity of the project was not acknowledged or even fully understood in 1986. The model on which the Souris Basin Development Authority was based was doomed to fail, if for no other reason than the animosity that existed between the bureaucracy and the Conservative government. Unknown to anyone at the time, a new operative principle of major project development was about to be developed. A proponent's ability to develop a project is only as good as the soundness of the environmental regulatory processes to which it is subjected, the strength of the regulatory bodies themselves, and the individuals therein. The looseness of the assessment processes at both the provincial and federal levels significantly contributed to Rafferty-Alameda's problems. It is said that changes in public opinion always precede changes in the law; this is certainly the case here. Oil spills, tire fires, chemical fires, concerns over drinking water quality—all occurred in the mid-1980s. They elevated concern about the environment among Canadians to an all-time high and, one way or another, they had an effect on Rafferty-Alameda.

The rules governing environmental assessment at both the provincial and federal levels were far from rigorous when the project was being considered. In the case of Saskatchewan, the *Saskatchewan Environmental Assessment Act*, passed in 1980 by the Blakeney government, was being administered a full seven years after coming into effect without any of the supporting regulations that were intended for it when it was passed. Instead, an informal set of guidelines was used, thereby exposing the proponents to unnecessary risk.

To compound the issue, having the same minister responsible for the environment also responsible for the agency that would ultimately own and operate the structures left the perception that there was conflict. It wasn't merely a perception, there was a conflict. At the federal level, the situation was worse. There, the agency responsible for the administration of the federal government's environmental assessment procedures didn't understand the legal status of the only process it was attempting to administer.

It was into this situation that increasingly active and integrated environmental interest groups intervened. They decided that the way the regulatory authorities were handling Rafferty-Alameda presented the opportunity to question, through litigation, the soundness of these processes. Differences between regulatory processes and the substantive impacts of the project—analytically distinct concepts—were lost in the complexity of the litigation. From this point on, the main participants, while using the same words in reference to the project, would mean very different things. The differences, in the public's mind, between matters of process and matters of substance sank into a technical morass of lawsuits. The situation created by the ambiguities in the process made it difficult for the media to cover and, with each court decision, less likely for the public to understand.

While many of the legal cases related to different aspects of environmental assessment processes, the common thread linking them was the Rafferty-Alameda project itself. If the public could not understand the nuances of environmental assessment law, what they could understand was that Rafferty-Alameda was in court again, and therefore it must be the cause of all this.

As the shortcomings of the environmental law became apparent, those responsible for its administration ran for cover. For Environment Canada, it was the worst of times and the best of times. It was the worst of times because the federal department was not staffed to deal with these kinds of issues. Lacking legal and economic expertise, not particularly respected by its sister agencies in the federal government nor by the provinces, the task of administering environmental policies was beyond the grasp of Environment Canada and FEARO. Its handling of the environmental assessment of the two Saskatchewan dams is a graphic demonstration of this. Being referred to as "silly and inattentive" by a federal court judge is somewhat less than a ringing endorsement of the capabilities of the department's officials. They were banking on the probability that the controversy created by their own misdeeds would pass quickly and that the proponent would take the flack; this cynical strategy worked for a time.

These were also the best of times for Environment Canada in that, with public concern over the environment reaching an all-time high, the Federal Court had created the opportunity for the department to do something it had been unable to do on its own—expand its bureaucratic turf. Such considerations are the currency of bureaucratic politics.

With the decisions of the courts would come an irreconcilable collision of interests. On the one side were the environmental lobby, Environment Canada, and the Saskatchewan NDP—all, for their own reasons, wanting to shift the blame onto the shoulders of the province. On the other side were the government of Saskatchewan, at least initially, and the area residents in support of the project. As the heat was turned up, the entire Cabinet save Berntson left the two Georges to twist in the wind. At the end, even Berntson couldn't help us, and Hill and I were left to defend ourselves.

The single scarcest commodity in politics is guts, and in the provincial Cabinet at the time there was none at all. For George Hill, who had spent most of his life passionately supporting the Progressive Conservative Party in Saskatchewan, it was a bitter pill to swallow. Caught in the middle were the federal Tories, between a tired provincial administration clearly going down to defeat on the one hand, and the entrenched position of their own officials on the other.

The debunking of myths is neither easy nor popular, particularly in an era of increased environmental awareness. This is particularly the case with Rafferty-Alameda. Much of the mythology surrounding the project has been premised on the environmental lobby and landowners—the Davids taking on the big impersonal Goliath in the form of the Saskatchewan government. At a superficial level, this explanation works, but at the more detailed and complicated level of political reality, it is simple sophistry.

The real power in all this did not lie with Saskatchewan. In the middle of the worst drought of the century, with the federal government pouring billions of debt-financed dollars into western Canada to offset the effects of the dry spell, Saskatchewan could not manage to convince Ottawa to do something as basic as take responsibility for its own actions. Saskatchewan's lack of influence is best seen by the federal government's decision to coerce the province into shutting down construction on two dams in order to maintain the integrity of the EARP Guidelines, and then within a matter of days exempting the Kemano hydroelectric project from the guidelines altogether and allowing the Oldman River Dam to be completed before a panel review could begin.

No, the real power on the Rafferty-Alameda issue was vested in the bureaucracy in Ottawa and in an increasingly powerful environmental lobby. So powerful was the bureaucracy that no official was ever dismissed, despite the egregious errors committed defending a policy that cost Saskatchewan millions of dollars. The demise of Robert de Cotret as federal environment minister lies at the feet of his own officials and his predecessor, Lucien Bouchard. De Cotret's position was undermined by his officials, who appeared steadfastly to refuse to implement the minister's instructions.

Biographer Robert Caro has written that "one of the first rules of power is that when power meets greater power, it does not oppose but attempts to compromise."[1] In the aftermath of the meeting of September 5, 1990, it was not the officials of Environment Canada who compromised, it was the minister. The officials are still there; Robert de Cotret isn't. Governments come and go, but the bureaucracy and the interest groups remain—to defend no one's interests but their own.

The relationship between the environmental lobby and the Environment Canada bureaucracy is particularly critical. Because the federal department has its own credibility problems, it depends for much of its policy support on its policy community, which is to say, from the institutionalized interest groups. Throughout all the distemper on the Rafferty-Alameda issue, the only relationship that was not characterized by tension and acrimony at one time or another was that between the interest groups and the bureaucracy of

Environment Canada. In the thousands of pages of newspaper copy and the hundreds of hours of radio and television tape dealing with this project, it is virtually impossible to find any public disagreement between these two interests. The reason is simple: they need each other. They knew that, after this issue had passed, there would be another, and their ongoing relationship is more important than any single issue.

The environmental lobby in Canada is shrewd and sophisticated. Most major project developers are amateurs by comparison. When opportunities arose to be critical of federal officials, it was always done by a representative of an issue-specific interest group. Vertically integrated strategies between and among institutionalized and issue-specific environmental interest groups have become common. As Rafferty-Alameda demonstrated, a proponent can be faced with a coalition of national interest groups holding a press conference in Ottawa, which you most certainly will hear about, or with quiet, behind-the-scenes lobbying of Environment Canada, which you almost certainly will not hear about.

Major project developers are thus faced with a considerably more difficult task than was the case even ten years ago. And they have done a poor job in recognizing the new reality. The rules have changed. Thirty years ago, the determining factors were technical and economic; ten years ago, environmental considerations were added; now it is a political game in which you have to recognize that all these previous considerations are on the table and perception matters more than reality.

The environmental assessment process in Canada is now so complicated—what with governments at the federal, provincial, regional, and municipal levels climbing all over themselves to get on the environmental bandwagon—that there is no such thing as someone else's problem. As Rafferty-Alameda demonstrated, the opposition will distort the facts because the generation of controversy is an end in itself. As Churchill said, "A lie travels round the world while the truth is putting on her boots."[2]

The more controversy generated, the more complex the review process. The more complex the review process, the greater the likelihood of stopping the development. What people think about your project matters, even if what they are saying isn't true. Environmental assessment is a political process that subsumes a scientific one. This is not without significance for other environmental issues. The current regulatory framework in Canada is not rigorous or sophisticated enough to determine in any definitive way whether developments are environmentally acceptable. The controversy surrounding the logging of old growth forests on Vancouver Island is typical. The rhetoric from both sides is such that it is impossible to determine who, if anybody, is telling the truth. The problem is further compounded because there is no government process that allows for a rational determination of the issue, largely because few people trust government any more. And if your project is being reviewed by a regulatory body with flawed procedures—and, as we have seen, most are—then as a major project developer, everything is your problem. If developers don't recognize these new rules, they will lose.

So the Rafferty and Alameda dams are built and the court cases are over. It is not unreasonable to ask, What is the legacy of this project? The residents of the Souris basin finally have the ability to manage this most peculiar river. Is there enough water? Will the reservoirs work as intended? Only time will tell. The environmental lobby presumably got what it wanted with greater clarity over federal jurisdiction on the environment. The project took longer than expected, cost more than it should have, and was definitely more rancorous than it should have been. Would the same thing have happened if the project had been situated in Ontario or Quebec? It's an interesting question.

After three environmental reviews, was there a consensus that the project should be built? No. This is arguably the most significant aspect to the entire Rafferty-Alameda legacy. After five years of virtual nonstop environmental reviews, all of which concluded that there were no overwhelming reasons this project should not be built, some parties still refuse to accept the results of the process they fought so hard to establish. That this is the case underscores the emotional nature of the environment as an issue, the difficulties inherent in regulating within this kind of subjective milieu, and why there will always be projects like Rafferty-Alameda that evoke these kinds of visceral responses.

It is worth noting one final irony. The program for mitigating the impacts of the Rafferty-Alameda project is now scheduled for completion in the year 2002— almost eighteen years after we got started. It was the Corps of Engineers in the basement of the Minot airport in 1985 who stated that it would take eighteen years to plan, design, and build a project the size and complexity of Rafferty-Alameda, while Saskatchewan claimed we could do it in three.

They were right.

NOTES

Unless otherwise noted, the information cited is from the Souris Basin Development Authority files. Researchers can find the author's personal papers and other material relating to the Rafferty-Alameda project in the Saskatchewan Archives, Saskatoon, Sask.

Preface

1. R.H.S. Crossman, *The Diaries of a Cabinet Minister* (London: Hamilton, Cape, 1975–77), and David E. Lilienthal, *The Journals of David E. Lilienthal* (New York: Harper and Row, 1964).

Old Water

1. *Wilkinson v Rafferty-Alameda Board of Inquiry* (1987), 64 Sask R 170 (QB).
2. Peter Gzowski, *The Private Voice: A Journal of Reflections* (Toronto: McClelland and Stewart, 1988), 91.
3. There is evidence that this region could have been subjected to much longer climactic fluctuations than are apparent from examination of Souris River flow data from the twentieth century. For greater detail see: J.T. Finnigan, *Souris Basin Heritage Study Summary Report on the 1984 to 1992 Archaeology Programs,* Western Heritage Services, Saskatoon, 1992.
4. Allan Turner, *Early History of the Souris River* (Saskatchewan Archives, 1958), 4.
5. *Ibid.,* 5.
6. Edward McCourt, *Saskatchewan* (Toronto: MacMillan, 1968), 7.
7. Marc Reisner, *Cadillac Desert* (New York: Penguin Books, 1986), 12.
8. Norman Ward, "Saskatchewan," cited in James Marsh (ed), *The Canadian Encyclopedia*, Vol II (Edmonton: Hurtig Publishers, 1985), 1637.
9. C.T. Shay, L.P. Stene, J.M. Shay, and L.C. Wilson, "Preliminary Report of Paleoecological Investigations in the Proposed Rafferty Dam Area, Southeastern Saskatchewan," in *Journal of North Dakota Archaeological Association*, Vol 4, 1990, 47.
10. Edgar Sawyer, cited in Olga Klimko and Michael Taft (eds), *Them Days: Memories of a Prairie Valley* (Saskatoon: Fifth House Publishers, 1991), 27.
11. Souris Basin Development Authority, Submission to the Rafferty-Alameda Federal Environmental Assessment Panel, Travelogue, 1990. See photos 81, 82, 230.
12. United States War Department, "Narrative and Final Report by Isaac I. Stevens, Governor of Washington Territory, upon the Route near the 47th and 49th Parallels," in *Reports of Explorations and Surveys to ascertain the most practical and economical route for a railroad from the Mississippi River to the Pacific Ocean, 1853–1855*, Vol XII, Part 1.

13. Edith Paterson, "Coal came in Barges Down the Souris River," in *Winnipeg Free Press* (Apr 4, 1970).
14. SBDA Environmental Impact Statement, *Summary Report* (Estevan, 1987).
15. Western Heritage Services, Oral History Transcripts, Estevan, 1990.
16. Klimko and Taft, 111. See note 10.
17. *Ibid.,* 116.
18. Souris Basin Development Authority, "Facts: The Rafferty and Alameda Reservoirs" (1988), #11.
19. "Estevan Dam Would Assure Steady Flow of Mouse in Minot," *Minot Daily News,* (Feb 20, 1932).
20. International Joint Commission, *Report of the Souris River Investigation* (Ottawa, 1940), 39. In Jan 1940 the Governments of Canada and the United States referred three questions to the IJC:
    1. . . . what apportionment should be made of the waters of the Souris (Mouse) River and its tributaries, the waters of which cross the international boundary to the Province of Saskatchewan, the State of North Dakota, and the Province of Manitoba?
    2. What methods of control and operation would be feasible and desirable in order to regulate the use and flows of the waters of the Souris (Mouse) River and of its tributaries, the waters of which cross the international boundary, in accordance with the apportionment recommended in the answer to question 1?
    3. Pending a final answer to questions 1 and 2, what interim measures of régime should be adopted to secure the foregoing objects?
21. *Ibid.,* 42.
22. J. Clark Salyer, quoted in International Joint Commission, *ibid.,* 30.
23. IJC 1940, 48. See note 20.
24. *Ibid.,* 49.
25. *Ibid.,* 51. As far as Manitoba was concerned in the 1940 reference, the IJC recommended a regulated flow of not less than ten cubic feet per second released from North Dakota to Manitoba during June, July, Aug, Sept, and Oct of each year. As will be evident when considering the 1959 Souris River Reference to the IJC and the interim apportionment decisions taken nineteen years later, in 1940 the members of the commission were extremely cautious recommending licenses for new uses. A factor in their deliberations may well have been that there was no large institutional demand for water within the Saskatchewan portion of the basin. The same could not be said within the North Dakota portion of the basin where the twenty-one dams were. By virtually maintaining the *status quo* on the Souris, the IJC gave American interests a tremendous advantage at the expense of both Saskatchewan and Manitoba. The ten cubic feet per second apportionment to Manitoba made in 1940 was doubled in 1959 to twenty cubic feet per second and still found to be inadequate. The recommendations of the commission and the subsequent decisions by the respective federal governments were not sufficient to satisfy Saskatchewan or Manitoba.
26. IJC 1940, 51. See note 20.
27. Letter from Saskatchewan Agriculture to External Affairs Re: Souris River Apportionment (June 10, 1957).
28. Letter to the International Joint Commission, Aug 1957, cited in George D. Hill, QC, *Remarks to the Senate Agriculture and Forestry Committee* (Sept 29, 1988).
29. Province of Saskatchewan, Department of Agriculture, Souris River Reference before IJC Hearing at Estevan, Sask., 1955, 3.

30. John E. Carroll, *Environmental Diplomacy* (Ann Arbor: University of Michigan Press, 1983), 184.

31. Rochon Memorandum Re: Rafferty/Alameda Project: IJC Interim Apportionment Measures (Department of External Affairs, Dec 12, 1988).

    During the negotiations leading up to the signing of the agreement between Canada and the United States in 1989, which made provision for flood protection for the city of Minot, ND, the question of inherent riparian water rights on transboundary rivers was raised by representatives of the Manitoba government. In the course of these negotiations, Manitoba officials indicated that, under the 1959 interim apportionment, that province was not receiving its fair share of the waters of the Souris River. Manitoba also stressed that it wanted to determine whether it had an inherent right to half the natural flow of the Souris as opposed to the twenty cubic feet per second that it was receiving. To this end the representatives of the government of Manitoba requested a legal opinion from the Department of External Affairs. The opinion received was that there was " . . . no basis in customary international law for the proposition that either a downstream state (in this case, Manitoba) or an upstream state (in this case, Saskatchewan) has an inherent right to half the natural flow of a transboundary river."

32. "A Brief Concerning Better Flood Control and Water Utilization in the Souris River Basin—Specifically From Weyburn to Oxbow" (Moose Jaw–Souris Water Association Area #4, June 12, 1970).

33. R.G. Trout. Interview with author (Nov. 7, 1993).

34. Grant Gross, "Voice of the Legislature: When Orlin Hanson talks, things happen," in *Minot Daily News* (nd).

35. Rep. Orlin Hanson, as quoted in Environment Canada, Rafferty-Alameda Project, Initial Environmental Evaluation, Vol II, Public Consultation Process, PA–181, Regina, Sask, 1989. Hanson claimed he was invoking the words of Winston Churchill.

Politicizing a Creek

1. Aneurin Bevan, cited in Chuck Henning (ed), *The Wit and the Wisdom of Politics* (Golden, Colorado: Fulcrum, 1992), 200.

2. David E. Smith, "Interpreting Prairie Politics," in Richard Allen (ed), *A Region of the Mind* (Regina: Canadian Plains Studies, 1973), 103.

3. George D. Hill, QC, cited in John Schreiner, "The power at SaskPower: George Hill shoots from the hip—but accurately," *Financial Post* (Nov 30, 1990).

4. Evelyn Eager, *Saskatchewan Government: Politics and Pragmatism* (Saskatoon: Western Producer Prairie Books, 1980), 181.

5. Byers to Blakeney Memorandum Re: Souris River Flood Prevention Citizens Association Meeting Sept 9, 1975 in Estevan (Sept 25, 1975).

6. George Hill, Q.C. Interview with author (Feb 21, 1992).

7. See note 5.

8. Mitchell to Bolstad Memorandum Re: Report on Souris Basin Study (Nov 28, 1978).

9. Blackwell to Mitchell Memorandum Re: Proposed Rafferty Meeting (Sept 6, 1979).

10. Kaeding Memorandum Re: July 6, 1979 Meeting with Souris Basin Action Committee (June 27, 1979).

11. Bowerman Memorandum Re: Souris Basin Action Committee—Proposed Meeting (June 28, 1979).

12. Bachorik to Bowerman Letter Re: Souris Basin International Involvement Group (Aug 30, 1979).

13. Hawkes to Norton Memorandum Re: Proposed Meeting on Rafferty Dam and Reservoir (Sept 14, 1979).
14. Mitchell to Bowerman Memorandum Re: Meeting in Estevan on Rafferty Dam Proposal (Oct 2, 1979).
15. Blackwell to Memorandum Re: Meeting with Bob Larter Group (June 14, 1979).
16. John E. Carroll, *Environmental Diplomacy* (Ann Arbor: University of Michigan Press, 1983), 184.
17. *Ibid.,* 182.
18. *Ibid.,* 192.
19. See note 9.
20. *North Dakota Journal of the Senate* (Mar 6, 1981), 1168; and *North Dakota Journal of the House of Representatives* (Mar 6, 1981), 1505.
21. Carter to Bowerman Memorandum Re: Rafferty Dam (May 12, 1981).
22. See note 8.
23. Peter C. Newman, *Renegade in Power: The Diefenbaker Years* (Toronto: McClelland and Stewart Ltd, 1963), cited in Marc Bosc (ed), *The Broadview Book of Canadian Parliamentary Anecdotes* (Peterborough: Broadview Press Ltd, 1988), 254.
24. Hill, cited in Schreiner. See note 3.
25. Roger Gibbins, *Prairie Politics and Society: Regionalism in Decline* (Toronto: Butterworths, 1980), 132.
26. Eager, 100. See note 4.
27. See note 6.

Undercurrents

1. Saskatchewan Power Corporation, *Generation 2000* (1985), 2.
2. While there were benefits that would accrue to Saskatchewan from the construction of the Alameda Dam and there was overwhelming support from the Alameda-Oxbow area residents, given that it was not detailed in the Souris River Basin Study, it does not appear that it was under active consideration until the issue of flood protection for the United States was raised.
3. John E. Carroll, *Environmental Diplomacy* (Ann Arbor: University of Michigan Press, 1983), 182. SaskPower was the provincial agency responsible for the Poplar River project, as well.
4. See Robert Caro, *The Power Broker* (New York: Vintage, 1974), 847.
5. From early on, there was a strong political bent to the project, even to the point of controlling how the environmental assessment would proceed. An October 24, 1985 memorandum from the deputy minister to the premier and secretary to the cabinet illustrates this point:

   This memorandum is to confirm the decisions taken at the October 23, 1985 briefing with the premier on the Rafferty Dam issue . . .
   7. That the environmental review process be permitted to begin as soon as the Environmental Impact Statement is submitted by Saskatchewan Power Corporation (February 2, 1986 estimated). It was decided, as well, that an open house process be utilized, if possible, in order to offset potential public opposition from a Board of Inquiry.
   - Cited from Riddell Memorandum Re: Rafferty Dam, October 24, 1985.
6. Hood to Harrold Re: Rafferty Dam U.S. Commitment and Assurances (Dec 18, 1985).

7. Ron Petrie, cited in Carl O. Flagstad, "Green Light Flashed in Province," *Minot Daily News* (Jan 30, 1986).
8. H. Laframboise "The Future of Public Administration in Canada," *Canadian Public Administration*, 25 (4) (Winter 1982), 513, cited in Alan Cairns, "The Embedded State: State-Society Relations in Canada," in Keith Banting (ed), *Canada in Comparative Perspective* (Toronto: University of Toronto Press in cooperation with the Royal Commission on the Economic Union and Development Prospects for Canada and the Canadian Government, Minister of Supply and Services Canada, 1986).

   As Laframboise has noted, albeit in the context of the federal government, the bureaucracy is becoming analogous to a mini-international system where a corps of diplomats engages in negotiations with other departments in the same jurisdiction: "This activity is becoming increasingly formalized through written contracts between parties as memoranda of understanding between ministers, and letters of agreement between deputy heads. The form and content of these various pacts and treaties have reached a fastidious level of refinement that would do credit to Talleyrand . . . This unfortunate trend toward formality reflects a prevailing and often unwarranted distrust of one another's motives within the same jurisdiction."

   The same phenomenon would appear to be occurring at the provincial level in Saskatchewan. What made the Saskatchewan situation unique is that the motivation for such an occurrence was also fueled by a fear of partisan elements within the Saskatchewan bureaucracy.
9. Author's Journal (Apr 15, 1986).
10. Saskatchewan Environment and Public Safety, "Major Deficiencies in Shand/Rafferty/Alameda EIS" (Aug 1986).
11. Don Curren, "Draft environment report poor, says government evaluation," *Regina Leader-Post* (Mar 13, 1989). Almost three years later, the comments from the meeting were leaked. Although the comments did not pertain to the actual environmental impact statement released to the public, those opposed to Rafferty-Alameda chose to paint both statements with the same brush.
12. Cited from memory.
13. *Saskatoon Star-Phoenix* (Friday, June 13, 1991), A–7.
14. Hood to Martin Re: Rafferty-Alameda project (June 21, 1989).
15. Dale Eisler, quoted in Jeffrey Simpson, *Spoils of Power: The Politics of Patronage* (Toronto: Collins, 1988), 270.
16. H.J. Michelman and J.S. Steeves, "The 1982 Transition in Saskatchewan," in *Canadian Public Administration*, Vol 28, No 1 (Spring 1985), 8–9.
17. *Ibid.*, 8.
18. Dale Eisler, "Hill firing had most impact," *Regina Leader-Post*, Dec 10, 1991, A2.
19. Scott to Devine Re: Environmental Impact Statement (Nov 19, 1986).
20. Hood to Walker Re: Saskatchewan-U.S. Negotiations and the Rafferty-Alameda EIS (Jan 20, 1987).
21. The majority from the 1986 provincial election, no doubt, played a role in this decision.
22. Souris Basin Development Authority, "Rafferty and Alameda Reservoir Wildlife and Fisheries Briefing for the Canadian Wildlife Federation," Environmental Management Associates (Sask), (Regina, 1988).
23. Re: Wildlife Mitigation Lands. A quarter section of land is a quarter mile square

and 160 acres in size. This meant that the SBDA acquired almost 10,000 acres of land and would plant 1½ to 2 million trees to meet the commitment of no net loss of wildlife habitat.

24. Souris Basin Development Authority, "Rafferty-Alameda Briefing Note: Funding for Environmental Conservation" (Estevan, 1988), 8a.

25. Re: *International River Improvements Act.* That a federal license was required did not mean that Environment Canada would use the licensing process as the means of assessing the environmental effects of the project. If one examines the IRIA licenses issued prior to Rafferty-Alameda it is readily apparent they are virtually devoid of conditions that would be construed as environmental protection measures and there are certainly none that apply to nonwater quantity and quality impacts. The same conclusion cannot be reached in considering the IRIA license issued after Rafferty-Alameda. This is an indication of how the federal government attempted to use its licensing authority to assert jurisdiction over the environment.

For examples of IRIA licenses with minimal environmental conditions see: Cora Linn Dam license (Kootenay Lake, July 11, 1956), Arrow Lakes Project license (Columbia River, Aug 1, 1965), East Poplar River license (Apr 29, 1975), Morrison Dam license (East Poplar River, Apr 29, 1980), Cora Linn Dam license #2 (Kootenay Lake, May 17, 1983). For an example in the post-Rafferty-Alameda period see: Pelican Lake Enhancement Project license (Pelican Lake-Pembina River, Manitoba, June 25, 1991).

26. See note 5. That a board of inquiry was held despite the deputy minister to the premier outlining a process in 1985 to avoid such a move reflected the growing controversy surrounding the project.

27. Author's Journal (Aug–Sept, 1987).

28. R.G. Trout, "Report on the Oilfield Mitigation Segment of the Rafferty-Alameda Dam Project" (SBDA, Sept 1992), 5.

29. Rafferty-Alameda Ministerial Approval, Saskatchewan Environment and Public Safety (Feb 15, 1988).

30. See Hood to Zukowsky Re: Compliance of Approval Conditions—Rafferty-Alameda Project (Dec 5, 1991).

31. The *Saskatchewan Environmental Assessment Act,* S.S. (1979–80), c.E–10.1.

32. Marie-Ann Bowden, *The Prairie Perspective: Environmental Law Update in Saskatchewan* (Canadian Institute, Calgary, 1988), F-3 – F-4.

33. *Association of Stop Construction of the Rafferty-Alameda Project Inc v Saskatchewan Minister of Environment and Public Safety and Souris Basin Development Authority,* 68 Sask R 52 (QB). In his decision, Mr. Justice Scheibel of the Saskatchewan Court of Queen's Bench noted:

In my view, it is open for the plaintiff among other issues to ask:

(a) What is an environmental impact assessment?

(b) What is an environmental impact statement?

(c) Can it reasonably be said that an assessment and a statement have been completed?

These issues raise serious questions. They are not ones inherently impossible to submit for judicial determination. The Act does not address the questions, therefore if the questions are to be addressed at all, the court is the only forum.

34. For a discussion of the problems related to multiple regulatory approvals, albeit in an Ontario context, see: James Rusk, "Impossible becomes more difficult," *The Globe and Mail* (Oct 27, 1992), A–12.
35. Naftel to Pepper Intradepartmental Memorandum Re: Fish Habitat Alteration Permit (Sept 7, 1988).
36. Gauley and Co, Written Legal Opinion Re: *Fisheries Act* (Sept 21, 1988).
37. *Ibid., 6.*
38. *Ibid.*
39. See note 22.
40. See note 35.
41. *Ibid.*

Substance and Procedure

1. For a good discussion of this see: Thomas Meredith, "Environmental Impact Assessment and Monitoring," in Bruce Mitchell (ed), *Resource Management and Development* (Toronto: Oxford University Press, 1991), 228.
2. *National Environmental Policy Act,* 102 (C), cited in Walter A. Rosenbaum, "The Bureaucracy and Environmental Policy," in James P. Lester (ed), *Environmental Politics and Policy: Theories and Evidence* (Durham, NC: Duke University Press, 1989), 216.
3. Lettie McSpadden Wenner, "The Courts and Environmental Policy," in *ibid,* 241.
4. Robert Connelly and Linda Jones, Federal Environmental Assessment Review Office. Interview with author (Sept 23, 1992).
5. P. Edmond, cited in Ted Schrecker, "Of Invisible Beasts and the Public Interest: Environmental Cases and the Judicial System," in Robert Boardman (ed), *Canadian Environmental Policy: Ecosystems, Politics and Process* (Toronto: Oxford University Press, 1992), 96.
6. See note 4.
7. G. Bruce Doern, *Getting It Green: Case Studies in Canadian Environmental Regulation* (Toronto: C.D. Howe Institute, 1990), 12.
8. M. Paul Brown, "Organizational Design as Policy Instrument: Environment Canada in the Federal Bureaucracy," in Boardman, 29. See note 5.
9. Larry B. LeBlanc and Robert G. Richards, "Environmental Assessment: Recent Developments and New Initiatives," in MacPherson, Leslie, and Tyerman, *The Law Turns Green: Environmental Law and Business* (Regina: MacPherson, Leslie, and Tyerman, 1991), 7–1.
10. David Vanderzwaag and Linda Duncan, "Canada and Environmental Protection: Confident Political Faces and Uncertain Legal Hands," in Boardman, 10. See note 5.
11. Norton James to Stan Gooch Re: Federal Government Involvement in Rafferty-Alameda (Mar 21, 1985).
12. Walker to Hood Re: Federal Involvement in Rafferty-Alameda EIA (Oct 27, 1986). The direction Walker received (re: not involving Manitoba and the federal government) resulted from the SBDA's concern about a possible trade-off between the two jurisdictions in the negotiations with the U.S. and on the environmental assessment. Both jurisdictions would eventually be involved in both processes.
13. Saskatchewan Justice Legal Opinion Re: Rafferty-Alameda Project—Federal Environmental Assessment and Review Process (Oct 30, 1986).
14. Sainte-Marie to Hood Re: Nonapplicability of the EARP Guidelines to the Alameda-Rafferty Project (Mar 10, 1987).

15. Hood to Walker Re: EARP Guidelines (Nov 10, 1986).
16. Berntson to McMillan Re: Federal Government and Rafferty-Alameda (May 19, 1987).
17. McMillan to Berntson Re: Federal Government and Rafferty-Alameda (July 27, 1987).
18. *Ibid.*
19. Hill Memorandum to Devine and Berntson Re: Federal Government and the Rafferty-Alameda Project (Nov 19, 1987).
20. For background to the *International River Improvements Act* see: Neil A. Swainson, *Conflict over the Columbia*, Institute of Public Administration of Canada (Montreal: McGill-Queen's Press, 1979).
21. Don Curren and Neil Scott, "Rafferty dam clears last hurdle before construction," *Regina Leader-Post* (June 18, 1988).
22. "Resolution No 11: Rafferty-Alameda Dam Project," Canadian Wildlife Federation (Autumn 1988 Meeting).
23. Kenneth A. Brynaert, "CWF Viewpoint: Rafferty Dam Approval Defies Law and Common Sense," *International Wildlife* (May-June 1988), 26.
24. In subsequent litigation, our legal counsel had the opportunity to question the executive vice-president of the Canadian Wildlife Federation. In this examination, the CWF's misunderstanding of the substantive aspects of the project became apparent. For greater detail see: *Canadian Wildlife Federation Inc et al v Minister of the Environment and Saskatchewan Water Corporation*, Cross-examination of Kenneth A. Brynaert (Ottawa: International Reporting Inc), Nov 9, 1989, 16–19.
25. *Canadian Wildlife Federation et al v Minister of the Environment and Saskatchewan Water Corporation*, Cross-examination of Denis Davis, Feb 17, 1989 (Ottawa: International Reporting Inc, 1989).
26. Don Curren, "Rafferty license decision delayed," *Regina Leader-Post* (Mar 31, 1989).
27. *Canadian Wildlife Federation et al v Minister of the Environment and the Saskatchewan Water Corporation*, 3 F.C. 309 (TD) (Apr 10, 1989), 327–28.
28. Geoffrey York, "Court lifts federal license for dam in Saskatchewan," *The Globe and Mail* (Apr 11, 1989).
29. "Work stops at dam site," *Moose Jaw Times-Herald* (Apr 12, 1989).
30. Dale Eisler, *Estevan Mercury* (Apr 19, 1989).
31. Don Curren, "U.S. funding becomes target," *Regina Leader-Post* (Apr 14, 1989).
32. Author's Journal (Apr 11, 1989).
33. Ross Howard, "Ruling on dam cheers environmental official," *The Globe and Mail* (Apr 17, 1989).
34. A. Paul Pross, *Group Politics and Public Policy* (Toronto: Oxford University Press, 1986), 117.
35. *CWF et al v Minister of the Environment*, 325. See note 27.
36. "Group says it can meet all concerns," *Regina Leader-Post*, (June 25, 1989).
37. Don Curren, "Dam meetings under way," *Regina Leader-Post* (June 23, 1989).
38. Environment Canada, Rafferty-Alameda Project, Initial Environmental Evaluation, Vol II, Public Consultation Process, Regina, Sask, 1989.
39. Vern Millard, "Moderator's Report," Initial Environmental Evaluation, Rafferty-Alameda Project, Environment Canada (1989), 3.
40. Hon Lucien Bouchard, Minister of the Environment, Remarks at Press Conference (Regina: Aug 31, 1989).

41. Dave Traynor, "Devine delighted dam project back on track," *Saskatoon Star-Phoenix* (Sept 1, 1989).
42. Don Curren, "Rafferty foes ponder moves," *Regina Leader-Post* (Sept 1, 1989).
43. Don Curren, "Devine lauds Rafferty decision," *Regina Leader-Post* (Sept. 1, 1989).
44. See note 42.
45. Cam Fuller, "Backers of dam flood into streets," *Saskatoon Star-Phoenix* (Sept 2, 1989).

Getting the Better of Them

1. For a discussion of the relationship between Environment Canada and environmental interest groups see: A. Paul Pross, *Group Politics and Public Policy* (Toronto: Oxford University Press, 1986), 68–69.
2. The conversation with Berntson is cited from memory.
3. "Opposition to dams steadily waning," *Weyburn Review* (Oct 4, 1989).
4. Trevor Sutter, "Dam supporters livid over new CWF lawsuit" *Regina Leader-Post* (Oct 6, 1989).
5. Trevor Sutter, "New challenge for dam project," *Regina Leader-Post* (Oct 5, 1989); Maureen Marud, "Wildlife federation at odds on dam," *Saskatoon Star-Phoenix* (Oct 5, 1989).
6. Author's Journal (Nov 9, 1989).
7. *Canadian Wildlife Federation Inc et al v Canada (Minister of the Environment) and Saskatchewan Water Corporation* (1989) 31 FTR 1 (TD).
8. Dalhousie University Professor M. Paul Brown has noted:
   . . . Mulroney appointed Lucien Bouchard, a long-time friend and high-profile Quebecker whom he had personally recruited into federal politics, as Minister for Environment Canada. Second, in what was described by the media as an attempt to "provide the bureaucratic muscle to back up Lucien Bouchard's growing political clout," he then shifted Len Good, the Deputy Secretary to Cabinet (via Energy, Mines, and Resources), from his position "near the centre of Ottawa's power structure" to Environment Canada as Deputy Minister. Together, these changes lifted Environment Canada from the junior to the heavyweight ranks in Cabinet and the federal bureaucracy.
   - Cited from: M. Paul Brown, "Organizational Design as Policy Instrument," in Robert Boardman (ed), *Canadian Environmental Policy: Ecosystems, Politics and Process* (Toronto: Oxford University Press, 1992), 37.
9. Thomas Meredith, "Environmental Impact Assessment and Monitoring," in Bruce Mitchell (ed), *Resource Management and Development* (Toronto: Oxford University Press, 1991), 228. Meredith is quoting from FEARO (1988), The National Consultation Workshop on Federal Environmental Assessment Reform, Ministry of Supply and Services, Canada.
10. Author's Journal (Jan 12, 1990).
11. *Ibid.*
12. One other issue that affected their relationship was the government decision not to privatize SaskEnergy. SaskEnergy, a spin-off of SaskPower, was a newly formed provincial crown corporation that controlled the supply of natural gas within the province. The principle architect of the plan to privatize SaskEnergy was George Hill. The rationale behind the privatization efforts was to maximize the economic benefits to the province through the increased diversification of the natural gas

industry due to private sector involvement. Hill had expended considerable effort readying SaskEnergy for privatization. In the spring of 1989, the government's plans were disrupted by a prolonged bell-ringing session in the Legislature when the NDP Opposition walked out of the House. What ensued was a highly acrimonious political fight between the government and the NDP over the issue. In late fall, 1989, the government blinked and shelved the plan to privatize the natural gas utility. Hill was livid, for he felt the government had failed to exhibit fortitude in the face of adversity, and that it had virtually lost the next election because of the shift in momentum. What happened with SaskEnergy irrevocably affected Hill's relationship with Devine and the Cabinet. It also had a very real affect on what we did on Rafferty-Alameda.

13. Author's Journal (Jan 22, 1990).
14. *Ibid.,* Jan 15, 1990.
15. *Attorney General of Canada v Saskatchewan Water Corporation and Souris Basin Development Authority,* Affidavit of George D. Hill, QC (1991), 1 WWR 426 (Sask QB), 17.
16. *Ibid.,* 19.
17. *Ibid.,* 19–20.
18. Author's Journal (Jan 25, 1990).
19. *Ibid.*
20. *Ibid.,* Jan 28, 1990.
21. *Ibid.*
22. *Ibid.,* Jan 26, 1990.
23. Environment Canada, News Release: "Work Stops on Rafferty-Alameda Dams (Jan 26, 1990) PR-HQ 090–06.
24. Saskatchewan-Canada Agreement Re: Rafferty-Alameda Dam Project (Jan 1990).

Straddling the Line

1. *Agreement Between the Government of Canada and the Government of the United States of America for Water Supply and Flood Control in the Souris River Basin,* Article II, paragraph 1. The agreement stipulates that:

   The Government of Canada shall expeditiously provide the Government of the United States of America with a minimum of 466,000 cubic decametres (377,800 acre-feet) of flood storage by:

   a. Completing construction of Rafferty Dam and including in that improvement a minimum of 327,100 cubic decametres (265,200 acre-feet) of flood control storage; and

   b. Constructing Alameda Dam and including in that improvement a minimum of 138,900 cubic decametres (112,100 acre-feet) of flood control storage.

   The agreement also stipulates that the Government of Canada designates the Government of Saskatchewan as the entity responsible for "the construction, operation and maintenance" of the dams and that Saskatchewan shall receive the American funding. Saskatchewan would enter into a separate agreement with Ottawa in which Saskatchewan agreed to construct the Rafferty and Alameda dams and, in return, the province indemnified and saved harmless the government of Canada from any liabilities resulting from entering into the agreement with the United States.

2. Hanson would eventually be hired as a consultant to the SBDA. The opposition to the project attempted to make much of the fact that he was being paid a monthly fee by the SBDA when it discovered this in 1989. However, Hanson's relationship with the Authority had been disclosed three years earlier. For greater detail see: Bob Laux-Bachand, "Hanson begins consulting," *Kenmare News* (Oct 8, 1986), 16.
3. Backes-Hanson to Gay Letter Re: Souris Basin Water Management (Aug 7, 1981).
4. Senate Floor Leadership to Quentin Burdick (Dec 13, 1985).
5. Carl O. Flagstad, "Burdick confident flood plan will work," *Minot Daily News* (Jan 2, 1986).
6. Five Party Letter to Senator Quentin Burdick Re: Agreement in Principle (May 1987).
7. Berntson to Clark Letter Re: Agreement in Principle (Oct 23, 1987).
8. Author's Journal (Dec 15, 1988).
9. Washington Talk, "Priority not threat," *New York Times* (Dec 15, 1988).
10. "Local Cooperation Agreement Between the Department of the Army and the Souris River Joint Water Resource Board for the Implementation of the Souris River Flood Control Project-North Dakota/Canada" (1989), 2.
11. Carl O. Flagstad, "Corps calls info meeting Tuesday," *Minot Daily News* (Apr 11, 1988).
12. Carl O. Flagstad, "Wildlife group requests stop to flood control project work," *Minot Daily News* (Jan 13, 1988).
13. Westmount Research Consultants Inc, "Estevan and Southeast Saskatchewan Survey Report" (Draft) (Regina: SaskPower, 1992), 2.

    Just how much this was so was evident from a poll taken by the Romanow government in 1992. The survey found that groups opposed to the project had been unsuccessful in gaining support from the Saskatchewan portion of the basin:

    For the final three groups and organizations, disapproval levels significantly exceed approval levels regarding their role in the Rafferty-Alameda project. Forty percent of respondents disapprove of the role played by the Friends of the Valley (twenty-three percent approve). Fifty-one percent disapprove of the role of the federal government (twenty-six percent approve). Seventy-five percent disapprove of the efforts of SCRAP (Stop Construction of the Rafferty-Alameda Project). Only seven percent approve of SCRAP's efforts.
14. Correspondence from the Saskatchewan Wildlife Federation, the North Dakota Wildlife Federation, and the Wildlife Society to Premier Grant Devine (Jan 21–22, 1988).
15. Vince Hilbert, "Little Solace from PCs," Letter to the Editor, *Saskatoon Star-Phoenix* (Apr 7, 1988).
16. Scott to Harde Re: Harde Committee Membership (Jan 20, 1988).
17. "Saskatchewan Wildlife Federation, Keith Harde, Honorary Life Membership."
18. Tom Loran, "Wildlife group has most to lose in dam decision," *Saskatoon Star-Phoenix* (Apr 19, 1989), B–10.
19. Schempp to Hood Re: Bismarck Meeting with Wildlife Groups (May 2, 1988).
20. North Dakota State Water Commission, "Resolution No 81–7–410 Supporting Memorandum of Understanding On Souris River Flood Control Project-Burlington Dam" (1981).
21. Richard Backes's submission to the Rafferty-Alameda Board of Inquiry (Estevan. Sept 17–19, 1987), 150–54.
22. Minutes of Meeting in Minot, North Dakota, on Proposed Rafferty Dam (Aug 21, 1984), H1–2–12.

23. *Ibid.* This is the reverse of the process Congress actually follows. It first approves a particular measure, then funds are appropriated. The error is probably attributable to the unfamiliarity with the American budgetary system of the individual who recorded the minutes of the meeting.
24. *Ibid.*
25. Dawson to Burdick Re: Corps of Engineers and Saskatchewan Dams (Nov 27, 1985).
26. Robert B. Smythe, "The U.S. Army Corps of Engineers," in W.J. Chander (ed), *Audubon Wildlife Report* (Academic Press, 1989/90), 13.
27. Lambertson to Burdick Re: US Fish and Wildlife Service and Souris River Flood Control (Nov 15, 1985).
28. Author's Journal (Nov 5, 1987).
29. For a discussion of the role of U.S. courts in environmental assessment see: Lettie McSpadden Wenner, "The Courts and Environmental Policy," in James P. Lester (ed), *Environmental Politics and Policy: Theories and Evidence* (Durham, NC: Duke University Press, 1986), 242.
30. Lawrence Mosher, "The Corps Adapts, the Bureau Founders," in *High Country News: Western Water Made Simple* (Washington, DC: Island Press, 1987), 17–22.
31. *Ibid.*
32. "US kicks in $55 million toward cost of Saskatchewan dams," *Montreal Gazette* (Oct 27, 1989).
33. *Ibid.*
34. "Canada-Saskatchewan Agreement" (Oct 1989).

Political Games and Verbal Deals

1. Author's Journal (Feb 8, 1990).
2. Environment Canada, *International River Improvements Act* License (Aug 31, 1989), clause 20; Saskatchewan Environment and Public Safety, Ministerial Approval for the Rafferty-Alameda Project (Feb 15, 1988), clause 1 (ii). The *IRIA* license contains a clause that states:

   The Licensee shall comply with the provisions of all federal statutes that relate to the improvement and the relevant provisions of any regulations made pursuant to such statutes. In addition, the Licensee shall comply with the specific terms and conditions which apply to the improvement contained in the provincial Ministerial Approval dated Feb 15, 1988, under the Environmental Assessment Act of the Province of Saskatchewan.

   The ministerial approval for the project issued by Saskatchewan Environment and Public Safety contains a similar clause:

   The proponent shall comply with all pertinent Canada and Saskatchewan legislation and regulations as same may be amended related to the construction or operation of the development. Where such legislation and regulations impose more stringent standards than those imposed by the specifications, mitigative measures and environmental protection measures described in the statement, the proponent shall comply with the more stringent requirements of the legislation and regulations.

   The letter accompanying the approval to construct the Rafferty Dam from the Saskatchewan Water Corporation stated that the "approval is subject to the applicant complying with the environmental conditions set out in the Feb 15, 1988 Ministerial

Approval of The Environmental Assessment Act." The approval to construct stated: "this approval is issued subject to the terms of the Boundary Waters Treaty (1909); as well as to any terms and conditions that may be imposed by a license under *The International River Improvements Act.*"

3. Author's Journal (Feb 15, 1990).
4. Robinson to Good Re: Construction (Mar 9, 1990).
5. Hill to Good Re: Rafferty-Alameda Review (Mar 14, 1990).
6. *Attorney General of Canada v Saskatchewan Water Corporation and Souris Basis Development Authority,* Affidavit of George D. Hill, QC (1991), 1 WWR 426 (Sask QB), 25.
7. George D. Hill, QC, "Remarks to the Minot Kiwanis Club" (Mar 13, 1990), 25.
8. Author's Journal (Apr 1, 1990; Apr 5, 1990).
9. Connelly to Bouchard Re: Continued Construction on Project (Apr 2, 1990).
10. Elizabeth May as quoted on *CBC Newsworld* (May 15, 1990).
11. Don Curren, "Invitation-only review upsets dam supporters," *Regina Leader-Post* (Apr 25, 1990).
12. Hill to Good Re: Invitation to Panel Briefing (Apr 20, 1990).
13. Bouchard to Martens Re: Continued Construction on Project (May 3, 1990).
14. Don Curren, "Rafferty project official critical of federal government," *Regina Leader-Post* (May 9, 1990).
15. Brynaert to de Cotret Re: Continuing Construction (June 5, 1990).
16. Hill to de Cotret Re: Continued Construction on Rafferty-Alameda Project (June 8, 1990).
17. Mitchell to Bowerman Memorandum Re: Meeting in Estevan on Rafferty Dam Proposal (Oct 2, 1979), 2.
18. Author's Journal (June 14, 1990).
19. Jack Fingler, President, Estevan Chamber of Commerce, quoted in "Dreams in the Dust" (Souris Basin Development Authority, 1990).
20. Hill to Devine Briefing Note Re: Rafferty-Alameda and the Federal Government (July 3, 1990).
21. George D. Hill, QC, "Comments Made at de Cotret Luncheon in Estevan" (July 26, 1990).
22. Rafferty-Alameda Environmental Assessment Panel, Information Request (July 31, 1990).
23. Devine to de Cotret Re: Panel Review of Rafferty-Alameda (Aug 10, 1990).
24. *Friends of the Oldman River Society v Canada (Minister of Transport)* (1990), 2 FC 18, 5 CELR (NS) 1 (1991), 1 WWR 352 76 Alta LR (2d) 289, 33 FTR 160, 68 DLR (4th) 375, 108 NR 241 (CA).
25. *Attorney General of Canada v Saskatchewan Water Corporation and Souris Basin Development Authority,* Affidavit of George D. Hill, QC (1991), 1 WWR 426 (Sask QB), 27.
26. Government of Saskatchewan, Briefing Note Re: Rafferty-Alameda and the Federal Government (Sept 4, 1990).
27. See note 25.
28. Hill Memorandum to File Re: Events of Sept 5, 1990.
29. CBC Radio Saskatchewan News (6:30 AM, Nov 2, 1990).

Dam Break

1. Author's Journal (Sept 24, 1990).
2. *Ibid.*, Sept 25, 1990.
3. *Ibid.*
4. *Ibid.,* Sept 28, 1990.
5. *Ibid.,* Oct 3, 1990.
6. Environment Canada, Draft Media Release: "Minister Accepts Resignation of Rafferty-Alameda Review Panel" (Oct 1, 1990).
7. Author's Journal (Oct 5, 1990).
8. Transcript of Robinson/Hill/Hood Phone Conversation (Oct 5, 1990).
9. *Ibid.*
10. Author's Journal (Oct 17, 1990).
11. Devine to de Cotret Re: Written Confirmation of the Sept 5, 1990 Agreement (Oct 10, 1990).
12. Rafferty-Alameda Environmental Assessment Panel to de Cotret Letter Re: Suspension of Operations (Oct 4, 1990).
13. Author's Journal (Oct 17, 1990).
14. Executive Council, News Release 90–703, "Work to Resume on Rafferty-Alameda Project" (Oct 11, 1990).
15. Murray Mandryk, *Regina Leader-Post* (Oct 20, 1990), A4.
16. Author's Journal (Oct 18, 1990).
17. Arthur Schlesinger, Jr, *A Thousand Days* (Boston: Houghton Mifflin Co, 1965), 289. Schlesinger cites John Kennedy using this maxim.
18. Souris Basin Development Authority, Media Release (Oct 12, 1990).
19. Souris Basin Development Authority, "Statement by George D. Hill, QC" (Oct 12, 1990).
20. SaskPower Land Department, Personal Communication (Jan 29, 1993).
21. Mark Hume, Peter O'Neil, and Phil Needham, "Alcan exemption on Nechako draws 'political fraud' charge," *The Vancouver Sun* (Oct 16, 1990). This issue would itself be the subject of a number of court battles that are not directly applicable to the discussion here. The important point is, whatever the rationale for the Alcan exemption, that the story broke when it did was not helpful to the federal government's position on Rafferty-Alameda.
22. "Review delayed until Oldman complete," *Regina Leader-Post* (Oct 24, 1990).
23. John Schreiner, "Dateline Regina: Saskatchewan lost patience," *The Financial Post* (Oct 23, 1990).
24. Robert Sheppard, "Ottawa's Prairie partner rebels," *The Globe and Mail* (Oct 25, 1990).
25. Ralph Hedlin, "How Ottawa reneged on Rafferty-Alameda," *Western Report* (Oct 29, 1990).
26. Brian Bergman, "The Clash over Rafferty," *Maclean's* (Oct 29, 1990).
27. Dan Oldfield quoted on CBC Radio, *Morningside* (Oct 31, 1990).
28. See note 15.
29. UCAL Management Consulting Ltd, *Water Conservation Study,* Regina (Dec 1990). The November 1990 province-wide poll was based on an extremely large random sample for Saskatchewan: 1,504 respondents. The most interesting results were that 78 percent of respondents expressing an opinion felt that Saskatchewan had been treated unfairly by the federal government; 92 percent of respondents expressing

an opinion felt that Saskatchewan was right to stand up to the federal government over its treatment of Saskatchewan on this project; and 79 percent of respondents expressing an opinion felt that the project was environmentally sound.

30. *Ibid.*
31. Legal counsel for the Tetzlaffs had been involved in preliminary discussions aimed at reaching an agreement whereby construction would be halted and, in return, the other parties would agree that no appeals would be filed. When negotiations on this front failed and we were forced to negotiate the January 26 Agreement with Ottawa, the Tetzlaffs filed an appeal. The action allowed them to protect their position and, until the announcement of the September 5 agreement, they sat on the appeal without perfecting it.
32. Glenn Kubish, "The judges wore green," *Western Report* (Feb 12, 1990), 27–28.
33. *Attorney General of Canada v Saskatchewan Water Corporation and Souris Basin Development Authority* (1991) 1 WWR 426 (Sask QB).
34. *Ibid.*
35. *Naskapi-Montagnais Innu Association v Canada (Minister of National Defence),* Fed TD, Reed J, unreported at date reference was made (1990) 35 FTR, 161, as cited in *ibid.*
36. See note 33.
37. David Roberts, "Judge criticizes Ottawa for flawed review process," *The Globe and Mail* (Nov 8, 1990.)
38. See note 33.
39. Author's Journal (Nov 22, 1990).
40. *Ibid.*
41. Mr. Justice John Urie. Interview with author (Sept 23, 1992).
42. *Ibid.*
43. *Canadian Wildlife Federation Inc et al v Canada (Minister of Environment) and Saskatchewan Water Corp* (1990) 121 NR 385 (FCA).
44. Lorne Scott, *CKTV News Service* (Dec 21, 1990).
45. Julia Langer, Friends of the Earth, *STV News Six O'Clock Report* (Dec 21, 1990).
46. *Attorney General of Canada and Edelbert and Harold Tetzlaff v Saskatchewan Water Corporation and Souris Basin Development Authority,* Saskatchewan Court of Appeal, File No 727 (Apr 9, 1991).

News and Truth

1. Barbara Robson, "Politics of dam project assailed," *Winnipeg Free Press* (Sept 11, 1988). Robson's views on the issue of whether journalists, on environmental matters, are observers or advocates are interesting, particularly in light of how the May story evolved and the absence of any solid confirmation of the allegation. Fletcher and Stahlbrand note, with respect to Robson:

    While she believes some of the best environmental journalism is done in an advocacy role, she says there is a place for objectivity. But she stresses that objectivity is much more than the old formula "on the one hand this, on the other hand that . . . You must give evidence its true weight. You can't balance a world expert with someone who isn't of the same calibre." Cited from Fletcher and Stahlbrand, "Mirror or Participant? The News Media and Environmental Policy," in Robert Boardman (ed), *Canadian Environmental Policy: Ecosystems, Politics and Process* (Toronto: Oxford University Press, 1992), 187.

2. Terry Collins, "No deal made on dam," Letter to the Editor, *Winnipeg Free Press* (Mar 23, 1989).

3. Don Curren, "McMillan steadfastly denies Rafferty-Grasslands link," *Regina Leader-Post* (Sept 24, 1988).

4. Randy Burton, "Rafferty said part of three-way swap," *Saskatoon Star-Phoenix* (Sept 14, 1988).

5. Dale Eisler, *Regina Leader-Post* (Sept 15, 1988).

6. "Federal adviser says she quit over Rafferty dam," *Regina Leader-Post* (Sept 12, 1988).

7. "Premier denies tradeoff regarding dam projects," *Estevan Mercury* (Sept 21, 1988).

8. Randy Burton and Dave Traynor, "Officials deny Rafferty part of trade-off," *Saskatoon Star-Phoenix* (Sept 16, 1988).

9. Terry Collins, quoted in Burton and Traynor, *ibid.*

10. See note 7.

11. "Deal on dam claims 'test all credulity,' parks minister says," *Saskatoon Star-Phoenix* (Sept 14, 1988).

12. Hon. Tom McMillan, former Minister of Environment and Consul General to New England, Letter to the Editor: "Facts about dam," *The Globe and Mail* (Nov 16, 1990).

13. "Senate will study two dam projects," *Regina Leader-Post* (Sept 28, 1989).

14. Mark Wyatt, "Rafferty work will rumble on while panel deliberates its fate," *Regina Leader-Post* (Apr 28, 1990).

15. "Dam opponents out to save invisible trees," *Regina Leader-Post* (June 2, 1990).

16. David Orchard and Marjaleena Repo, Letter to the Editor, "Rafferty dam not for irrigation," *Battlefords News Diplomat* (Oct 31, 1990).

17. *International River Improvements Act* License for the Rafferty-Alameda Project (Aug 31, 1989), Clause 10.

18. Ror to SBDA Re: CBC Filming (July 13, 1989).

19. Memorandum to File Re: CBC Film Crew (Sept 14, 1989).

20. *Ibid.*

21. Bart Johnson, "CBC drama shows dam fight," *Regina Leader-Post* (Oct 29, 1990).

22. *Ibid.*

23. Chris Wattie, "Politics stalled dam-fight film, producer charges," *Regina Leader-Post* (Jan 30, 1991).

24. *Ibid.*

25. David Wilson, "Lament for a valley," *The Observer*, Vol 55, No 2 (Aug 1991), 20–24.

26. D.V. Johnson, Letter to the Editor, *The Observer*, Vol 55, No 5.

27. Wilson, 24. See note 25.

28. Proposals for alternate developments were put forward during the public meetings. The alternate proposal most frequently recommended was the construction of a series of small dams along the Souris River and Moose Mountain Creek. In view of the frequent references to this proposal, the board considered it further:

> The advocates of the small dam proposal agree that such structures would provide the flood control required by residents along the river at a reduced cost, both monetarily and in terms of environmental disruption. Small dams, it is said, will take up less area and hence cause less disruption to farms along both waterways. Clearly certain multi-use objectives such as large scale recreation developments and water provision for industrial development would not be achieved; however, to residents supporting the alternate proposal, these objectives are not a priority.

The Board duly considered the reduction in potential uses with the overall cost of building small dams. In analyzing the alternate proposal the Board found that small dams are less efficient than large dams for the following reasons:

1. small dams flood a greater area to achieve the same storage volume—that is, more land would be required with greater negative impact on wildlife, archaeology, and agriculture;
2. surface area-volume ratio would be changed resulting in proportionately greater evaporation;
3. small dams are more costly to maintain;
4. small dams increase the potential for "breaching" in major floods;
5. small dams allow limited recreational and fisheries potential;
6. small dams offer poorer water quality;
7. small dams would not have an adequate water supply for irrigation.

If both proposals serve to guarantee the same amount of flood protection, and as such, start from the same base, they must then be analyzed on the basis of other benefits and their relative cost. Viewed in these terms, the SBDA proposal is more efficient since it provides greater benefits at similar or lower costs. The small dam proposal will not result in lower construction or disruption costs, and will not provide benefits to the same extent. [Saskatchewan Environment and Public Safety, "Report of the Rafferty-Alameda Board of Inquiry (Regina, 1988), 100–101.]

29. "Former PC minister decries Rafferty work," *Regina Leader-Post* (June 14, 1990).
30. Maxwell to Brynaert Re: Rafferty-Alameda (June 11, 1987).
31. Souris Basin Development Authority, "Media and the Mega Project: A Case Study of Media Coverage of the Rafferty-Alameda Water Conservation Project" (1991), 1.
32. Don Curren. Interview with author (Dec 7, 1992).
33. "The Media's eco-failure," *The Globe and Mail* (Dec 18, 1991).
34. "Build It and Be Damned," *Western Report* (Oct 29, 1990), 12.
35. "Ottawa University group tour Rafferty Dam site," CKCK Radio (May 2, 1991).
36. CBC Radio, *Ideas*, "Rivers of Change" (Mar 8, 1993).
37. UNBC Political Scientist Mary Louise McAllister has noted:

The public's perception of resources is more complex and multi-faceted than the debates in the media would have one believe. In his analysis of North American values regarding natural resources, Alan Ewart points out the emergence of a set of attitudes in North America including

• a reduced level of understanding, coupled with an elevated level of interest in natural resources, particularly forests and wildlands;

• a growth in the appreciation that forests and wildlands are a source of non-commodity values such as wildlife, recreation, water and non-urban experiences; and

• a growing reluctance to accept professional authority as objective or even accurate.

- Alan Ewart, "Wildland Resource Values: A Struggle for Balance," in *Society and Natural Resources*, Vol 3. (Oct–Dec 1990), 386. As cited in Mary Louise McAllister, *Prospects for the Mining Industry: Exploring Public Perceptions and Developing Political Agendas,* Centre for Resource Studies (Kingston, Ont., 1992), 17.

38. Eric Malling, "James M. Minnifie Lecture," University of Regina (1991).
39. Dale Eisler, "Media, Motherhood and the Environment," Speech Delivered to Environment and Mining Conference, Saskatoon (Nov 21, 1991).

40. I am indebted to Dr Roger Needham of the University of Ottawa, Department of Geography, for this description of the various levels of abstraction in media coverage of environmental issues.
41. Walter Lippman, as cited in Chuck Henning (ed), *The Wit and Wisdom of Politics*, expanded edition (Golden, Colorado: Fulcrum, 1992), 152.

Conclusion

1. Robert Caro, *The Power Broker* (New York: Vintage, 1974), 277.
2. The quotation is ascribed to Winston Churchill but likely originated with Charles Haddon Spurgeon (1834–1892), cited in M. Hirsch Goldberg, *The Book of Lies* (New York: William Morrow and Company, 1990), 5.

INDEX